Jack Duckworth and Me

Jack Duckworth and Me

BILL TARMEY
with Alan Hart

**SIMON &
SCHUSTER**

London · New York · Sydney · Toronto

A CBS COMPANY

First published in Great Britain by Simon & Schuster UK Ltd, 2010
A CBS COMPANY

1 3 5 7 9 10 8 6 4 2

Simon & Schuster UK Ltd
1st Floor
222 Gray's Inn Road
London WC1X 8HB

www.simonandschuster.co.uk

Simon & Schuster Australia
Sydney

Pictures provided courtesy of the author, excluding pictures 14, 15 and 18
and all pictures in Plate Section 2 © ITV Granada Picture Archive.

A CIP catalogue record for this book
is available from the British Library.

Hardcover ISBN: 978-0-85720-236-9
Trade Paperback ISBN: 978-0-85720-240-6

Printed in the UK by CPI Mackays, Chatham ME5 8TD

Contents

Acknowledgements

In writing this book, I've had to delve deep into my jumbled box of memories to recall events spanning sixty-nine years. If I've made mistakes, don't be too hard on a poor old pensioner who's done his best. To all those friends whose names have slipped my mind, I apologise. You know how it is: one moment it's there as clear as day; the next moment it's disappeared again.

My family have been a great help in reminding me of dates, people and places, and I'm extremely grateful to them. My pals from the music business and the building trade have also added to my pile of recollections. Some have confused me, but that's not hard to do these days.

As far as *Coronation Street* memories are concerned, I'm deeply indebted to Daran Little, whose book *40 Years of Coronation Street* reminded me of what Jack Duckworth had been up to between 1979 and 2000. I'm also obliged to the current archivist, Helen Nugent, for filling me in on the storylines from 2001 to the present day. Other help was provided by Dave Woodward, the picture archivist, who spared his time to provide a photographic record of my *Corrie* career.

My greatest thanks go to all those writers who invented marvellous adventures for Jack to pursue, and the production team for putting up with me. I'd also like to take this opportunity to apologise to all my talented cast colleagues for testing their patience while I was struggling to get my acting together.

Finally, I'd like to thank my friend Alan Hart for taking a break from his tough job as a travel writer to ghost-write this book and put my thoughts into words. He seems to have arranged my random memories into some semblance of order. I hope the story of my life so far will make sense to you; it's never made much sense to me.

Preface

The crazy world of *Coronation Street* was brought home to me soon after I joined the show as Jack Duckworth. I wasn't a regular in those early days, so I was allowed to take on other work as well.

In 1982 I was an extra in a Granada TV production of *King Lear*. It starred Sir Laurence Olivier and John Hurt, among other top-notch actors. I'd been for a pub lunch with two of my mates, who were cast as non-speaking soldiers in the Shakespeare play. By coincidence we returned on foot to the main doors of the Granada Studios at the same time as Sir Larry and John got out of a taxi. The crowd of autograph hunters outside went wild. As they surged forward with books and biros in hand, they yelled, 'Jack, Jack, Jack.' Sir Larry and John, two of the finest actors of my generation, were able to walk past unchallenged as the mob surrounded me. I'll never forget the look on Sir Larry's face as he smiled and winked at me as he entered the building.

It taught me an early set of lessons about the fame game. First and foremost, those two seasoned actors had enjoyed *not* being spotted – that was something to think about. And I had been recognised as Jack Duckworth. In the eyes of *Corrie* fans, Bill Tarmey didn't exist.

Like many other *Street* stars have done over the years, I developed a split personality. At home, with my family and friends, I was the same old Bill I'd always been. Outside my front door, even with my wife Ali at my side, I was Jack Duckworth. And I had no choice in the matter.

Fans would jab me in the chest with their fingers, telling me I should stop cheating on screen wife Vera. I was annoyed at first. Can you imagine going out with your wife and people accusing you of being a womaniser? But it was Ali who always calmed me down. They were referring to Jack's on-screen affairs, she explained. These had been played out twice a week in 20 million living rooms across the country. The fans knew what Jack had been up to even if Vera didn't, and they thought I deserved a piece of their minds.

Nothing prepares you for the *Coronation Street* effect. I wasn't a young actor just starting out in the profession; I'd had a variety of jobs and had been trying to make my way as a club singer. The thought of becoming an actor hadn't even crossed my mind. Fortunately, I had a loving family around me to keep my feet on the ground and together we learned to deal with the amazing changes in our lifestyle.

It's been more than thirty years since I first trod the famous cobbles of Weatherfield as Jack Duckworth. It's been a white-knuckle ride, taking me to far-flung corners of the old empire, where *Corrie* topped the viewing charts. Apart from all the other *Street* legends I used to watch on our tiny black-and-white telly, I've met Hollywood movie stars, not to mention prime ministers and Her Majesty The Queen. The role of

Jack led me to appear on *This Is Your Life*, where I sang a musical tribute to my darling wife Ali. That, in turn, led to a recording contract with EMI and some best-selling albums and gold discs.

My life hasn't been a bed of roses all the way – not by any stretch of the imagination. My dad was killed during the war by a German mortar bomb when I was just three years old. My widowed mum married another war hero and I had a new family with two brothers and two sisters.

I was hopeless at school so I had to choose jobs that involved more brawn than brain. There were fun times, but I thought having a decent singing voice was my best hope of making a better life for my family.

I was singing on a pub stage in 1976 when I collapsed with a heart attack. If it hadn't been for a quick-thinking mate who rushed me to hospital, that would have been the end of me. Three years later, I made my first appearance as Jack Duckworth at the wedding of Brian Tilsley and Gail Potter. Just before filming started, I was introduced to Liz Dawn, who went on to play my screen wife Vera for the next twenty-eight years.

Since then I've survived two heart bypass operations and been in a variety of scrapes as my own other half, Jack Duckworth. Perhaps I'll be best known as the idiot who burned down the Rovers Return.

It's been an incredible journey. As it comes to an end, I'd like to share it with you.

CHAPTER 1

Lucky Horseshoe

It's only when I look back that I see how lucky I've been. Don't get me wrong – I've had more than my share of misfortunes. But being chosen to play Jack Duckworth in *Coronation Street* has been like winning the pools and the lottery in the same week. And like almost everything in my life, it came about without any planning on my part.

I suppose it all started at a nightclub in Ashton-under-Lyne, a former mill town seven miles east of Manchester, the city where I was born and raised. I was a regular singer and compère at the Horseshoe Club, where the disc jockey was a pal called Ian Raven. Sadly, he died while I was writing this book.

I was there one day in the mid-1970s setting up equipment when Ian's manager arrived for a chat with him about future bookings. I was on the edge of the conversation when they discussed some extra work at the Granada TV studios in

Quay Street, Manchester. Curiosity got the better of me and I asked what they were talking about. Ian's manager explained there was good money to be earned by people with Equity cards who were free in the daytime. Granada needed men and women in various productions to wander around in the background of crowd scenes while professional actors played the main roles.

At that time I was trying to earn a living as a singer, appearing at the hundreds of pubs, clubs and nightspots around Manchester which employed cabaret artists. With a wife and two young children to support, it was always a struggle to make ends meet. By earwigging the conversation, I'd spotted a possible opening.

Ian's manager was a friendly guy and suggested I join them on a trip to the studios next day. I figured I had nothing to lose so I went along. At the studios I was given a form to fill in. Among the questions it asked was whether you could ride a bike or a horse, drive a car or swim. I was advised to tick 'Yes' for everything and worry about the consequences as and when they arose.

A few days later I started working as an extra and soon discovered that half my mates from the cabaret circuit were there too. There were singers, comics, jugglers, conjurors, musicians of every description, wrestlers and even circus clowns who were trying to earn a bit of extra money. I was doing OK with my singing but it was hard to get off the lower rungs of the ladder, and the fees for being a face in the crowd were a godsend. After a few weeks I became a regular and soon I was appearing in a load of TV programmes, including *Coronation Street*. Britain's most popular soap series was being screened twice a week in those days. The twenty main characters then were Len Fairclough, Elsie Tanner, Ray Langton, Billy Walker, Maggie Clegg, Jerry Booth, Annie Walker, Alan Howard, Stan and Hilda Ogden, Ernie and Emily Bishop, Betty Turpin, Ken Barlow, Bet Lynch, Norma Ford, Lucille Hewitt, Ena Sharples, Minnie Caldwell and Alf Roberts.

If you had extraordinary eyesight, you might just have seen me chucking darts in the corner of the Rovers while the stars were chatting in the foreground. Later I graduated to speaking parts, which paid more. Classic lines, such as 'Taxi for Barlow' and 'Pint of bitter, please', tripped off my tongue. I was also the man who knocked the bar hatch over and broke Ernie Bishop's piano-playing fingers. Actor Stephen Hancock and I had to stage the 'accident' so when the hatch dropped it hovered an inch above his hand.

I liked to joke later that these were the cameo roles which showed the directors what a talent they had hidden in their midst. Joking aside, I did like to take an interest in the technical side of filming. I'd ask if I could stay behind to watch how and why certain things were done. Singing at night was still my great love, but I was developing a fascination for the world of television.

I'd also got used to the extra money. Occasionally, when work dried up at Granada, I'd ring the casting director and howl down the phone. When he asked what the noise was, I'd say, 'That's the wolf at the door.'

Looking back I was quite shameless in putting myself forward, but I was building up a good set of contacts while earning and learning. I guess I'll never know whether any of these things led to my hitting the jackpot – no pun intended – but I like to think they helped.

I was at my home in Gorton, three miles from the centre of Manchester, when my phone rang one day in the late summer of 1979. One of the *Corrie* casting directors asked me if I'd be available on certain dates to play a new character they'd created. He was called Jack Duckworth and he was the husband of loud-mouthed machinist Vera Duckworth. Jack was going to make his first appearance at the church wedding of Brian Tilsley and Gail Potter.

My first question was: 'Will this affect my other extra work?' There had been an ITV strike earlier that year. The *Street* had been off air from 8 August until 24 October 1979. I didn't want to accept anything which would jeopardise working elsewhere.

Having been reassured that it was just for two episodes initially, I accepted the role of Jack. It never occurred to me for a moment that this was going to be a life-changing decision for me – that I would still be playing Jack thirty years later.

Of course I was nervous on that bitterly cold day in November 1979, when the cast assembled outside St Boniface's Church, Salford, to record the ceremony. Everyone was shivering so it was easy to hide the butterflies. I'd seen Liz Dawn, who'd been playing Vera since 1974, at the studios and we were already on nodding terms. Outside church one of the crew introduced us, telling Liz, 'This is Bill.'

I'd like to pretend that the first meeting between Jack and Vera was something out of *Brief Encounter* or *Gone with the Wind*, but the conversation went like this:

ME: 'I'm playing Jack.'

LIZ: 'Oh! That's nice.'

It was a little later that our smouldering passion burst into flames in a scene which could have come straight out of the script of an Ealing comedy.

After those brief introductions, we were rounded up to take our places in the church. During a break we had to go back outside, where the crew had provided heaters to keep us warm. Liz was wearing a thin Crimplene skirt so she huddled up with her back to the fire as we waited to be called for the next shot. We were both sucking on cigs so I didn't spot the smoke at first, but then the smell of burning Crimplene hit me. Without further ado, I hurled Liz to the ground and started slapping her backside to put out the flames which were starting to spread.

Liz screamed. She must have thought I was a maniac. I carried on spanking her while saying, 'I'm sorry but you're on fire.' Fortunately, the only damage done was to the dress, which was replaced. It certainly broke the ice between Liz and me.

My first episode as Jack was screened on 28 November 1979, three weeks after filming. In the second episode, I was given an earbashing from Vera for getting drunk at Brian and Gail's reception. It was to be the first of many.

Unknown to me, it seems the background team had seen a spark between Jack and Vera that they thought they could develop. Scriptwriter John Stevenson, who became a good friend, was the main man who spotted the potential to develop these characters.

John was an ex-*Daily Mail* showbiz writer who lived in the Manchester area and had seen confrontational couples like the

Duckworths having a go at each other in pubs and shops. With my background, I'd also come across husbands and wives who behaved like Punch and Judy, bickering away and fighting in public. You had to wonder why on earth they stayed together. I suppose that like Jack and Vera they were hiding a secret love they would hardly admit to themselves, let alone anyone else.

I gradually built up the character of Jack by taking bits from various people I knew. These were the folk I'd seen and heard in my younger days. So let me take you away from the cobbled streets of fictional Weatherfield to the real cobbled streets of central Manchester where I was born and raised.

CHAPTER 2

From Tuppenny Rabbit
to Churchill

The cobbled streets of Manchester where I grew up were just like the Coronation Street you see on TV, but not half as posh! They've all been swept away now in the slum clearance programmes of the 60s and 70s – good riddance, I say.

Some folk feel nostalgia for those homes, but the truth is they were built quickly, cheaply and badly to cram as many people together as possible during the Industrial Revolution of the nineteenth century. Nearly 100 years later families were still living there like too many sardines squashed into too few tins. And as if that wasn't bad enough, we were being bombed by the Luftwaffe.

I was born on 4 April 1941 in a rented terraced house in Tiverton Street, Ardwick, about a mile from Manchester Town Hall. I was named William Piddington after my father, William Piddington Senior. He and my mum had married in

1940. By the time I came along, Dad was in the army. Although he saw me as a baby and held me, I'm afraid to say I have no memory of him. He was killed in October 1944, while serving as an ambulance driver on the Dutch–Belgian border following the D-Day landings in Normandy. I'll tell you more about that later.

My mum, Lilian, and her parents, John Willie Smith and his wife Adelaide, known as 'Addie' to most people and 'Grannie Smith' to me, kept the news of his death from me. They probably thought I was too young to understand and there was no point in upsetting me.

Because he was an absentee dad anyway, fighting abroad in the war, I didn't know him to miss him. By the time the war ended, my widowed mum had married a sailor called Bob Cleworth and he became the only dad I ever knew.

By then we'd moved a mile and a half from Tiverton Street to 41 Butterworth Street, Bradford. When she made the move in 1942, Mum reckoned we'd be safer from Hitler's bombs away from the city centre, but Bradford was in the heart of east Manchester's engineering industry. The loco-motive, wire and gas works, three giant coolers for the electric power station and Bradford coal pit provided prime targets for bombing raids. Well done, Mum!

The sounds of the air raid sirens and the subsequent all-clear are still vivid memories from my dim and distant past. The most dreaded noise was the hooter to signal an emergency at Bradford Pit. It would be followed by the sounds of men's boots and women's clogs as miners, their wives, mothers and sisters made their way to the mine entrance to offer assistance and find out what had happened. Many houses

8

were destroyed by what's now known as collateral damage during those air raids on the factories that surrounded our homes. Along with the casualties among our soldiers, sailors and airmen, it must have been a time of terror and tragedy for everyone involved. I never noticed. I think people just accepted the horrors as part and parcel of an unavoidable war, and I'd never known anything different.

When the war ended, I remember there was a lot of celebrating and dancing in the streets, but I didn't really know what it was all about. Food and clothes rationing continued for many years. Even though we'd won the war, the country was in a right state. There were ruined, bombed-out buildings everywhere. Millions of men came back wanting homes and jobs. Some of them had arms and legs missing, and later I'd see limbless men selling matches in shop doorways.

The war ending coincided with my first days of school. Bradford Memorial School was only a few yards from my home, and its most remarkable feature was that it had a playground on its roof. My parents told me that on my first day there, when the classroom emptied for mid-morning playtime, I thought school had finished for the day. Consequently, I walked home – much to the surprise of my Grandma Cleworth.

She was known to all and sundry as 'Fairy' because she was so tiny. She was one of a close-knit gang of relatives who all lived within a stone's throw of each other and raised the family's children as and when required.

It was Fairy who gave me my lifelong love of music. She would sit me on her knee and teach me the songs of the day, such as 'Lily of Laguna'. As I sang the words, she would do the harmonies. Then we'd swap, with her singing and me harmonising.

Granddad Cleworth was an asphalt potman who got up at the crack of dawn, sometimes while it was still dark. His job was to reach the building sites around 5.30 a.m. and get the asphalt ready for men like my dad to spread when they arrived a couple of hours later. He'd melt solid blocks of asphalt in an iron pan by gently simmering them at just the right heat. Because of his early starts, Granddad Cleworth knew the times and numbers of every bus and train that ran around Manchester and beyond. He was a walking time-table.

His unofficial job was as a bookies' runner. He used to collect bets for an illegal gambling round operated by a shady character called Mr Pogson. Every now and again the police would tell him they were going to carry out a raid and somebody would have to be arrested. Granddad was the fall guy. They'd give Mr Pogson a day or two to make arrangements, and he'd ask Granddad if he'd take the blame. Granddad didn't mind because it was his way of earning a bonus. He'd be arrested with betting slips in his possession and held overnight in the cells. Next morning Granddad would plead guilty to illegal betting and he'd be fined £5 or £10 by the magistrates. Mr Pogson would pay the fine and give Granddad ten shillings (50p) for his trouble. He reckoned it was a bargain in return for a cosy night in a police cell.

Granddad's other unusual source of income was the money he earned for docking dogs' tails. He used to charge three-pence (1½p) and would bite them off with his teeth. I'm not sure what the RSPCA would have had to say about the practice and I certainly don't recommend it.

My mum worked in a munitions factory in Gorton when I was a baby, leaving me in the care of my Aunty Maggie. One day Mum came home and found me sitting in a dolly tub, which was a non-automatic washing machine. Aunty Maggie said it stopped me getting into mischief and saved her having to keep a constant eye on me. Mum wasn't impressed and Aunty Maggie got her marching orders, but the story of my dolly tub prison became part of family legend. I blame that time in the dolly tub for a lot of the many stupid things I did later in life.

Grannie Smith lived three-quarters of a mile away in Princess Street. I used to call on her on schooldays for my lunch. When she wasn't around, I'd visit Uncle Walter and Aunty Ada five doors away. They had an upright piano, which I loved to bang around on. I made such a terrible din that Uncle Walter feared one day I'd break the piano. He locked the lid and bought me a mouth organ by way of compensation. I loved it. Within three months I could play any tune on that little instrument. Only later did I discover that I'd been playing it upside down.

My new dad, who had served in the Royal Navy, was given a gold medal by the Russians in the 1990s. He was one of many British sailors who had kept their convoys of the Baltic Fleet safe from German U-boats. During the 1940s he was promoted to leading seaman and issued with a whistle but was demoted again for some misdemeanour and had his whistle confiscated.

At various stages during the war, Dad served on the *Marne*

and the *Nelson*, as well as French minesweepers. He came home with an Italian-made accordion, or squeeze-box, which he took to the pub on Saturday nights.

My mum was a decent singer. I used to stand on a ledge outside the Duke of Edinburgh in Mill Street so I could watch her through the window. Then my dad would sing 'Don't Laugh At Me 'Cos I'm A Fool'. He was a lovely bloke but a dreadful singer. It was hard to tell whether his voice put the accordion out of tune or vice versa. People used to groan when he stood up to sing and play. I'm not sure whether he didn't notice or didn't care.

Granddad Smith used to play the drums at the Salvage pub, and promised me I could have his set when he died. Just before he passed away, when I was eleven or twelve years old, he told me with tears in his eyes that he'd had to sell his drum kit to make ends meet.

After his death, Grannie Smith married a binman called Mansel Williams and they moved to Wales with his two kids. When he died, Grannie came back to Manchester, where she lived in Yew Tree Road, Northenden.

Our two-up and two-down house would have been small even for the three of us, but over the years we became seven. I was six years old when Robert Cleworth Junior came on the scene, followed by Linda, Annie and Alan.

Downstairs there was a kitchen at the back and a front room. Upstairs there were two bedrooms. Outside there was a privy in the backyard. The house leaned so we had to lock the front door to stop it from swinging out into the street. You couldn't open the windows because they wouldn't shut again.

As the family grew, my mum and dad shared the front bedroom with the two girls and baby Alan in a cot. I shared a single bed in the small back bedroom with my brother Robert. At first we had bare floorboards and many's the time I had to pull splinters out of my feet. Eventually I was given a piece of oilcloth to put at the side of the bed. With all those nappies in the house, it's a wonder we didn't have a rainbow on the landing when the sun was shining.

We had a gas oven for cooking food and a copper boiler for laundering clothes. We kept our coal under the stairs. Every fortnight the coalman would deliver one bag of coal and one of 'nutty slack', and we had to remember to cover the chip pan. A cloud of black dust would settle everywhere, and if we forgot about the chipper, we'd have to scrape off the sooty top layer and throw it away.

The front room contained a two-seater couch, an armchair, a table, three dining chairs and a tallboy. It was so small you had to shimmy round the furniture to get in and out.

The toilet was a brick building in the tiny backyard. There was a gap a foot wide under the door and another two feet wide above it. In the winter it was bitterly cold and we'd take old newspapers to light while we were in there to create a bit of warmth. Mum and Dad always had first use of the toilet. Then came the youngest children upwards because they had less warning of when they needed to go. That put me in last position but at least I was guaranteed to avoid an icy experience: a swinging chain meant a warm seat.

For toilet paper we had squares of newspaper spiked through a nail on the wall. There was no lock on the door so if you were shy you had to be good at whistling – not that you could afford to be shy in our family, living cheek by jowl as we did. If anybody lingered in the khazi, it wouldn't be long before somebody asked the question: 'Are you going to be much longer?' Occasionally you'd hear the desperate shout of 'What on earth are you doing in there?' I don't suppose they really wanted a precise answer.

There was no bathroom. I used to go once a week to the public baths at Barmouth Street, Bradford. At first the entry fee was a penny, but once I'd learned to swim and got my length certificate at the age of seven or eight, I got in free. After that I'd go in as often as I could. A bloke known as Roger the Shepherd supervised with a long stick. You were allowed to stay for 1½ hours. When Roger saw your skin starting to go crinkly from the water, he'd hook you out.

Before you were allowed into the main pool, you had to rinse off any dirt in a smaller pool about one foot deep. That was disgusting because you were sitting in everyone's dirty water. It's a wonder we didn't all go down with dreadful diseases; I suppose a few did. All we had to revive us were Fennings' Little Healers for chesty coughs, Beecham's Pills for headaches, and Fennings' Fever Curer for just about everything else.

Bombed-out derelict houses were the adventure playgrounds of our day, and a croft opposite was where games of 20-a-side football with coats or piles of bricks for goalposts took place. There seemed to be little in the way of organisation but a great deal of fun. You just turned up, asked one of the bigger boys if you could play, and joined in. It took a while to know who was on your side; sometimes you had to guess from which way they were facing.

The croft also had a water tower. I would occasionally throw one of my boots into it. I could never explain why I did this. It always earned me a clip round the ear. I think I just liked the sound of the splash it made. One of my first pair of Wellington boots, or wellies, ended up in the water tower. When I wore them, they rubbed against my calves and made red marks on the backs of my legs. If I'd thought about the consequences (being smacked on the backs of my sore legs), I might have behaved differently, but I always tended to act on impulse.

Cars were still a novelty in those days, so the cobbled streets were safe for games. Lamp-posts were also great for converting into swings with a length of rope. All the kids played outside in the streets and on the derelict sites. There was no spare room in our houses and the only time we went home was when we were hungry.

Lots of men in the area kept pigeons in their backyards, just like Jack Duckworth. There was a man who lived round the corner in Moody Street who used to go mad if we were making a racket when his pigeons were coming back to the roost. They'd circle round after a race to make sure everything was peaceful and safe for their return. If there were a bunch of young lads yelling and running around, the birds would keep circling. Once the pigeons had landed, the owners had to race down to the clocking-in point in Kenyon Street half a mile away. There was a small amount of prize money at stake, so my mates and I earned many a clip round the ear for being too noisy in the wrong place at the wrong time.

I had various chores to perform. Lighting the fire was my biggest responsibility. This involved carefully spacing pages of old newspapers under the coal, then balancing a sheet of paper across the front of the chimney and holding it in place with a shovel. When the fire was lit, this ensured a flow of air under the grate and up the chimney. The great danger was that your sheet of paper would catch light and get sucked up the chimney, where it would cause a fall of soot. This was a problem I was later to re-enact as Jack in *Corrie*. It ended with Jack and Vera looking like renegades from *The Black and White Minstrel Show*.

There were no idle times in those days. I had to be up at seven o'clock every morning for a breakfast of toast and dripping. It was my job to keep the house tidy for Mum, who worked in munitions during the war, then at Johnsons' Wire Works and later the UCP tripe and cowheel factory 100 yards from our house. The tripe had to be boiled, washed, scrubbed and cut. I remember the premises used to attract the biggest bluebottles I'd ever seen.

I'd set the fire next door at 39 Butterworth Street, the house Fairy shared with Granddad Cleworth and their daughter Margaret. Then I'd take the kids to nursery and school before going myself.

I was hopeless in the classroom. There was a teacher called Mr Standren who seemed to hate children in general and me in particular. He seemed to be always giving me backhanders or screaming down my ear. I didn't like school and school didn't like me. I could never understand why they would chalk things on the blackboard and then, just as I was starting to understand what they were getting at, the teacher would rub them off again.

Another source of irritation was the fact that they insisted on calling me Piddington. I refused to answer to my name. I wanted to be called Cleworth like my mum and dad and my brothers and sisters. It was an embarrassment being the only one called Piddington. If anybody had ever asked me what I would like more than anything for Christmas, it would have been to change my name to Cleworth. Nobody ever asked.

Looking back, I suppose teaching us was a thankless task. The only lessons I enjoyed were art and history. Our art teacher was a Mr Hines. He showed us how to draw. I had a great deal of enthusiasm but precious little talent. I remember being very proud after I had sculpted an Indian brave and a Roman general out of clay, but whether anyone else was able to recognise my finished products is doubtful. I think Mr Hines was more impressed with the effort than the talent when he patted my head and said, 'Well done, lad.'

I got the impression that most of the teachers and pupils at the school were just going through the motions. In our deprived area, kids had enough chores to carry out for the family without having to work at school as well. It all seemed irrelevant because they were churning out factory fodder by and large. My assessment informed my parents: 'This boy is wasting space.' I wouldn't argue with that verdict.

You learned to live on your wits from an early age. There was little time for daydreaming but we always enjoyed particular shows on the wireless. Our imaginations were fuelled by listening to programmes such as *Dick Barton – Special Agent* and *Journey Into Space*.

For visual treats there was a cinema called the Princess in Grey Mare Lane, Bradford, where we'd go on Saturday mornings. One of our gang would pay the 2d (1p) to get in.

Then, as soon as the lights went down, he'd crawl to the toilets. There was an emergency exit there which was opened from the inside by a push bar. We took it in turns to be the bar pusher. It had to be done as quietly as possible. Then the rest of our mob would come in and emerge one or two at a time from the toilets. Sometimes the cinema would be full of about a hundred kids. Only half had paid the entrance fee. The usherettes, or torchy tarts as they were known, were fighting a losing battle to keep order among this rabble of noisy, excited children.

We'd cheer on our heroes, such as Flash Gordon, Tarzan, Zorro and Superman. The Wild West was ruled by cowboys like Roy Rogers, Tom Mix, Hopalong Cassidy and Gene Autry. When the bad guys came on the screen — always wearing black hats in the westerns for ease of identification — we would hiss, boo and stamp our feet. Flash Gordon's archenemy was Ming the Merciless. There were also creatures called the Clay People, who had a scary habit of coming out of walls.

On the way home, I'd try to copy my heroes' performances by wearing my coat back to front so it looked like a cloak. Then I'd gallop down the streets smacking my backside as if I were a horse and shouting meaningless words like 'Shazam!'

More scary than the screen monsters was the threat posed by our own personal bogeyman. It was actually a bogeywoman and her name was Ginny Green Teeth. Whenever we misbehaved, we were threatened with the dreaded words 'Ginny Green Teeth will come to getcha.' It was never clear exactly who this lady was, where she came from or what she was likely to do to us. Fear of the unknown was a far greater terror, but I had the impression that biting would be involved.

While I was playing out or running errands, back home the older generations were listening to *ITMA* (*It's That Man Again*) with Tommy Handley, cheerful Charlie Chester, *Workers' Playtime* and *Two-Way Family Favourites*.

Outside the lads of the neighbourhood would meet to swap comics. I remember a time when one of my mate's mother contracted some contagious disease. I was reduced to tears – not in sympathy for the poor woman but because my mum burned all the comics I'd got off her son in case they were infectious.

The lad who'd given me the comics was called Graham King and his mum died. Graham was one of four boys and he had to leave the area to go into a children's home in Styal, Cheshire. There was nobody to look after the boys while their widowed father was working so the kids were all shipped out to this home ten miles away. You didn't have to rob banks to be taken into care in those days. Many kids who'd done nothing wrong would end up there.

Graham was about ten years old, and his brothers were younger. I remember being sad when I heard what had happened because he was one of my closest pals. We got into a few scrapes together. Once we were caught lowering his baby brother out of a bedroom window in a bucket tied to a piece of rope.

By an extraordinary coincidence I saw Graham again a few months later. I'd joined a mixed children's choir called The Songsters. It was organised by a bloke called Stan Ball. We used to visit old folks' homes and perform for them. One day we went to a children's home in Styal, and Graham and his brothers were in the audience.

When I look back on what sounds like a life of drudgery, when you could wake up some winter mornings to find ice on the *inside* of the windows, I'm surprised at what a happy childhood it was. Perhaps it was the deprivation which made life's simple pleasures so much more enjoyable.

There was sweet rationing until well after the war ended, but we would invest our coppers in sticks of Spanish liquorice root. You could keep it in your pocket and take it out to chew on all day long. Those of us who'd developed a liquorice habit were easily identified by our brown teeth, gums and lips. Many shopkeepers bought in home-made sweets, which they stored in huge jars. Other sweets, like Uncle Joe's mint balls, were the height of luxury.

The best time for sweets was Bonfire Night on 5 November, when all the neighbourhood handed out treacle toffee, fudge and parkin as we played with sparklers. The older boys would torment each other by hurling bangers and rip-raps at each other. It caused a few visits to the hospital burns unit, but in those days that was generally regarded as the price you occasionally paid for your fun. The male adults were entrusted with the job of lighting the bonfires and setting off the rockets, Catherine wheels and Roman candles which brought screams of appreciation from the delighted audience.

We would earn a few coppers days earlier by stuffing old clothes with newspapers and propping this rather pathetic attempt at a model of Guy Fawkes outside the pubs with a scrawled note urging passers-by to contribute 'A penny for the Guy'. For a couple of weeks we'd have collected wood, including broken boxes from the market, to create our own 'bonny' on the croft. From time to time other kids would try to plunder our pile for a rival bonfire but screaming hordes of us would rush out of our homes to drive the invaders away.

I don't think for a moment any of us understood the political significance of Bonfire Night, why Guy Fawkes was being burned or knew there'd been an attempt to blow up Parliament 300 years earlier. It was just a much-loved carnival-style party enjoyed by Protestant and Catholic kids alike.

Christmas was another time to look forward to. I used to hang my pillowcase at the end of the bed. One year I was sure I'd seen Father Christmas in his red suit at the end of my bed. I still don't know whether I'd been dreaming.

I used to joke that in my day one year you'd get the toy gun and the next Christmas you'd get the caps so you could fire it. That wasn't so far from the truth. Mum and Dad did the best they could for me with their limited means. I remember one year getting my Roy Rogers gun, a *Beano* or *Dandy* annual, an orange and some nuts. I was absolutely thrilled because expectations were so low in those days and we all appreciated things more.

There was never a turkey for Christmas lunch. It would be a chicken and most of the breast would go to my dad because he was a working man and needed to keep up his strength. For me, whose only experience of meat was corned beef or Prem (a cheap version of Spam), a chicken wing was a real treat.

Distant relatives and friends would visit each other's houses for a drink and a sing-song, and sooner or later Dad would bring down the dreaded accordion. After my brothers and sisters were born, we started to have a Christmas tree in the front room, which made the house even more cramped. But with a tree, presents and a chicken dinner we felt like kings.

By then I was earning extra pocket money by going on errands, although I'm told my success rate left a lot to be desired. After being carefully told what was required in the way of bread, tea, sugar, flour and vegetables, I'd invariably return with a pound of carrots and a bundle of wood. It seems that the list of things to buy would always end with carrots and firewood. I could never remember the whole list – just the last two items. This put me in the doghouse when I came back from my expeditions.

Granddad Cleworth was my staunchest supporter in such times of trouble. He used to call me 'Churchill' and would sit on his doorstep with me. I must have fattened out a bit to lose my first nickname. I was such a skinny baby they'd called me the Tuppenny Rabbit.

To say Granddad Cleworth enjoyed a drink would be something of an understatement. In his cups, he would chat away to me as we looked out from our perch at 39 Butterworth Street. Fairy would fetch two pots of beer from the pub. By the time she returned, Granddad would hand her two empty pots for refills. Eventually Granddad would ask for an eggcup to give me a mouthful. Then he'd shout to my mum next door, 'Lil. He'll sleep tonight.'

Granddad Cleworth had been a boxer in his youth and he taught me how to defend myself. He put these massive gloves on me and showed me how to land a straight left. I tapped him in the face, but he kept shouting, 'Harder, lad.' It was awkward for me because I'd been brought up to respect older people, especially my own grandfather. But he was a tough old bloke who used to accept challenges to fight in fairgrounds for beer money. He certainly wasn't bothered about taking punches from a little boy.

His lessons proved useful when a lad started bullying me at primary school. I used to walk away and ignore him most of the time, as my mum had told me to. One day I was sitting in the library when he hit me over the head with a book. The red mist descended and the next thing I knew a teacher was pulling me off the school bully. He'd taken a right pounding and he never bothered me again.

I was about eleven years old when Granddad Cleworth died from cancer in his mid-fifties. Just before his death, he'd suffered a really painful injury at work. He'd been carrying a bucket of hot asphalt across a plank when he slipped and dipped his elbow into the scalding mixture. My mum used to dress his bandages for him. We suspect that shock from the injury might have set off the cancer which eventually killed him. It was tragic to see a big strong man turn into a skeleton in a few weeks.

In his dying days, a gang of Irish navvies were digging drains outside the house and Fairy asked if they could keep the noise down. Those men broke off from working outside his house out of respect and started digging around the corner until they heard he'd passed away. I'll never forget their kindness at a sad time for our family.

Granddad Cleworth had been a great character and was sorely missed. Fairy would get lonely sometimes and ask me to come next door and stay at her house. One night I said I didn't want to sleep in her bed because she snored. It caused so much upset that I never objected again. I'd rather put up with the noise than hurt her feelings.

She was an avid movie fan and took me with her to watch films at the Princess. I remember I only went to watch the action pictures starring Jimmy Cagney and Edward G. Robinson. I didn't like the kissing movies because I thought they were soppy.

One day I'd been out playing and lost track of time. Fairy had promised to take me to the pictures, as movies were called in those days, but I got home late. Mum told me Fairy had set off for the Princess on her own. I ran over the croft, past the tripe works and the market just in time to see her disappearing into the cinema on the other side of Grey Mare Lane. As I ran across the road without looking, I was hit by a motorbike.

The collision knocked me out cold and I was rushed to hospital. Luckily, I'd landed on my head, and where there's no sense, there's no feeling. Apart from scrapes and bruises and some concussion I was none the worse.

By the time Fairy got home from the film, I'd returned from the hospital a bit battered and bruised but with no bones broken. She was shocked to hear what had happened to me. She'd assumed I'd forgotten we were going to the pictures.

The one time Dad took me to the pictures was when we went to watch *The Cruel Sea*. As a Royal Navy sailor, Dad was anxious to see a film about naval battles. At one point in the movie the captain, played by Jack Hawkins, ordered his ship, the *Compass Rose*, to ignore the British sailors from another ship which had been torpedoed by a German U-boat. He couldn't risk stopping to pick up survivors because he would have lost his crew too. As I turned to my dad, I could see tears running down his cheeks. I'd never seen him cry before or since.

I asked him, 'Was it like that, Dad?'

He said, 'It was like that and worse.'

The subject was never mentioned again.

My best pals in those days were Johnny Taylor, Graham and George King, Albert and Alan Waterworth, Frank Farriker and Eddie North. We weren't exactly a gang, but we hung out together and always watched each other's backs.

An older lad who lived on our street was called Frank Pearson. He'd been a boxer in his early teens and was working in clubs and pubs as a singer who told gags between songs. He later became a legend in Manchester as Foo Foo Lamarr, a drag artist and club owner who was known throughout the city for his charity works. He was a staunch Manchester United fan and counted the Beckhams and the Giggs family among his firm friends. Sadly, Frank died of cancer in 2003 and attracted a host of local celebrities to his funeral.

There was also a girl called Gladys Stubbs, whose dad was a painter and decorator. I wasn't really bothered about girls at that age, but Gladys was special – she had a bike! I used to go round there and borrow it whenever I could. Being seen on a bike round our way in those days made you feel special.

The only other person I remember seeing on a bike was the rent collector. He'd come round once a week and sometimes my mum would hide behind the couch and tell me to say there was nobody at home. We always paid up eventually.

My dad fell out of work from time to time but he'd find some way of putting food on the table.

On one occasion he drove a horse and cart round the streets as a rag and bone man. He'd blow a bugle to warn people to get their unwanted stuff ready. In return for people's scrap, he'd hand out plastic windmills or donkey stones for cleaning your front step.

One of my mates recognised him and asked, 'Isn't that your dad?' I was ashamed to admit it. I pretended it was someone who looked like him. Now I realise there's no shame in a man taking any job to feed his family. It was one of the lessons I learned as a child.

Like I said at the start of this chapter, I don't miss those slums being demolished. It's just unfortunate that so many close-knit communities got broken up too. Lots of people look back and think those were the good old days. They've forgotten now about the harsh life we led, with poverty and poor health everywhere around us. Nobody bothered to lock their doors, but there were two reasons for that: one was that we had nothing much worth stealing; the other was that if you were in trouble, you only had to ask for help. The slums were disappearing by the time Tony Warren wrote the first episodes of *Coronation Street* back in 1960, but the spirit of those working-class families lived on.

CHAPTER 3

Growing Up

It's always a bit of a shock when you move up to big school. After gradually becoming the biggest boys at primary school, you immediately became the smallest boys at secondary school. This could lead to a more violent form of bullying if you didn't learn either to avoid trouble or to fight your way out of it. I suppose it's all part of the learning curve which helps you to deal with the wider world later.

My mum had told me to walk away from trouble and not get involved in fights. If you ran away, you would be showing fear and that would encourage the bullies. Granddad Cleworth had taught me what to do with my fists so I was able to fight if cornered.

Queen Street School, or Queenies as it was known, later became Philips Park Secondary Modern School. I can't remember taking an 11-plus examination or even whether they existed in 1952, but there was no possibility of a dunce like me passing any exams. John Hobby was our headmaster, and he was a man who could strike fear into his pupils with a withering stare. When that didn't work, you got hit with a leather strap across the palm of your non-writing hand.

The first shock I got on my first day there was when they read out the class register. By this time I'd got used to being called Piddington, despite my wish to be a Cleworth like the rest of the family. But when the teacher called out 'Piddington, W.', two of us stood up. The teacher asked which of us was called W. Piddington and we both answered, 'Me, sir' simultaneously.

The mystery was solved when it turned out that Wilfred Piddington was the brother of my late father, William Piddington. As was common in those days, he'd named his son after himself like mine had done. So Wilf Piddington and I were cousins. He lived in Gibbon Street, Bradford, about 300 yards away from me. We'd never met nor known of each other's existence.

If that seems strange to you, it seems odd to me now as I look back. I can only imagine my mum and her parents hadn't wanted to upset me with news of the death of my natural dad. Then, as time went by, they didn't want to unsettle me by introducing his relatives. So many dads had gone off to war and never returned, for a variety of reasons, that lots of families chose not to talk about it. They just got on with their lives and buried the past.

Death was a taboo subject in our family. I remember Granddad Cleworth had a black-and-white mongrel dog called Teddy. The dog idolised him – apart from those times when Granddad took him to the canal with soap and a scrubbing brush to clean him. He'd throw Teddy in the canal, soap and scrub him when he came out, then throw him back in to rinse off. Teddy hated being washed but loved Granddad.

One day I asked Granddad Cleworth where Teddy was.

He replied, 'Dead.'

I asked what he meant.

He just repeated, 'Dead' and I knew not to ask any more.

In the same way I sensed I shouldn't ask about the father killed in the war. Wilf and I became best pals at school, but we never discussed Bill Piddington Senior, my late father and his late uncle. Years later we visited his grave in a military cemetery in Holland, but that's a story for another chapter.

The change of school didn't change my academic progress. I was still slow to learn subjects in which I had no interest. I was average at English and learned to read OK but my handwriting was appalling. There were always blots and smudges over my work. This confirmed the general opinion of the teachers that I was a hopeless case, wasting my time and theirs. I still enjoyed history and art, and engineering drawing was fun once I'd got the hang of it, but maths remained a mystery to me. Counting past ten with my shoes on was quite a struggle.

I fancied myself at woodwork, but that proved to be another disaster. I told Grannie Smith we were all making photo frames and I'd make one for her. She gave me 9d (4p) for the materials. When mine was finished, it looked such a mess the teacher binned it. I didn't want to disappoint Grannie Smith, so I had a brainwave. I used 9d of my pocket money to buy a decent frame made by my classmate, Graham Smith. It took pride of place on the mantelpiece with a family photo inside it.

I used to blush with embarrassment when Grannie Smith pointed it out to family and neighbours, announcing with great pride, 'Our Bill made that.' She went to her grave believing that lie and it's only now I've had the courage to confess.

In the early days at Queenies I was still a member of The Songsters, a mixed choral group. Stan Ball organised the bookings and transport to venues. Bill Verity, who played piano, accompanied us. His daughter Jean went to the same school as me and sang in the cathedral choir. Mr Verity bought me a harmonica to replace my lost mouth organ.

With overcrowded houses and no televisions, we spent our time doing chores, earning money where we could, playing sports and joining clubs. I played soccer occasionally, but wasn't much good at it. I was a bit like a charging bull – plenty of speed and power but no finesse. They stuck me in goal where I could do least damage.

Some boys joined the cubs and scouts, the army and sea cadets or took up sporting activities. I joined a mixed youth club attached to the Ebenezer Methodist Church on Princess Street, Bradford. I also joined the Lads' Brigade at St Paul's Church, Philips Park, when I was twelve or thirteen. I'd tried to join the brigade at Christ Church, Beswick, but was turned down, probably for looking too scruffy. I absolutely loved the music and fun at the Church Lads' Brigade. It had nothing to do with religion. I'd been to Sunday school and sung in the choir but by then I was lapsed C of E.

I learned to play side drum and bugle (not simultaneously, you understand). We had rehearsals on Thursday nights at the church hall opposite a croft. We played football outside on fine nights before and after band practice. On wet nights, when the adults weren't around, we'd play indoors.

There were anything between twelve and twenty of us in the band. I remember there was my cousin Wilf, Ian Ball, Frank and Derek Young, Billy Taylor, Dave Dutton, Len Harris and a mate called Derek Wren. Derek had been born with a twisted foot and had his leg amputated at the knee. They gave him a pot leg and Derek did everything the rest of us could do. He played in goal at football and you certainly knew about it if he crashed into you with that pot leg.

The band was run by Bill Reece, whose son Billy was also a member. Normally we marched as an all-male group, but for special occasions, like the Whit Walks, we'd link up with the Church Girls' Brigade. Whit Walk processions were a big thing in those days. People would line the pavements waving flags as we marched proudly by. They had one day for Anglicans and another one for Catholics. There was also a separate walk at Whitsun for the Italians, who had a large contingent living in Ancoats, near where I was born. The Italians were very popular because they knew how to make the best ice cream.

I used to love taking part in the Whit Monday parade through our streets. The only thing I dreaded was the sight of Grannie Smith, who'd come to watch us go by. She'd be in her Sunday best, but would overdo the celebration and turn up the worse for wear. She would wave a flag. I tried to pretend I hadn't seen her by looking at the feet of the marcher in front of me. But Grannie Smith would shout, 'Cock your lily up, our Bill.' It meant keep your chin up. I had to nod and smile at her to the giggles of my mates.

In the midst of this hectic social scene, my schoolwork and my chores, I used to earn a few shillings at weekends by helping out at the local market in Grey Mare Lane. A fairman called John Seldon had a kiddies' carousel, which I helped to put up for him. If light bulbs needed replacing, I'd go and get them. As I got older and bigger, I'd turn the wheel by hand for him. He'd give me about three bob (15p), which I'd pass on to my mum. She'd give me a tanner (2½p) back to spend on sweets, comics or the pictures.

This was my bit for the family income. I'd tried doing a paper round but it lasted only one day. A lot of customers didn't get the newspapers they'd ordered and others got papers they'd never asked for. So, at the age of eleven, I was sacked for the first – but by no means the last – time.

During school holidays, I'd also help out Mr Seldon at Conran Street Market, just off Rochdale Road, and at Ashton Market. It's a chilling thought that a few years later the notorious Moors murderers, Ian Brady and Myra Hindley, would hang around these self-same markets looking for potential victims.

They lived at addresses within a mile of me in the Gorton district of Manchester. They'd moved from Gorton by the time they were captured and tried for torturing and killing innocent children they'd abducted and buried on Saddleworth Moor. At the time of their arrest in October 1965, Brady and Hindley shared a council house at 16 Wardle Brook Avenue, Hattersley, near Hyde. It was there they killed their last victim, a 17-year-old lad called Edward Evans. By then I was working as an asphalter and had helped to build a tower block of flats in Hattersley which overlooked the murder scene.

When the gruesome story emerged, it caused both anger and shame in our neighbourhood. We were angry at what had been done to those poor, innocent kids. And we felt ashamed that the people who had done such dreadful deeds had come from within our own community. Brady had originated from Scotland but he'd lived at various addresses in Gorton and Longsight for several years. Hindley was a local girl. What they did was beyond belief. I remember the tears rolling down my cheeks when I read in the newspapers how they'd made tape recordings while they tortured their victims. Like the vast majority of people, I wished we'd never got rid of hanging so they could have paid for their crimes with their lives.

At the time I was doing odd jobs in the market like a lot of my young mates, among them Billy Taylor, Ian Ball and Tommy Jones; it was assumed we were perfectly safe. Kids played out all day long without any supervision. We'd never heard of paedophiles.

Although I went to a mixed school where certain romances blossomed, I was a bit shy with girls. Some of my classmates would be spotted holding hands from time to time and teased mercilessly. I must have been a slow starter.

Then, one Tuesday night, as my fifteenth birthday was approaching, I saw a lovely girl at the youth club. She was fourteen years old, tall and slim with brown hair in a shoulder-length bob. She had blue-grey eyes and the most beautiful smile. As I stood admiring her, she asked if I fancied a game of table tennis.

I was a decent player and she was a girl, younger than me, so I thought I might have to take it easy on her – far from it.

She was a terrific player and absolutely battered me. So much for my chance to impress, but at least it got us talking. Her name was Alma Short and it turned out her elder sister Beryl was at the same school as me. Alma was one of the few bright sparks from our area who'd passed her 11-plus and went to Ducie Avenue Technical School in nearby Moss Side.

I didn't think she'd want anything to do with a blockhead like me, but I plucked up the courage to ask when I might see her again. There was a dance the following Monday at St Paul's church hall. When Alma agreed to go, I was on cloud nine. As she left that night, she said, 'By the way, call me Ali. Everyone else does.' And that was the start of a love affair that's lasted more than fifty years.

It didn't get off to the most promising of starts, though. Ali came to the dance with her pal, Barbara Ryder. I was sitting with a group of other girls I knew, feeling shy and embarrassed. After a while, Ali came over, kicked me on the shin, and said, 'Are you dancing with me or what?'

The music was provided by an old wind-up record player, and I think it was a barn dance. I managed to stumble my way through it. Afterwards, Ali and I chatted the night away. Until then I'd always felt more comfortable with my mates than with girls, but talking to Ali was different. I'd been afraid that with her being clever and me being a thicko, we'd have nothing in common, but we got on like a house on fire.

From that night on we'd keep meeting at church dances. Sometimes it was St Paul's; sometimes it was the Ebenezer Methodists; and sometimes it was a church which Ali's pal Barbara attended. One night, at the end of the dance at Ebenezers, we went outside and found it had been snowing.

People were chucking snowballs at each other, so Ali and I joined in. At one stage I was trying to put snow down the back of her neck as she tried to escape. We slipped and both finished up rolling in the snow. It was one of those moments when you wonder whether you've gone too far and blown it, but Ali was laughing her head off and I knew I'd found my soulmate.

This was confirmed a few weeks later when there was an incident during another dance at the church hall. There was rarely any trouble at these dances, but it flared up one night while I was there with Ali, cousin Wilf and some other pals.

One of the lads had punched a girl, which was totally out of order. Another lad called Chris had biffed him. As the lad who hit the girl went away with his tail between his legs, he threatened to bring some mates back from a nearby club. I didn't believe him and said we weren't scared. An hour later this lad returned with about fifteen or twenty mates. I told my pals they didn't need to stay because this was my problem. To my horror, instead of saying, 'We're with you, Bill,' they thanked me and ran off. That left just Wilf, me and Ali. I told her to go home but she wouldn't.

The mob approached and said, 'Who's Piddy?'

Once again Wilf and I answered simultaneously, 'I am.'

Then, in a moment of mad bravado, Wilf said, 'Your mate hit a girl. He got what he deserved. If you're going to do anything about it, do it now.'

My heart was in my mouth because we were in for a good hiding, but this other gang had a brief discussion and wandered off. Ali and I walked away hand in hand.

In those days, a real date was when you paid to take a girl

somewhere and she then became your girlfriend. My first date with Ali was a romantic occasion. I took her to watch the Belle Vue Aces' speedway team! Unknown to Ali, I'd got free tickets from Grannie Smith, who worked in the canteen. That was in the days of speedway legends like Peter Craven, Jack Parker and Louis Lawson, who attracted huge crowds. We had to leave before the races ended because Ali was under strict instructions from her dad to be home by 9 p.m. So I walked her to the bus stop and we had our first kiss.

Ali's family had moved four miles away to Failsworth, between Manchester and Oldham, when she was twelve. Luckily for me she still came back to the church youth club in Bradford to keep in touch with her friends.

Ali's parents, George and Alice Short, had had six children, but their eldest, Jean, died young before I knew the family. Ali's surviving sisters were Mavis, Beryl and Margaret, and they had a brother, Norman. Ali's father was a baker, who used to make birthday cakes at home.

As our courtship began, I reached fifteen and left school. I remember seeing girls weeping on that final day. They were hugging each other as if they were grief-stricken. I was over-joyed. I finished school on the Friday and started work the following Monday.

CHAPTER 4

The Boy from the Blackstuff

My dad, Bob Cleworth, was a master asphalt spreader. He worked for a firm called Limmer and Trinidad, who had offices in Pottery Lane, Gorton. Like many fathers of his day, he saw it as one of his duties to make sure his sons found work. This often meant boys followed in their father's footsteps, and that's what happened to me.

Although I'd been pretty hopeless at school, I was never lazy or workshy – it wasn't an option in our house. As soon as I became a teenager, my big ambition was to leave school and start earning a living. Thoughts of a career as a singer lay in the distant future. The idea of becoming an actor never occurred to me.

When Dad told me he could get me a trial as an apprentice asphalter, I was chuffed to bits. I wasn't afraid of hard work or early starts. Besides, what else could I do? I'd met some of the men I'd be working with when they called on

Dad. I couldn't wait to join the grown-ups in a proper full-time job.

The work could be anywhere within a 70-mile radius of Manchester and we started at 8 a.m. It was our responsibility to get there on time. This could involve getting up at 5 a.m. and catching a series of trains or buses. My foreman was a man called Roy Burtoft. He was a distant relative.

On my first day he asked me if I knew his name.

I said, 'You're Uncle Roy.'

He said, 'No, I'm not. I'm Burtoft the Bastard and don't you forget it.'

He'd been a physical training instructor in the army so he wasn't a man anybody crossed.

Another member of our asphalting team was my mum's brother, Jim Smith.

He said, 'Hello, Billy boy. So you've joined the lunatics.'

Uncle Roy had a powerful Norton Dominator motorbike. He could take a pillion passenger clinging on behind him and he had the chassis of a sidecar attached to the machine. This consisted of planks of wood on the floor and a metal frame. The sidecar was often my lift to work in places like Sheffield and York. We had no helmets in those days, so I used to cling on as if my life depended on it – and it did!

I saw Uncle Roy smile only once. I'd been working with him for a couple of years and we were doing a job at a new housing estate in Little Hulton, near Bolton. I'd caught at least two buses to get to the site by 7.45 one morning. The minute I arrived, Roy asked if it was true I played the silver drum for the Church Lads' Brigade.

'Yes,' I said.

'And you're a soloist with the 1st Battalion?'

'Yes, I am.'

'Why didn't you tell me?' he demanded to know.

I explained that the subject of the Church Lads' Brigade hadn't come up at work. He then told me for the first time that he was an officer with another battalion and he was short of a drummer for that afternoon. Roy told me to go home, put on my kit, pick up my drum and be at a church in Droylsden for a 1.30 p.m. performance. It was clearly not up for discussion, so I caught a series of buses back home.

For parades I used to wear a suit with a white shoulder sash leading to a bag on my hip and matching white gloves. When I told my mum what had happened, she looked embarrassed. Then she told me that because Dad had been working away, she'd run out of money. She'd had to pawn my suit at Morris's on the corner of Mill Street and Ashton New Road to raise the cash for food until Dad came home.

I managed to find a double-breasted jacket, a clean pair of jeans, a shirt and a tie among my clothes. Then I picked up my drum and caught the bus to Droylsden to face Uncle Roy. When he saw the state of me, Roy looked me up and down and asked what had happened to my suit. I told him the story and he just nodded. Then he said, 'You're the soloist. You'd better be good.'

The parade went pretty well and afterwards I was talking to the band members when Roy approached. He said, 'Thanks,' and I thought I spotted the flicker of a smile. It might have been wind. From a tough taskmaster like Uncle Roy, this was the highest praise.

On the site, three or four of us would work together,

preparing and laying asphalt on the floors or roofs of houses. The potman would mix the ingredients – solid blocks of bitumen, sand and a special form of grit – in an iron pan. Then the asphalt would be run over the prepared surface.

My dad's labourer was a guy called Pete Tennant. He was built like a cross between Garth and Superman – a modern-day Schwarzenegger. Those buckets weighed forty about pounds before the hot asphalt was poured in. You needed tremendous strength to carry them up a ladder on to a roof. We had great respect for our labourers. They were as tough as old boots and fit as butchers' dogs. It was a sight to see them walking with a full bucket in each hand. They had a way of swaying as they walked so the molten asphalt didn't spill. A lot of young recruits weren't strong enough and had to give up.

The work was hard but we had our fun moments too. I remember Pete's party piece was to get a whole orange inside his mouth without breaking the skin. Don't try this at home, kids, because on one occasion he got it stuck and we all had to tear chunks of it out from between his teeth to stop him from choking. Uncle Roy could walk across roofs on his hands without any ladders. I don't think anybody gave a thought to health and safety in those days.

At the start, my job was to brew up, go to the chippie for the lunches and generally make myself useful. It didn't always go according to plan. I remember once dropping a bag of egg custards I'd brought from a baker's shop. The men ate the custards anyway, but I had the cost deducted from my wages. I was soon learning how life could be unfair.

Once Roy Burtoft sent me from Cheetham Hill about three miles to our yard in Gorton for some paraffin wax. I had to go on a rickety old bike. Mr Taylor, the storeman, said they had no wax left so he gave me a tin of paraffin instead. I wobbled back to the site on my bike through pouring rain. I explained what Mr Taylor had said but Roy wasn't having any of it. He said the paraffin was no use and neither was I. During the row that followed, the tin of paraffin slipped from my hands on to the asphalt which they'd just laid.

When I saw the expression on Roy's face, I decided I'd best make a speedy exit. As I ran away, he threw my toolbag after me. Cliff Sheffield, our asphalt machine operator, saw Roy's face too and shouted, 'Keep running.' My dad had been working thirty miles away in Sheffield but he'd heard what happened along the grapevine before he got home. He told me, 'You're an idiot.'

It was another six months before I could work there again. Fortunately, I got fixed up with another gang. Between Uncle Roy and my dad, brothers called Dick and Harry Palmer, and a potman called Georgie Clowe, they knocked me into shape.

On Thursdays I used to go to building school in Ancoats. It was a day release for apprentices in the building trades. There were brickies (bricklayers), chippies (joiners), sparks (electricians), painters and decorators, plasterers, plumbers and asphalters like me. Later we moved to St John's Technical College near the Granada TV studios in central Manchester, and I carried on studying at night school.

I was still a slow learner in the classroom, where they'd teach about quantities and dimensions, but I was learning the hard way during the rest of the week. Many's the time Uncle

Roy or my dad would order me to rip up the asphalt I'd laid because it wasn't neat enough. Sometimes I'd do it three, four or even five times before it came up to Roy's high standards. I used to resent the constant criticism.

At the age of eighteen I was named Best Apprentice in the North and gained my City & Guilds certificate as an asphalter. I thought I might burst with pride, and realised how all the carping by my older workmates had been for my own good and had finally paid off. It seemed they'd turned me into a decent asphalter. I was working 5½-day weeks with Saturday afternoons and Sundays off.

At the same time, I was courting my girlfriend, Ali Short. You needed money to take a girl out, and I never seemed to have much of it, but Ali didn't appear to mind. That's what I loved about her: she was happy just to walk around the park holding hands and chatting.

Grannie Smith was still supplying free tickets for the speedway. She also got me passes for the wrestling and the boxing at King's Hall, Belle Vue. Ali wasn't interested so I'd go to the wrestling with my dad and we'd watch the stars of the day, such as Cowboy Jack Cassidy, Kendo Nagasaki, Jackie Pallo and Mick McManus.

I don't think Cowboy Jack had ever been to the United States or ridden a horse. Wrestling was all baloney but great fun. Kendo Nagasaki was a masked wrestler, apparently from Japan, but if you checked the local newspapers he'd be appearing at eight different venues hundreds of miles apart on any given night. Jackie Pallo wore his wavy blond hair in a ponytail, which was a bit daring in those days. And Mick McManus was billed as 'the man you love to hate'. I got the shock of my life one night when I booed him on his way to the ring. He turned and booed back right in my face.

The boxing was more serious and I remember watching Billy Walker, a good-looking heavyweight from London known as 'The Blond Bomber'. He knocked his opponent out with a right hook that lifted him two feet off the canvas.

Ali preferred the pictures. We'd go to watch the films of the day at the Popular, near her home in Failsworth, or at the Roxy, nearby in Hollinwood. If Ali visited me, we'd go to the New Royal or the Mosley in Beswick. Apart from being close to Ali's home, the Popular also had the advantage of being lit by gaslights. We'd go to the back row and turn the light right down so we could have a kiss and cuddle.

Some nights Ali would catch the bus and meet me in Bradford, where she still had friends, and sometimes I would get the bus up to Failsworth. Sometimes, to save money, I'd run the four miles up Oldham Road. That's how I came to have another set of friends in the Failworth area as well as my old pals in Bradford, Beswick and Gorton. One of my new Failsworth pals was Dave Bailey. His dad, Bill Bailey, played piano in the Church pub next to the Popular cinema.

Officially you weren't allowed to drink alcohol until you were eighteen, but the age limit has always been a challenge to growing lads. I'd been introduced to the odd mouthful of beer by Granddad Cleworth as a little boy, but my first real taste of beer was provided by a mate when I was fourteen. At that age I couldn't have got away with being served in a pub.

By the time I was sixteen, with a bit of stubble on my chin, I could just about pass for an eighteen-year-old. So I started drinking pints of bitter in the Church. They cost about a shilling (5p) in those days. If I were taking Ali to the pictures, she'd wait outside while I had a swift one with Dave Bailey and my other mates.

Because Ali's dad knew I drank, she'd added a year to my age. So it came as a shock to George when he bought me a pint for my birthday. As he wished me a happy nineteenth, I told him it was my eighteenth. 'But you've been drinking for a year,' he said. George, Alice and all their children were brought up to stick to the letter of the law. Drinking under age was against the law so they just didn't do it.

George didn't hold my unlawful behaviour against me. He's dead now but I've kept his memory alive by giving one of his mannerisms to Jack Duckworth. When George was concentrating, he used to do a combination of singing and whistling at the same time. I started to do it as Jack. Now I've got Alan Halsall, who plays Tyrone Dobbs, doing it too.

I guess many people's singing careers began in the church as choirboys and girls. The second phase of mine began at the Church in Failsworth, where I was drinking under age and anything but a choirboy. My membership of The Songsters had fizzled out when I started work at fifteen but I was still banging the drum and blowing the bugle for the Church Lads' Brigade until I was twenty-four. It was in the Church, however, that my great love of singing developed.

Bill Bailey would organise a group of us into a male voice choir. Although I had a deep gravelly speaking voice by then, I was a tenor when I sang. Bill showed us how to harmonise among the tenors, baritones and basses and he often drew magical sounds from this rough, tough bunch of working-class lads.

Occasionally I'd sing solos, such as 'I've Got You Under My Skin' by Frank Sinatra and 'Moon River' by Danny Williams. I also sang 'A Certain Smile' by one of my idols, Johnny Mathis. Many years later I played golf with him. Can you imagine how amazing that seemed at the time? As a matter of fact, it still seems amazing now.

Encouraged by my success at the Church, where I'd received some enthusiastic applause for my efforts, I decided to try for a career as a pub singer. I'd heard they were holding auditions at the Bradford Miners' Club in Grey Mare Lane one Sunday afternoon. It was a chance to showcase your talent in front of pub landlords and club secretaries who booked acts.

Unfortunately, because I was unknown, they put me on last. I'd had a couple of pints to steady my nerves, but as the afternoon wore on I was getting more and more drunk. By the time I wobbled on to the stage and tried to sing 'More' by Bobby Darin, I was as pissed as a newt. The audience clearly decided they'd have preferred less. I was emptying the place, and when I'd finished the booking agents weren't interested. So that was the end of the second stage of my singing career.

Who could have guessed that later I would earn two gold discs for albums which each sold more than 100,000 copies? And guess what else? 'More' was on one of those CDs.

Despite the disappointment, at least I had a pretty shoulder to cry on, because Ali always had faith in me. My mum loved me dearly as only a mother can, but she could never understand what Ali saw in me.

Ali was clever and beautiful, and always looked smart,

whereas I was a thick, scruffy bugger who spent half his days covered in muck. We must have looked like Lady and the Tramp when we stepped out, with her in a suit, hat and gloves, and me trying to make the best of clothes I was always growing out of. Sometimes I'd meet her from work, covered in sweat with holes in my jeans, a scruffy toolbag slung over my shoulder and stinking of asphalt. Ali would insist on holding my hand as we walked through the city centre. I was embarrassed, but she was proud to be my girlfriend, even if I was dirty, scruffy and smelly.

It was another miracle that Ali's parents, George and Alice, allowed our relationship to grow. They must have been hoping for someone better than me for their daughter. If they did feel that way, they never showed it. Perhaps they realised we were teenagers in love, and had the common sense to trust their bright, lovely daughter to know what she was doing.

By the time I was eighteen, in 1959, we'd been dating for three years and had started talking about getting married. I wanted to do things properly so I asked Mr Short if he would do me the honour of giving me his daughter's hand in marriage. I was a bag of nerves, but he and Alice said they were very pleased and couldn't have made me feel more welcome to their family.

Ali's sister Mavis had a gift catalogue, and I ordered a diamond engagement ring costing £17, which I paid for in weekly instalments. It was the smallest solitaire you've ever seen, and would just about glint if you caught the light at the right angle. But Ali was so proud as she put it on the third finger of her left hand that she made me feel like a king. We knew we'd have to wait a few more years for the wedding but we were on our way.

Another big development in my life at that time occurred when Mum and Dad were finally told they were going to be re-housed. They'd been on the council waiting list for donkey's years. Finally Butterworth Street had been condemned under the slum clearance scheme and they were given the keys to a council house at 16 Deepdale Avenue, just off Mauldeth Road, Withington. It was only a three-bedroomed semi but it seemed like a palace to us. It had an inside bathroom and toilet, with gardens at the front and back, and hot running water. My brother Robert and I still had to share a bedroom, but at least we had separate beds.

Back in Butterworth Street, Dad had bought an old second-hand TV set. It was black-and-white with a 12-inch screen. The horizontal hold was always slipping, but Dad knew just where to bang it with his fist. In our new home, we had a rented telly which didn't need any of Dad's attention. We used to sit round watching it in our big posh front room. Just before Christmas 1960, a new twice-weekly drama series came out and soon everyone was talking about it. I wonder if you can guess the title?

Our families were among *Coronation Street*'s fans as we watched the lives of Jack and Annie Walker at the Rovers Return, where Ena Sharples, Martha Longhurst and Minnie Caldwell held court in the Snug, among other regulars such as the Barlows, old Albert Tatlock and single mum Elsie Tanner. It never occurred to me for a moment that I'd be rubbing shoulders with them one day as a *Coronation Street* regular myself.

Our wedding day was set for 17 March 1962 at the Ebenezer Methodist Church in Bradford, Manchester, where Ali was a lifelong member. Two days before the wedding, Terry Whitelegg and John Pearson took me out for my stag night. It was traditional to go out for your last night as a bachelor on the night before you got married but I wasn't taking any chances – a good job too.

We started off at the Church in Failsworth, where I drank a few pints of bitter with all my mates. I'm sure someone must have spiked one of my drinks. I could normally hold my beer quite well, but when we left the pub to head for the bright lights of Manchester, my head started spinning as soon as I breathed the fresh air. Terry and John managed to get me on to the bus with them, but when we got into the city centre, none of the doormen would let me in. I could hardly speak or stand.

They got me back home to Withington and somehow I managed to get to work at a job eight miles away in Irlam on the Friday morning. I was working on a roof fifty feet up and still feeling the effects of the night before. Within a couple of hours I'd dropped two trowels off the roof and then a wooden float used for levelling. The chargehand, Dick Palmer, must have decided I could be next to fall. He suggested I go home and get to bed.

After catching the wrong bus, I finally got back to Withington at 3 p.m. Mum gave me a cheese butty and a cup of tea and packed me off to bed. The following morning, I woke up early feeling fine and thanking my lucky stars that I'd had my stag night a day early.

Ali's younger brother, Norman Short, was my best man.

We were picked up and dropped off at the church in a car driven by Malcolm Wiltshire, the husband of Ali's sister Beryl. I was wearing my only suit, which was lovat green, and a pair of fashionable soft leather black slip-on shoes. They were scuffed across the toes where Terry and John had dragged me home on the Thursday night.

Ali arrived by limo and walked down the aisle on her father's arm in a traditional white wedding dress. She looked just like a princess. The bridesmaids were my sisters Anne and Linda, Ali's sister Margaret, her cousin Pauline and her best pal, Barbara Ryder. To add a bit of comedy to this scene, Ali's nephews, Stephen and Paul, and my baby brother, Alan, were dressed in satin sailor suits.

Terry had volunteered his services as official photographer, and took two rolls of film with his brand-new state-of-the-art camera. The colour film had to be sent off to Germany for processing. It was supposed to take two weeks, but we're still waiting for it to come back. Luckily, one of Ali's teachers turned up and took two or three shots or we'd never have had any wedding day souvenirs. A few weeks later we all put on the same clothes for a re-enactment of our special day.

The reception was held at the church hall which held the youth club where Ali and I first met. Ali's parents did the catering, and George made a magnificent four-tiered wedding cake for us. It was a terrific spread and Norman made a lovely speech. The only thing lacking was booze. Because it was a Methodist church, they didn't approve of drinking. The lack of booze didn't seem to bother many of Ali's relatives and friends, but I noticed my family and friends kept

49

disappearing from time to time. It may just have been a coincidence there was a pub 100 yards away.

You may have read in some wedding reports that the bride and groom left for their honeymoon at an undisclosed destination. It usually meant that to prevent any practical jokes they didn't want people to know where they were going. In our case, we left for an undisclosed destination because *we* didn't know where we were going. We'd decided to spend our wedding night up in the Lake District but hadn't made a booking.

The plan was for Norman to drive us and his girlfriend up to the Lakes in his old black Wolseley and we'd choose somewhere once we got there. When it got dark, I told him to stop in the next village. The four of us went into a fish and chip shop and I spotted a police sergeant outside. I told him we'd just got married and were looking for a place to stay. He pointed to a house across the road, where he told us a lady did bed and breakfast. If we mentioned his name, she'd look after us.

So that's what we did. We rented three rooms for the night and left straight after breakfast. To this day, none of us knows the name of the village where Ali and I spent our wedding night. Ali fretted on the way back because she'd left her nightie under the pillow. When we got back to our new home as Mr and Mrs Piddington, I had 7s 6d (37p) left in my pocket.

George and Alice had converted a room in their four-storey Victorian terraced home at 495 Oldham Road, Failsworth, into a bedsitter for us. It was quite roomy, with a double bed, three-piece suite, a tallboy and a telly. We shared the bathroom and kitchen with the rest of Ali's family, but compared to what I'd been used to, it was sheer luxury.

CHAPTER 5

New Career; New Name; New Baby

After our one-night honeymoon, Ali and I went straight back to work. She was employed as a secretary at Jack Chadwick's, a textile wholesaler, with offices in Brazil Street in the centre of Manchester. I returned to asphalting, but my days at Limmer and Trinidad were numbered.

I'd fallen foul of a supervisor called Mr Skelly, who'd deducted money from my wages for being late for work. I felt he had it in for me. One day he came on site and went to the top of a ladder to talk to one of the other lads. I pushed the ladder away from the wall with him stuck at the top of it like a cat up a tree. His fate was in my hands.

I shouted up at him, 'What now, Skelly? What now?' He went as white as a sheet.

My dad shouted, 'Leave it, Bill.' He thought I was going to kill him.

After a few dramatic seconds, I pushed the ladder back

against the wall so he could climb down. Unknown to Skelly and my dad, who thought I'd gone mad, I'd lined up a better-paid job with Wimpey, the builders. This had just been a chance to show the boss what I thought of him before I left – and to scare the crap out of him at the same time.

Working as an asphalter for Wimpey took me further afield to Yorkshire and Birmingham. But one Sunday we were helping to build a 14-storey block of flats in Spotland Road, Rochdale, which Ali could reach in her car.

All the rest of the lads used to go for a pie and a pint at lunchtime, but Ali drove out six miles with a plated roast dinner and all the trimmings for me. I put it on top of the asphalt machine to keep warm. She'd also make sandwiches for me to take to work. They'd have three different fillings and each one was individually wrapped.

Ali brought me the prettiest teacup with a floral pattern. You can imagine how the others used to take the piss out of me unmercifully over my girlie cup. Whenever I let it out of my sight, it got 'accidentally' smashed to pieces. I kept telling Ali there'd been an accident and she kept replacing the cup with a pretty new one. I hadn't the heart to tell her a plain mug would stand a better chance of surviving.

Ali was a wonderful cook. The truth is that my dear mother wasn't a hard act to follow. She had a talent for serving food that was raw on the inside and burned on the outside. Mum had lots of good points, but cooking wasn't one of them. My dad used to come back from the pub, mix all the food together on his plate, shower it with pepper, sneeze, then smother it in sauce to disguise the taste. He'd tuck into it and say, 'Just the job, love.'

Now I was getting food I'd never seen before, like thick pork chops with kidney, and fillet steak. My pretty young wife was spoiling me rotten.

I still enjoyed singing in pubs. I was paid in pints rather than cash at the start. Then, one day, the entertainment secretary of a club in Salford heard me sing and asked if he could book me. He was offering me 7s 6d (37p). It was to be my first professional appearance!

After I'd pretended to consult my diary to see what night I might be free, a date was fixed. Six of us went that night. Apart from me and Ali, there was Terry Whitelegg and his girlfriend, and Bob Tracey and his girl Pam. They'd come to give me moral support.

The first setback came when the pianist asked if I'd brought any music. No. Then he asked what songs I was going to sing. I thought I'd do five or six, but they wanted six for my first spot and eight for my second. I went away to write down the songs I thought I knew on the back of a Park Drive fag packet. The pianist didn't seem too impressed. Did I know what key I sang in? No. I invited him to pick a key and I'd find him somewhere along the way.

Needless to say, despite the loud applause from five members of the audience, I went down like a lead balloon. At the end, I joined them for a drink and the secretary slammed 7s 6d on our table and issued the old rejoinder, 'Don't ring us. We'll ring you.'

A lesser man might have taken the hint and given up – not me. Ali had huge faith in my voice so I went back to singing for drinks to get more experience and learn some more songs. I used to swap pints with a guy called Doug Worsley in the Church at Failsworth. Doug was an international ten-pin bowler and a salesman for Granada TV. He had a shop in Oldham and would get me to stand outside watching the new colour TV sets in the afternoons. A curious crowd would gather round me and I'd say, 'I can't believe how cheap these are. I'm paying the same rental for my black-and-white set.' This would get him two or three new customers a time.

It was Doug who told me about a great trio who were playing at the Stockport County Social Club. The club held regular talent nights with prizes for the winners. The Mike Timoney Three had Mike on an electric accordion, Paul Atherton on guitar and George Walker on drums. They were proper musicians who knew their stuff. A singer called Dave Blakeley was the compère and he was a pro too.

I entered three or four times, singing Sinatra songs, such as 'I've Got You Under My Skin' and 'The Lady Is A Tramp', but there was one man who kept beating me. He was singing a popular song called 'Maria' from *West Side Story*. Whenever I asked if I could sing 'Maria', I was told he'd already picked it and I'd have to sing something else. So one night I got there early and pinched his winning song. The guy arrived with his mum and he was taken aback when they told him he could-n't sing 'Maria'. His mum wasn't just taken aback – she burst into tears. When I was pointed out to them as the man who was going to sing 'Maria', I couldn't have it on my conscience that I'd reduced a sweet lady to tears. I said, 'Let him do it.' So he did. He won. I came second, and there was no prize for coming second.

One of the great things to come out of this lack of success was the friendships I formed with Mike Timoney and Dave

Blakeley. I'd talk to them for hours about arrangements, keys, timing and which songs suited my voice and which didn't. The things I learned from them were invaluable but they didn't pay the gas bills.

To earn money I had to start at the bottom at pubs and work my way up. Doug Worsley told me about a charity night his brother George was organising at Stockport Bus Club. George had heard me sing with Dave Bailey on piano and wanted us to take part. When we got there, I saw the names of all the acts had been chalked on to a blackboard, but there was no Bill Piddington. I checked my diary to make sure I'd come on the right night and then asked the concert secretary why my name was missing. He told me Piddington was too long for the blackboard. He thought he'd give me a name like the American crooner 'Mel Tarmey'. He was referring to Mel Tormé, of course, but there, on the blackboard, was 'Bill Tarmey'. So that's how I got my stage name. We had a good response that night so I've stuck with Bill Tarmey ever since.

But there was far more exciting news on the home front than a name change: Ali had fallen pregnant. It was the most wonderful news. We'd had a spell of looking after her nephews and nieces when they called to see George and Alice. When they returned to their homes, it left a gap in our lives. We realised we wanted kids of our own, but it still came as a pleasant surprise when Ali told me she was expecting.

The baby was going to be born at Oldham District General Hospital. Ali had to go in three weeks early because of complications. The gynaecologist was Patrick Steptoe, later to achieve worldwide fame for creating the first test-tube baby. Now he was having to deal with a baby who wouldn't stay in the right position. As the delivery date got nearer, they realised they'd have to carry out an emergency Caesarian section.

I was working at Mixenden, near Halifax, at the time, ringing in whenever I could for any news. When they told me Ali had had a healthy baby boy on 4 August 1966, I rushed to the hospital, expecting to see my wife sitting up in bed cradling our newborn son. Instead, I found her semiconscious with her legs raised off the bed and no sign of a baby. Ali's stomach was sewn together like an old football. The nurse told me what had happened and I felt sick. I had to leave the room. Later the nurse told Ali what a caring husband I was, thinking that I'd been fighting back tears rather than vomit.

We'd already chosen the names Carl William for a boy. When I saw him I really did shed tears. He looked quite chubby for a baby – nothing like the tuppenny rabbit his father had been. Ali had suffered from a twisted womb, which was why Carl had been in difficulty finding his way out. But he was a beautiful, healthy boy, and after a week or so Ali was fit enough to come home with him.

The house in Failsworth would not be our home for much longer. George and Alice, and their son Norman, had a shop in Clayton, Manchester, selling groceries, greengroceries and hardware. They'd found another one in Kirk Street, Gorton, which they thought we could run for them. There was a house next to the shop so Ali and I would have a place of our own. Ali thought it was a great idea.

My life as an asphalter ended in 1967 at the age of twenty-six. It was time to start my new career as a singing grocer. The shop was called Short's and it was next to the Vale Cottage pub. I'd take a list to buy from the markets, deliver the main stuff to Clayton and bring the rest back to our shop, which Ali ran while looking after our lively baby.

Carl was walking at nine months and at that age he escaped once when the milkman left a gate open. He'd managed to totter over the road to the newsagents opposite before Ali realised he was missing. It was a huge relief when he turned up safe and sound.

Thanks to Mike Timoney's recommendations, I'd had a chance to sing with some top musicians. The Jack Anderson Band and the Pete Boston Band were made up of professionals who played with the Northern Dance Orchestra and the National Radio Orchestra. They were heard regularly on the BBC Light Programme. In their spare time they'd play in these dance bands and I was given a chance to perform with them. It was a great honour to play with musicians who'd also backed top American artists, such as Buddy Greco and my near namesake Mel Tormé, when they toured Britain.

For all the pleasure and experience I was getting, it still wasn't paying the rent. So I found myself back at a Sunday afternoon showcase. This time it was a working men's club in Openshaw, Manchester, and I had nothing to drink before I went on stage – I'd learned my lesson.

It led to two bookings and some advice from Ali. 'Don't just sing the songs you like,' she said. 'Sing something the audience will like. They're the ones who are paying.' So I stopped concentrating on swing and jazz numbers. On Ali's advice, I started incorporating songs by Elvis Presley and Tom

Jones, updating my repertoire in the 1970s with popular new songs like 'Yellow River' and 'Tie A Yellow Ribbon Round The Old Oak Tree'. I still managed to slip in one or two of my personal favourites and that seemed to keep everybody happy.

Dave Blakeley had put my name forward as his deputy compère at the Warren Club in Bredbury, Stockport, where big stars like Tony Bennett would appear. The club manager once asked me if I'd stand in and work the following spotlight on one of his shows. At a pinch I could claim to have worked with Tony Bennett.

The club scene was booming in the Swinging Sixties and I was getting bookings at nightspots throughout the north of England. Soon my diary was full and I was having to turn down work.

Ali was running the shop while I was singing for our supper, but then she had some more good news for me: she was expecting another child. This time it was a beautiful girl.

CHAPTER 6

Singing with the Stars

Sara Anne Piddington was born on 18 March 1970. Once again Ali had to go through the pain of a Caesarian section but our daughter was a lovely healthy little girl.

We had a scare, though, when she was six or seven months old. Carl had been ill with a touch of scarlet fever, so when Sara started crying and her temperature shot up, we thought she was going down with the same thing. Then she came out in a spotty rash and had difficulty with her breathing, so we sent for the doctor. By the time he visited on his rounds a couple of hours later, the rash had disappeared and Sara's breathing had eased. No sooner had he gone than the rash and breathing problems returned.

I took Sara down to the surgery, where the doc said, 'I'm so sorry. I didn't realise it was so serious.' He called an ambulance and Sara was whisked away to Monsall Isolation Hospital for a series of tests. We were allowed to see her only from behind a glass partition in case she was contagious. We were sick with worry. Sara was allowed home after three weeks but she was still listless. It turned out she'd suffered a complication of the measles, and once they'd sorted out her medication she started to recover. In later years she became quite a tomboy, climbing trees, but she always liked to play rough and tumble in pretty girlie dresses.

With a beautiful wife, a son and a daughter and a blossoming career as a singer, I couldn't have been happier. It's always at times like these that life seems to kick you in the teeth. That's what happened to me.

After a couple of years, we'd moved to a bigger shop on the other side of Kirk Street. Then, with Sara on the way, we'd given up the second shop and bought our very first house in the same street. So we'd moved twice without needing a removal van; all we did was transfer the furniture on a trolley.

When I came home from a gig one night in the early hours of the morning, I didn't want to wake our new baby by sliding open the garage door. I left my car parked on the street outside. It was a purple Morris Oxford estate in those days. I crept in quietly at 1.30 a.m. without disturbing Sara and went to sleep.

The next morning I discovered my car had been broken into by thieves. They'd not only nicked my performance suits, shirts, ties and shoes, but they'd also stolen the case containing all the music I'd accumulated over the years, specially arranged for me and written in my key. That music would have had no value to anyone but me. It's also doubtful whether the clothes and shoes would have fitted the thieves unless they dropped lucky. Besides, they were stage suits which would have looked a bit odd in a pub vault. It's more than likely everything finished up in a skip somewhere. But the loss to me was devastating. All they'd left me was a tambourine with three bells on it. I had to cancel my gigs for the next three weeks.

Paul Atherton, guitarist from the Mike Timoney Three, did me a huge favour by writing me ten arrangements so I could start working again. I had to sell all my golf equipment to buy replacement clothes. Then I had to pray that my stand-ins hadn't shone too brightly while I was out of the game. Fortunately, the clubs stood by me in my hour of need and I was able to carry on singing.

I employed three or four agents over the years to get bookings for me. They charged around 10 or 12 per cent. The money was usually paid to them; you got your fees, less the commission, about ten days later. There were some dodgy agents around who would claim they'd got you a booking for £20 when instead they'd negotiated £30. Not only would they fiddle you out of the £10 difference but take the commission as well if you let them. Sometimes it felt like I was walking around with someone's hand in my pocket.

Some clubs had a reputation for taking any opportunity to cut your fees. It happened to me only once, when I was appearing at a pub in the Bardsley area between Oldham and Ashton. I was booked to do two 30-minute spots. My first, where I'd tell a few jokes between songs, overran by ten or fifteen minutes. So I kept my second spot down to twenty-five minutes. They told my agent they'd only pay half the £30 fee because I was five minutes short in my second spot.

What can you do? I wasn't going to sue them for fifteen quid but I made sure I never worked there again, and put the word round to other performers.

Another time I was paid off – but for the best possible reason. I'd been booked to open the show at the Batley Variety Club in Yorkshire. It was a massive venue, which attracted top artists like Shirley Bassey. The night I was due to appear, Engelbert Humperdinck was topping the bill. After I'd been rehearsing with the resident band, playing a Blood, Sweat & Tears number called 'Spinning Wheel', Engelbert's management told the club owners I was too much competition, so they paid me off. It meant I got my fee but didn't have to perform.

During this time I also got a chance to record a song for the Pope! It happened when Pope John Paul II was visiting Britain, and Mike Timoney rang to ask if I could sing a song. It was called 'Il Papa' and had won a competition. Mike had been chosen to arrange the music, and he picked me to sing the words.

During that tour, it seemed to me that every time a photo or film of the Pope was shown, you could hear my recording of 'Il Papa' in the background. If my memory serves me, I got £64 from the BBC for that recording session. I was very pleased to have helped Pope John Paul with his gig. He seemed a charming man and brought a lot of pleasure to many people – not just Catholics.

There were loads of us working the north-west clubs in those days. I shared stages with well-known local comedians, such as Al Showman, Bunny Lewis, Jack Diamond and Jimmy Gordon.

Some of the guys I worked with, such as Bernard Manning, Colin Crompton, George Roper, Jos White and Charlie Williams, went on to become famous nationally through a weekly TV programme called *The Comedians*. They had a resident band called Shep's Banjo Boys. Johnny Hamp produced the show at the Granada TV studios in Manchester. Later there was an offshoot called *The Wheeltappers and Shunters Social Club*, with Colin Crompton hosting it as chairman.

All the stand-up comics, including the black ones like Jos White and Charlie Williams, told racist jokes in those days. It was considered acceptable. There was a sitcom, *Love Thy Neighbour*, starring Jack Smethurst, about black and white families living next door to each other. That, and programmes like *Till Death Us Do Part*, with Warren Mitchell playing loud-mouthed bigot Alf Garnett, wouldn't be tolerated today.

I compèred shows in which up-and-coming stars of the future appeared. There was Les Dawson, Little and Large, Cannon and Ball and The Grumbleweeds. There was also a glamorous singer called Lynne Perrie, who went on to play Ivy Tilsley, later Ivy Brennan, in *Corrie*. She worked in Mike Baldwin's clothing factory.

I compèred a band called Mud at the Horseshoe Club in Ashton one week and they were performing their chart-topping hit 'Tiger Feet' on *Top of the Pops* the next week. Then there were singers with Top Ten hits, such as Dave Berry, Shane Fenton (who became Alvin Stardust), Wayne Fontana, Solomon King and P. J. Proby.

Jim Proby was a wild character who could put away a bottle of bourbon before breakfast. He had a wonderful voice but became more famous for the fact that he once split his tight trousers when he leaned towards fans during a stage performance. You could never relax when Jim was around. He would be slurring and staggering, completely out of it, then go on stage and seem sober for an hour. He had a sensational voice and the audience lapped him up. When he finished, he'd be pissed again. I don't know how he did it. Plenty of practice, I suppose.

It's always surprised me how some people succeed in show business and other artists fail to make the big time. There doesn't seem to be any rhyme or reason to it. Just the luck of the draw, I suppose, and I've been a lucky sod.

I've worked with some remarkable singers who deserved far better than they achieved, like Maggie Cole, Molly Coogan and Nina Brent, who all had fabulous voices. Another was Chris Marlowe. She'd sung with all the local dance bands and we'd performed duets together. I'd worked with her ex-husband, Max Beesley, who was a brilliant drummer and a terrific impersonator. He did an especially good take-off of Marlon Brando in *The Godfather*. He was full of fun and would have the bands he worked with in stitches. Before they parted, Max and Chris had a son, Max Beesley Junior, who now stars in the TV series *Survivors*.

The vocalist Jo Lester was the daughter of musician Art Lester, and she started singing solo with dance bands at fourteen. We were both appearing at the Ritz Dance Hall in Manchester one night with the Jack Kirkland Band and were chatting away when Jack asked me to choose a quickstep for the next number. In my haste, I handed four different numbers to the section leaders and they started playing different songs. I started scat singing to disguise my cock-up until I could mouth, 'Tramp in C' to my confused bandleader. Without a pause, he switched and I was into 'She gets too hungry for dinner at eight . . .' Jo was laughing her head off and I think the audience sensed what had happened because they applauded generously at the end.

There were great male vocalists too. A blind singer guitarist called Billy Hall had a terrific voice and he could play guitar like Clapton. Billy liked to feel the faces and bodies of his friends so he could get a mental picture of them. Afterwards he had a sixth sense of who was in a room with him before they even said a word.

I once asked Billy, who'd been born blind, what he'd like to have done if he could see. He told me he'd like to have seen an elephant, so I arranged for us to call at Belle Vue Zoo so he could 'feel' one.

He also fancied driving a car. There was a croft opposite the club where we worked, so I let Billy have a go in my old Ford Cortina. I let him sit behind the steering wheel, feeling the pedals with his feet, while I sat in the passenger seat. I told him how everything worked and switched on the engine. Then I told him to let the clutch out slowly while pushing gently on the accelerator. Seconds later I was screaming like a schoolgirl as the car shot forward and I was hurled back in my seat. Eventually I managed to knock it out of gear and stop the car with the handbrake. As this was happening, the band was arriving at the club for that night's show. Their faces were a picture as Billy, with his dark glasses and white stick, climbed out of the driver's seat. I nearly wet my pants but Billy said it had been great fun.

David Lane, who married Mary Mudd and was one of The Mudlarks trio, was another fine singer. When The Mudlarks split up, Dave became a soloist and he was a great pal of mine. He died while I was writing this book.

Apart from working with the rich and famous, I also compèred at stag nights where there'd be a men-only audience and half a dozen striptease artistes. It was on these nights you had to have your wits about you to deal with hecklers. They'd come to see women get their kit off so singer-compères like me were given a rough ride.

My job was to keep some semblance of order, sing louder than the audience could talk and then accompany the strippers as they performed. They didn't have tapes in those days, so I had to sing stuff like 'The Girl From Ipanema' to a bossa nova beat while the girls pranced around. Sometimes I'd have to sing an extra verse if they still had their bra and pants on. Then, when they'd finished, I'd go round the stage picking up exotic articles of clothing to take to the dressing rooms. There were plenty of men from the dirty-mac brigade on the front row who'd offer me a fiver for the privilege. They thought I'd got the best job in the world.

With male hecklers, you could come out with a witty insult. Standard responses were: 'Last time I saw a mouth that big it had a hook in it.' Or 'Is that your own brain or are you trying it out for a friend?' The lads would usually take it in good part and try to get the better of you with a funny reply.

The stag night audiences were tame compared to women-only hen nights. They went completely bonkers when male strip nights became popular. The women hecklers came back with unbelievably foul-mouthed insults. It was quite an eye-opener for a well-brought-up young chap like me. Trying to sing while 500 excited women shouted, 'Off, off, off' was quite a challenge. I bet Frank Sinatra and Tony Bennett never had that problem.

I was offered well-paid work on cruise ships, but I always turned it down because it involved weeks at sea away from the family. If I could fill my diary with local work, I'd do so.

Sara must have been about eighteen months old when I started to earn money in the daytime from extra work provided by Granada. My first role on telly was as a newspaper reporter in the *Crown Court* series. I sat there pretending to scribble notes as the witnesses gave evidence.

Calls would come directly to my home in Gorton from Pam, Eric or Suzie in the casting department at Granada TV. They wanted me to be a face in the crowd or sometimes the back of a head in the crowd. *Crown Court* was the most fruitful source for extras. They needed jury members or solicitors or probation officers or prison warders or people in the public gallery. I remember once, when work and money were short, asking if there were any vacancies on *Crown Court*. Eric laughed and said, 'Not for you, Bill. You've played everyone but the judge.'

These were exciting times, as I started to rub shoulders with the TV stars of the day, including those from *Coronation Street*. Most of the extras on *Corrie* were professional entertainers like me. It was like our own private club. The money was OK – about £25 a day in the mid-70s , with an extra £6 if you had to say a few lines.

I soon learned the ropes from the regular extras. It was important to be quiet, pay attention and react to what was going on in the scene. The biggest crime was to stare at the camera. It's surprising how some newcomers made this mistake — they didn't last long. Your own mum might want a clear view of your face on telly but the director certainly didn't.

It was also important not to become over-friendly with the stars. While they were trying to remember their lines, they didn't want anything in the way of chitchat. You may want to tell an actor that you once worked with his brother, but there's a time and place. I just kept my head down and got on with it.

My fellow extras continued to be mates after I gained fame as Jack. I advised any newcomers to follow the lead of the older hands like I did — until I became an old hand myself.

Despite my efforts to keep a low profile, I once earned an icy stare from Doris Speed, the veteran actress who played Rovers' landlady Annie Walker. I was chucking darts at the back of the Rovers during a take when one of my darts bounced off the board and landed near her hand on the bar.

The director yelled, 'Cut.'

I said, 'Sorry, Miss Speed,' as I retrieved the dart.

Doris gave me that withering look and said, 'There are long queues at Aytoun Street these days.' She was referring to the dole office in the centre of Manchester.

It must have been the early 70s when family, neighbours and friends all gathered round the telly to watch my first appearance. I was one of a crowd of extras in the Rovers, and my proud mum shouted out, 'There. That's our Bill's arm there.' Unfortunately, we didn't have a video recorder in those days so there wasn't a chance for those who'd blinked to get a second chance to see my arm.

Slowly I graduated from an arm to a full body. I first appeared behind the bar of the Rovers in 1978. The episode centred on the wedding reception for Alf Roberts and Renee Bradshaw. Alf's friends, Annie Walker and Bet Lynch, were invited to the reception in the Select room. A man was sent from the brewery to help Betty out behind the bar. The man never spoke and wasn't given a name, but it was me.

Then I was given my first speaking part as a taxi driver. Thrusting my head through the door of the Rovers, I shouted, 'Cab for Barlow.' Bill Roache, who's been playing Ken Barlow since God was a boy, said, 'Can you wait five minutes?'

I said, 'Yes,' entered the Rovers and said, 'Pint please, Betty.'

It was never going to win me an Oscar, but I managed to deliver my lines without tripping over the furniture. My mum was over the moon.

Another time I was told to bump into the serving hatch so it dropped and broke the fingers on the hand Ernie Bishop was resting on the bar. Stephen Hancock, who played Ernie, could play piano in real life and wasn't keen to sacrifice his fingers for his art. I suggested that if we left a telephone directory next to his hand, it would absorb the blow without hitting him. After a couple of runs with his hand well out of the way, we went for a take and it looked great. Of course, when Ernie screamed in agony and held his hand in pain, I had a few anxious moments until the director shouted, 'Cut', and Stephen smiled at me.

It was about this time that Betty Driver told me she thought the writers ought to find a part for me. She said, 'You're a natural, Bill.'

Betty's such a nice lady, I wasn't sure whether it was the sort of thing she said to everybody. Either way it was kind of her to say so. It made me think for the very first time about the possibility of a stint in *Corrie*.

Betty had been a top singer before she joined the *Street*. She'd worked as a soloist with the Victor Silvester Orchestra. They were famous for their 'slow, slow, quick, quick, slow' dance numbers on the BBC's Light Programme. Betty had also worked with bands in the United States. I've actually got a song sheet with Betty's face on the front cover. It's called 'I'll Walk Alone', with words by Sammy Cahn and music by Jule Styne, two of the finest writers of the twentieth century, whose songs included 'Three Coins In The Fountain' and 'Let It Snow, Let It Snow, Let It Snow'.

During the long waiting times between shots, when a lot of the extras would be in card schools, I'd ask the floor managers if I could watch the action. I learned to stay out of the actors' sight-lines and picked up the technical jargon they used.

By now telly was my day job and I sang at nights. I'd landed a four-nights-a-week booking as singer-compère at the Condron Club in Salford, run by a businessman called George Williams. The resident trio were John Marsh on keyboards, Billy Hall on guitar and vocals, and my old pal George Walker on the drums. John could play by sight only and was note perfect when the music was in front of him. Billy was a marvellous guitarist and had a terrific voice. He should have gone on to stardom. George was everyone's favourite drummer. We were so popular among our fellow musicians that some of them would come along to watch and listen as we rehearsed. We kept refreshing our repertoire with the latest songs of the day.

The family was well, happy and settled. I was established as a singer and I was earning good money from TV. Something had to go wrong – and it did.

CHAPTER 7

A Matter of Life and Death

For some people, bad luck comes on top of bad luck. In my life it always comes when things seem to be going well. That's how it was in 1976, when I had the four-night booking each week at the Condron Club, with other gigs here and there, and my extra work for Granada TV.

One Monday I went to the club in Salford for rehearsals when I felt a pain in my chest. I thought it was a bit of wind and presumed it would disappear if I burped, but it didn't go away. When I got home, I told Ali I wasn't feeling well and went to bed for an early night. The next day I was still feeling the worse for wear. The pain was still there but I'd got used to it.

The lawn needed mowing, but I hadn't the strength to push the mower because the grass was too long. I'd borrowed a scythe from the band leader Jackie Anderson when I'd seen him to discuss the new arrangement of 'The Look Of Love', and set about my lawn like the Grim Reaper. The blade broke so I drove to the shops to get a new one. When I got back into my car, my left arm just dropped. The pain in my chest was now crippling. I had to sit still in the driver's seat until it passed.

Once I'd made it back home, Ali looked at my ashen face and told me I should send for the doctor. I didn't want to make a fuss over a bad case of indigestion so I said I'd see how I felt after a lie down. At the top of the stairs I felt a sudden rush of nausea and had a bout of projectile vomiting into the toilet. That made me feel a bit better and I thought the problem was solved.

I had a gig that Tuesday night with the Jack Anderson Band at the Well Green Hotel in Hale Barns, Cheshire. Ali wanted me to cancel but I explained that I couldn't because I had the public address system in my car. The show couldn't go on without me.

I didn't know this at the time but Ali asked our next-door neighbour, Dave Livesey, to go with me to make sure I was OK. It was a decision that saved my life. I'd no idea I was the victim of a plot when Dave said he wanted to come and watch me perform. He even offered to drive me in my blue Ford Cortina.

When we arrived, about 7 p.m., Dave carried in the PA system and I discussed the music with Jackie. I wasn't feeling too good, but I thought I'd be able to manage a couple of songs. The show started at 7.45, and I began singing the new arrangement to 'The Look Of Love'. I was in the middle of the song when I suffered a heart attack.

It was just like being punched hard in the chest. Somebody

was taping my performance and you can actually hear the pause when the coronary struck. Somehow I managed to finish the song and stay on my feet but I knew I couldn't continue. Jackie took one look at me and said, 'You look rough. Go home.'

As I was leaving, Dave Blakeley walked through the door. I told him I wasn't feeling well and asked if he'd take over from me. I also asked him if he'd like to finish a pint of beer which I hadn't touched. Dave didn't realise how bad I was, and said jokingly, 'It must be serious if you're leaving a pint, Bill.'

As we walked out of the front door of the hotel, I was violently sick. Dave Livesey was holding me up and I heard a passing customer say to his mate, 'Look at the state of him – eight o'clock and he's pissed already.'

Dave led me to the car, propped me in the passenger seat and drove me at top speed to Wythenshawe Hospital. It was just over the border in Manchester, two miles away. Luckily Dave had grown up in Wythenshawe and knew the quickest way. He carried me in and the next thing I knew I was on a trolley. I remember looking at my watch and thinking that if they gave me a tablet to make me better, I'd have time to get back for the second set at the Well Green.

The rest of that night is a blank. I woke up in the early hours of the morning in a hospital bed in the intensive care unit. I had a drip pumping something into my arm and a TV screen monitoring my heartbeat.

I really thought I was a goner. I was thirty-five years old with a wife and family. All I could think was: 'What a waste.' OK, I smoked and enjoyed the odd pint but I'd always thought of myself as a fit bloke. Now I realised I was at death's door. I'd not recognised the classic symptoms of heart failure and I was paying the price. For forty-eight hours it was touch and go. But, thanks to the skill and care of the doctors and nurses, I pulled through. After eight days I was allowed home and warned to take it easy.

The weight fell off me and I wasn't able to work for eleven months. For six weeks George Williams carried on paying me for four nights' work at the Condron Club. It was a wonderful gesture from a man whose clothing business was in financial trouble.

When I thanked him, he said, 'You're all right, cockaloo. You're a good lad.'

Not long after that, he lost a Ministry of Defence contract to supply raincoats. He lost his business and had to sell the club. I'm sure it was the strain which brought on a stroke. I visited him in hospital afterwards. George couldn't speak so I chatted to him about old times. As I talked, I could see his heart monitor changing its rhythm, so I like to think he could hear me. He died two days later. He was in his sixties.

During my eleven months off work, I had to sign on to claim benefits. It was hard to find work as a club compère in those days. James Anderton, Chief Constable of Greater Manchester, was having a crackdown on pubs and clubs. Any breaches of the licences were being punished ruthlessly and many nightspots went out of business.

They were desperate times for a singer-compère with a heart defect. I remember one day an assistant at the Job Centre was trying to arrange an interview for me to work at an iron foundry. Then a woman I knew told me that Frank

Ford, the compère at the Manchester City Social Club, had just quit. It was the break I was looking for.

I took some tapes of my singing and went to see the manager, Roy Clarke. He was a former City player and a Welsh international with a lilting voice from the valleys, look you now. I'd only been there two minutes when one of my boyhood idols, Bert Trautmann, the former City goalkeeper, walked in. After Roy heard the tapes, he offered me a two-week trial. Then he took me for lunch along with Mike Summerbee and Joe Corrigan, two of Manchester City's England internationals.

I've never been much of a soccer fan. In fact, I'm one of those rare Mancunians who want *both* City and United to do well. But I have to say that by offering me the job of compère at their social club, Manchester City saved my sanity. It came when I was at my lowest ebb.

My family was suffering too. My son Carl was a promising footballer when he was eleven years old. God knows where he got his talent from. He played in goal for Manchester Boys. One day I went to watch him and he was on the substitute's bench. I asked the manager why Carl had been dropped. It was because he wouldn't take goal kicks.

After the game I asked Carl why he'd started handing the job of taking goal kicks to one of the fullbacks. He blushed with embarrassment and said it was because he'd outgrown his boots. They were hurting him and he knew we couldn't afford to buy him new ones. It broke my heart to think he'd suffered in silence like that. Needless to say, when I told Ali the story she somehow found the money to replace the boots. Carl went on to play football at a decent level and became a ball boy at Manchester City, which restored his pride. So we both owe City a debt of gratitude.

Roy Clarke gave me the freedom to sort out my own sound system and I spent a happy year at the social club. Soon after I'd started, though, I had another health warning. I'd opened the show one night and, while I was backstage, I had a strange feeling down the left of my face, my left side and my left leg. It was a sort of tingling sensation.

My friend Chris Marlowe, the singer, had a boyfriend who was a doctor at Wythenshawe Hospital. I rang him for advice. When I told him my symptoms, he told me to jump in a taxi and get straight to hospital. I explained that I couldn't come immediately because the main act was on stage and I needed to close the show when he finished.

Despite the doctor's insistence to the contrary, I closed the show and drove to the hospital. They gave me tests and he told me I'd had what they called a minor embolism. In non-medical language, I'd had a minor stroke. He told me to go home and lie down for a few days.

I carried on feeling the effects of that stroke for about four years, even after I'd joined *Corrie*. It took the form of a strange icy feeling down the left side of my face and a tingly feeling in my left leg. It gradually got better and, touch wood, it has now disappeared.

After a couple of days of bed rest I was able to carry on at the City Social Club as though nothing had happened. Roy and I had our disagreements occasionally, but he was always a perfect gentleman and we parted amicably.

A few years later, by the time I'd become famous as Jack Duckworth, I went back to the club to take part in its annual pantomime. It had become part of local folklore because top City internationals, such as Colin Bell, Joe Corrigan, Francis Lee and Mike Summerbee, dressed up in outrageous costumes to take part.

Due to restrictions in my Granada contract, I wasn't allowed to appear in *Jack and the Beanstalk*, but I was allowed to be the voice of the giant. I'll never forget how my booming voice as I shouted, 'Fee, Fie, Foe, Fum, I smell the blood of an Englishman' had the young kids in the audience screaming with terror.

I'd left the City Social Club so I could work with Mike Timoney and his trio at Deno's Club in Princess Street, Manchester. This was a famous nightspot on the fringe of Manchester's red-light district. The ladies of the night used to come in when they were on their tea breaks or had just finished their shifts. They were tolerated as long as they didn't try to drum up any business inside the club.

I remember when Ali's churchgoing parents, George and Alice, came with her to watch me one night. George was a man of the world, but Alice said, 'Look at those lovely girls, all dressed up and on their own. They must be waiting for their husbands.' Nobody had the heart to put her right.

It was great fun working at Deno's on Thursday, Friday, Saturday and Sunday nights, but I had to make sure everyone got paid before the owner raided his till for a trip to the casino. Another feature of Deno's was the number of stray cats which lived in the eaves of the club. I'm sure the health and safety people would have had a field day if they'd raided us. But Mr Denos was too kind-hearted to have the cats put down, so we shared the facilities with our feline friends.

After my two-episode debut as Jack Duckworth at the Tilsleys' wedding in November 1979, I carried on with my work as an extra for Granada. I worked on *Strangers*, starring Mark McManus, who later became even more famous as Scottish detective Taggart. I also appeared in the follow-up to *Strangers* called *Bulman*, which starred Don Henderson. If you think I've got a deep voice, it was nothing compared to Don's. He made Paul Robeson sound like a tenor. I was usually just a face in the crowd, but I had minor speaking parts as a cab driver and a policeman.

It's also my claim to fame that I introduced Don to the actress who became his wife. I was playing the husband of actress Shirley Stelfox in *Bulman*, and Bulman, played by Don, wanted to see me. My wife said, 'He's on the toilet.' I had to utter a few lines out of vision as if I were behind a toilet door. After the scene, Don asked me who the beautiful actress playing my wife was. I introduced him to Shirley, they started dating and I heard later they'd got married. Don sadly died in 1997, but Shirley is now a regular in *Emmerdale*, playing Edna Birch.

On one occasion I was working for a Canadian director on a crime series. He wanted me to drive a car up to a grave at Moston Cemetery, Manchester, where thieves were retrieving some buried jewellery. He asked me to drive a Jaguar automatic at high speed up to a bend surfaced with shale. It looked a bit dodgy to me, but I said I'd give it a go. As I reached the bend, the rear end fishtailed and I cracked a gravestone and put a big dent in the Jag. I was expecting a bollocking, but the director was delighted. He said it looked very realistic. He said, 'Thank you. Good job. You're free for the day.'

I also did extra work for a kids' comedy called *The Ghosts of Motley Hall*. Actor Freddie Jones was the most brilliant storyteller. He had us in fits with his anecdotes about his life in the theatre. And I had a tiny part on a live show called *Glamour Girls*, hosted by Duggie Brown, the real-life brother of actress Lynne Perrie, who played Ivy Tilsley in *Corrie*.

I worked on *The Mallens* saga, and on *A Family At War*, set in the north-east during World War Two. Colin Douglas and Barbara Flynn headed the family. Other parts were played by John Nettles, who went on to star in *Bergerac*, and Patrick Troughton, who had been in the title role of *Doctor Who*. It was always a thrill to work alongside these household names. I tried not to stare at them or pester them for autographs.

On one occasion three members of my family appeared on telly on the same day. Son Carl was working as a ball boy at Maine Road when the Manchester City game was featured on *Match of the Day*. Daughter Sara was singing with The Ramblers' choir from her school in Gorton. They performed 'I'm Only A Poor Little Sparrow' on *Tiswas*, hosted by a young Chris Tarrant. The same night I was appearing in a *Play For Today* entitled *Thicker Than Water*. It was a drama about black puddings and I played a slaughterman.

That was one of the most sickening scenes I've ever had to shoot. We did them at a real slaughterhouse in Chorley, Lancashire. As a live pig was heading towards me with its legs hooked on a rack, I had to step aside. Then a real slaughterman stepped forward and slit its throat with a knife. I stepped back for the next shot and I could see the life go out of that pig's eyes. I was assured the pig hadn't suffered, but I noticed the slaughterman had a scar across his mouth. He told me a pig had bitten him as he killed it. The whole process was being monitored by health and animal welfare people, but I found it very disturbing. I couldn't eat bacon butties for a couple of months afterwards.

Jack Duckworth still wasn't a regular in *Corrie* in 1982 when I got the chance to work alongside a real galaxy of stage stars in *King Lear*. Jack had made a few fleeting appearances after the Tilsleys' wedding, but he hadn't been involved in any long-running storylines. This meant I could accept the offer of work on *King Lear* – as long as I wore a beard! Among the cast were Sir Laurence Olivier, John Hurt, Diana Rigg, Robert Lindsay, David Threlfall, Leo McKern, Anna Calder-Marshall and Dorothy Tutin.

I'd pretended years earlier, when I filled in my application form to work as an extra, that I could ride a horse. In fact, my equestrian skills were limited to donkey rides along Blackpool beach as a child. Now they were calling my bluff. They wanted me to play a mounted servant of King Lear; it was a non-speaking role.

In panic mode I spoke to Ali's brother, Norman, to see if he could put me in touch with my old mate, John Pearson, who ran a stables and bred horses for Yorkshireman Harvey Smith, the internationally famous showjumper.

I arranged to see John at his stables near Chorley and told him I needed to learn to ride a horse. 'No problem,' said John. Then I told him he had just three days to knock me into shape. John shook his head and smiled. From no problem it went to no chance. I said I didn't need to do anything fancy because it would be filmed in a studio. If he could just show me where the accelerator and the brake were, I'd muddle through.

John whistled and a magnificent hunter some seventeen hands high came over to see what he wanted. John introduced me to James, who gave me the once-over. After I'd got on board the horse, he kept looking round at me to see what on earth I was playing at. John explained that I was confusing the animal by giving it conflicting signals. Eventually, with a lot of patience from James, I learned how to get him started, pull him up, go backwards and shuffle sideways. I also learned how to slide off the saddle. What a pity the horse they provided for me three days later didn't have the same easygoing temperament as James!

Sir Larry had met me in earlier scenes and knew by now I was being recognised by viewers as Jack Duckworth from *Coronation Street*. He even asked me for tips on how to land a part in *Corrie*. It seemed unreal to be chatting like this to one of our greatest actors. He was so friendly and welcoming. I wish I could say the same for my horse.

He was a 14-hand gelding called Bracken and he took an instant dislike to me. First he tried to bite me; then he tried to stamp on my feet. The floor manager told me to keep my horse quiet. I suggested he should have a word with the horse. Sir Larry was chuckling as I finally mounted Bracken and took up my position next to him with two other extras.

One of the giant studios at Granada had been converted into a hill for the scenes we were shooting. Although it was indoors, they'd created a dark atmosphere with fine rain. Bracken decided to take off up the hill. His sudden spurt made me drop one of the reins. I heard Sir Larry's distinctive voice shout, 'Bye, Bill' as we disappeared. Eventually I managed to pull Bracken up with one rein, got off and dragged him back to our marks. Sir Larry was roaring with laughter, which probably saved the day for me.

If he'd objected to working with a rank amateur, I could have left the set in disgrace. But I managed to keep Bracken under control after that and we completed the scenes. It was such a privilege to work with the great man. I was amazed at the way he could slip in and out of character as King Lear in between asking me what was happening next in *Corrie*.

Later I watched a sword fight scene in which Robert Lindsay and David Threlfall were going at it hell for leather. It was brilliantly staged by the fight director. It looked so fierce I thought they were really trying to kill each other. In fact, they were looking fierce because they were concentrating on not hurting each other.

During the filming of *King Lear* I was also the official ciggy supplier to Diana Rigg, the glamorous actress who had earlier become famous for her leather-clad role as martial arts expert Emma Peel in *The Avengers*. Patrick Macnee played her boss, the bowler-hatted English gent John Steed. Diana's poster was on many a wall in factories, barracks and schoolboys' bedrooms. Now here she was in Manchester, cadging fags off a one-time asphalter.

I kept my cigs and lighter in the hidden pockets of a caveman-style outfit which I'd been issued by the wardrobe department as part of my costume. My smoking jacket had the name of handsome American actor Doug McClure written inside it. He was known to me and millions of other cowboy fans as Trampas in the TV series *The Virginian*.

Apparently he'd worn the jacket in a movie filmed in 1975 called *The Land That Time Forgot*. How that fur jacket got from Hollywood to Manchester is a mystery to me, but its pockets were very handy.

During any breaks in shooting, Diana would ask me to light her a cigarette. She'd take a few puffs and then hand it back to me to finish off while she shot the next scene. Rubbing shoulders with Sir Laurence Olivier and sharing cigs with Diana Rigg – I didn't think life could get much better for the Tuppenny Rabbit, but I was wrong.

It was around this time that Bill Podmore, *Coronation Street*'s executive producer, sidled up to me on set one day and had a casual conversation with me that changed my life.

CHAPTER 8

Idle Jack the Lad

As executive producer, Bill Podmore was the Godfather of *Coronation Street*. He decided who lived and who died. It was his job to oversee the smooth running of the show within his budget allowance. He was responsible for the actors, the scriptwriters and the technicians. To do all those things well was hard enough. To do them well and be loved at the same time might seem impossible. Somehow Bill managed both.

Known by everyone as Podders, Bill was a Lincolnshire lad who had worked his way up the ladder at Granada from assistant cameraman. As a result, he knew how to do all the jobs performed by the technicians. He also had a terrific sense of fun, which rubbed off on the people around him. As well as *Corrie,* he produced sitcoms such as *Nearest and Dearest,* starring Jimmy Jewel and Hylda Baker, *Brass,* starring Timothy West, and *The Brothers McGregor.*

After a period of political correctness in the 1970s, which

saw the *Street*'s popularity on the slide, Podders brought comedy back to the cobbles of Weatherfield and sent the viewing figures soaring again. He introduced colourful new characters to spark off the much-loved early cast of Annie Walker (Doris Speed), Ena Sharples (Violet Carson), Albert Tatlock (Jack Howarth), Len Fairclough (Peter Adamson), Stan and Hilda Ogden (Bernard Youens and Jean Alexander), Rita Littlewood (Barbara Knox) and, of course, Ken Barlow (Bill Roache). Podders also persuaded Pat Phoenix to return as the much-loved Elsie Tanner when he took over in 1976. She'd been touring the country's theatres in stage shows for three years.

Over the following years Bill brought in Peter Baldwin as dithering Derek Wilton, Johnny Briggs as Cockney wideboy Mike Baldwin, hunky Chris Quinten as Brian Tilsley, Sue Nicholls as Audrey Potter, the vivacious mum of Gail, glamorous Amanda Barrie as Alma Sedgewick and veteran actress Jill Summers as Phyllis Pearce.

Now here was Podders telling me, a school dunce, asphalt spreader and singer, that he wanted to make me a TV soap star. He said the scriptwriters had persuaded him there was scope to develop the sparky relationship between Jack and Vera. There were no guarantees or long-term contracts at that stage, but Podders was confident that Liz Dawn and I could pull it off. 'I think this is going to work out well for you, lad,' he told me. I had to pinch myself to make sure I wasn't dreaming.

He said they wanted me to sign an initial three-month contract. This involved not appearing anywhere else for those three months.

Bill asked, 'Are you going to sign it?'

I said, 'Yes.'

He laughed and said, 'God help you' as he walked away.

Other regulars, such as Julie Goodyear, who played Rovers barmaid Bet Lynch, and Bryan Mosley, who played corner-shop owner Alf Roberts, urged me to go for it. My old pal Betty Driver, who played barmaid Betty Turpin, said, 'I knew it. What did I tell you?'

All I had to do now was break the news to my wife and family. I needn't have worried. Ali was delighted for me. She told me to enjoy it.

I was concerned I might make a fool of myself and be an embarrassment to my family. Carl was about sixteen and Sara was twelve at the time. I was especially worried about Sara in case she got teased at school. Carl was a handy lad who knew how to look after himself, but Sara was at that sensitive age for girls when they don't want anything to draw attention to them. They both dealt with it really well. They were each proud of me but didn't boast about having a dad on the telly. They were very mature about it and I was equally proud of them.

None of that stopped me from being terrified of letting people down. They'd put a lot of faith in me, but I was no actor. I didn't have any formal training; I'd picked it up as I went along. Learning where to stand and deliver the odd line was one thing. Now I'd be expected to memorise long scripts. And I was the lad who couldn't even remember a shopping list. What had I let myself in for?

My family and mates all told me the same thing: just go for it. So that's what I did.

Remembering the dialogue has always been a problem for me. It was five years before I found an alternative to memorising the written scripts, but in those early days it was torture. Ali would read all the other parts while I tried to remember my lines. We would go over and over them and I'd be muttering the words in my sleep.

Other actors had learned how to remember lines since stage school and they tried to help me. But you can't teach an old dog new tricks and I struggled. Gradually I improved, but it seemed I was having to put in a lot more effort than the more experienced cast members. It was second nature to them. I'm just grateful they had patience with me.

As Jack's character was developed by the scriptwriters, he didn't have a lot going for him. He was lazy. He was a thief. He was a liar and a womaniser. Any illusions I might have had of Jack cutting an heroic figure were soon shattered. I hadn't really expected that, but nothing prepared me for the reaction of *Corrie* fans when I was out and about.

There was a big up side to being in the *Street* financially. Even on a short contract, the money was good compared to what I'd been earning. And Podders had told me to carry on singing. Even though the contract said otherwise, he told me I wouldn't be punished if I sang at clubs. My money as a singer suddenly shot up from £35 to £100 for a 45-minute gig in Leeds as a result of appearing on *Corrie*. That was exceptional. Normally my average fee had gone up to about £55. There was a price to be paid though, as I discovered at a club in Irlam, Lancashire.

In the *Street* earlier in the week, viewers had seen Jack dipping into Vera's handbag and nicking a fiver. I was on stage singing as Bill Tarmey when this middle-aged woman with a fierce expression on her face stormed towards me.

She started swinging her handbag at me and shouting, 'You thieving swine.'

I was saying, 'It's only a play' but she wouldn't listen. She kept hitting me and screaming abuse.

The club committee members had to drag her off the stage before I could continue with my disrupted song. The rest of the audience were laughing at what had happened, but I was stunned.

At first I was baffled by the way fans talked to me as if I were really Jack. I didn't understand how rational people could chat as if I were a character in a soap opera. Surely they knew it was only pretend.

It's a funny feeling when people start staring at you. It's a bit unnerving at first. You wonder why they're staring, but often it's because they're trying to place you. They're wondering where they know you from or they want to make sure they really have seen Jack Duckworth in their local shop.

Most of the fans are delightful. If I had a pound for every time someone's asked, 'Where's your Vera today?' I'd be a multimillionaire. It's often nervousness on their part. They want to say something but they don't know what. So they talk to me as if I'm Jack. I soon got used to it. I also got used to the autograph hunters who expected me to carry pens and paper so I could sign for them. A tiny minority can be really rude though. They'll interrupt your conversations and thrust bits of paper under your nose. I try to be polite, but some people push too far.

I can laugh at the ones who ask for an autograph and,

while you're signing for them, insist on telling you, 'It's not for me.' Some go further and say, 'It's for my missus. She thinks you're great. But I think you're crap.'

There was one guy who wouldn't take no for an answer after I'd been signing photographs at a charity bash for more than an hour. My wrist was throbbing and the queue wasn't getting any shorter, as some were coming round for the second or third time. When I got to my last three photos, I said wearily, 'Just three more and that's it. I'm knackered.' Despite being fourth in the queue, this man stood his ground until he got in front of me. I repeated that I could scarcely hold a pen, but he started prodding me in the chest and causing a right old scene. He complained, 'I've been waiting in the queue for an hour.'

It got to the stage where I wondered whether I should hit him before he hit me, when my son Carl intervened. He picked the guy up from behind, pinning his arms to his side, carried him outside and shut the door on him. I breathed a sigh of relief. Granada TV doesn't like their soap stars getting involved in punch-ups with their viewers.

When I was out with Ali, the fans often acted as if she were invisible. On one occasion Ali was knocked off a chair by a couple and landed on the floor. As I went to help Ali to her feet, I told them angrily, 'That's my wife you've just knocked over.'

The man replied, 'I'm sorry. I didn't realise it was *your* wife.' Presumably he thought it would have been OK if she had been someone else's wife.

Liz Dawn, who had started playing Vera five years before Jack appeared on the scene, was having similar experiences when she was out with her husband, Don Ibbetson. Sometimes the four of us would attend an event together and Don and Ali would be shoved aside. It's a good job they learned to take it so calmly, otherwise we wouldn't have been able to go out anywhere in public.

There have been plenty of good times too, of course. During a holiday in the South Pacific, I noticed our Fijian waitress was staring at me. I asked if something was wrong.

She said, 'I cannot believe you are before me, Mr Duckworth.' It turned out she had a friend in New Zealand who sent her tapes of *Corrie*, which was her favourite TV programme.

It's nice to enjoy that kind of recognition, but there's a lot to be said for anonymity. The irony is that you go into showbiz hoping to find fame and fortune. But you soon learn that once the spotlight's on you, there's no turning it off again.

Liz and I used to swap stories about the crazy things fans would do. I was once asked for an autograph while I was standing in the gents. I told the over-eager fan, 'I'm afraid I've got my hands full at the moment.'

Liz had a similar tale. One fan followed her into the ladies and when Liz went into a cubicle, this woman's hand appeared under the door holding a pen. 'Can I have your autograph?' the fan asked.

'Have you got any paper?' asked Liz.

'No, but you should have some in there,' she replied.

People are always asking me what Liz is like so I'll tell you . . .

CHAPTER 9

My Other Wife

Liz Dawn landed her role as Vera Duckworth in *Coronation Street* in August 1974, five years before I appeared in the show. She was brought in as a machinist at the Mark Brittain Warehouses in Weatherfield. In that same year Gail Potter (Helen Worth), Jerry Booth (Graham Haberfield) and Eddie Yeats (Geoff Hughes) also made their debuts, Betty Turpin's husband, Cyril, died from a heart attack and Lucille Hewitt, one of the original cast, played by Jenny Moss, left the show after appearing in 749 episodes.

Liz's route to the show was similar to mine. Her maiden name was Sylvia Butterfield. She was married to an electrician called Don Ibbetson and was the mother of four children. She'd just had her second child, Dawn Elizabeth Ibbetson, when Don put her name forward as a singer in a talent competition. Don decided that Sylvia Ibbetson was too much of a mouthful so he reversed their baby daughter's

names and called her Elizabeth Dawn. This was later short-
ened to Liz Dawn and became not only her stage name but
also the name she was known by everywhere. Similarly, only
my close friends, family and the postman knew my real name
was Bill Piddington.

Liz won the talent competition and started working as a
singer in the pubs and clubs around Leeds, West Yorkshire,
where she was born. She shared stages with some of the same
people I was working with around the late 60s and early 70s.
We could have met on stage but we never did. She mostly
worked on the east side of the Pennines and I worked mostly
on the west side.

With an Equity card for her singing, Liz was also able to
work as an extra in TV and films. Like me, she'd never imag-
ined a future as an actress. At first it was just a bit of extra
money.

Ironically, it was a TV advert for Cadbury's cookies which
launched her career. She had to play a mum trying to coax
her young son out from under his bed by offering him a bis-
cuit after a disappointing day at football.

'Come on, Tim,' she said in that distinctive voice of hers.
'I'm sure all goalies let in ten goals at some time in their
career.' The ad was very popular and it must have sold a lot
of cookies.

There was another famous ad for Formica in which Liz's
character insisted a salesman should wear a lie detector
machine that fitted round his head. Whenever he claimed a
product was made from Formica, the alarm would go off.
Eventually, the salesman showed her the real thing.

After that Liz was in demand for cameo parts in TV plays

and films. They led to what started as a minor part in *Corrie*. She and Ivy Tilsley were involved in a union dispute at the clothing factory. Playing a machinist wasn't much of a stretch for Liz because she'd worked in the rag trade as a teenager in Leeds.

By the time I was introduced to the show, Liz was established as a familiar face. She told me later that she was a bundle of nerves when she started out in *Corrie*, acting and mingling with the soap stars she'd watched on TV at home. She said she got round it by putting on a bold front.

I took a different approach, keeping a low profile and hoping to earn some pity. But I found, just as Liz had done, that the *Street* stars couldn't have been more helpful or friendly towards me. It's something you remember and try to pass on to any newcomers.

After that incident at the Tilsleys' wedding, when I hurled Liz to the ground and smacked her bum, we got on, you could say, like a house on fire. When I made my debut, Violet Carson and Jack Howarth, who'd been playing Ena Sharples and Albert Tatlock from the beginning, were at the church with me. They didn't appear in the show much after that. I hope it wasn't something I said.

Top of the appearance charts in 1979 were Gail Potter-Tilsley with 61 episodes, followed by Elsie Tanner (60), Len Fairclough (60), Hilda Ogden (57), Ivy Tilsley (56), Suzie Birchall (55), Rita Fairclough (54), Stan Ogden (52), Betty Turpin (52), Deirdre Langton (51), Brian Tilsley (51), Annie Walker (49), Ken Barlow (47), Alf Roberts (47), Bert Tilsley (46), Fred Gee (45), Eddie Yeats (44), Bet Lynch (43), Mike Baldwin (42) and Emily Bishop (41).

After working as an extra for so long, I was still too shy to go into the Green Room. This is the inner sanctum, the hallowed ground where *Corrie*'s actors sat around, learning their lines, drinking coffee and playing cards.

I was sitting on a window ledge trying to memorise my script when Julie Goodyear walked past. She turned and said, 'What are you doing out here, kid? Would you like a coffee?' And with that she led me into the Green Room. It felt like I was entering a new world. These icons from Britain's favourite TV programme were all around me. Some were talking to walls as they ran through their lines. Others would stamp their feet to indicate they were going to open a door. Others were just chatting away like normal people.

Liz came over and said, 'Hiya, kid. How're you feeling?'

I said, 'Petrified.'

She said, 'You'll be all right. Don't worry.' Easier said than done.

My biggest fear then — and even now thirty years later — was that I'd forget my lines and cock everything up. People like Annie Kirkbride, who plays Deirdre, seemed to be able to read the dialogue once and remember it. I know I'm just a Manchester lad playing a Manchester lad, but learning anything always came harder to me than the rest of the world. Eventually all those famous people helped to calm me in one way or another and I'll always be grateful to them.

One time I was at the bar of the Rovers and I kept spoiling a scene because my hand was shaking. Jean Alexander, a fantastic actress who played Hilda Ogden from 1964 to 1986, asked me what the matter was. I explained that whenever I tried to pick up my pint to take a sip, I couldn't stop my hand from shaking. She patted my hand, and said, 'Then just leave the pint on the bar in front of you.' It was such an obvious solution to the problem, but it hadn't occurred to me.

Another time, Julie Goodyear noticed that I would be able to do a certain scene when we rehearsed it but I became a stuttering wreck as soon as the director shouted, 'Let's go for a take.' Unknown to me, she whispered to the director to pretend we were rehearsing.

We were playing the scene at Bet Lynch's flat after a night of passion. Julie had even playfully dropped a pair of knickers on my shoulder, which I casually shrugged aside, little knowing the scene was being filmed. We got through the scene perfectly, and I heard a voice shout, 'Checking that.' Followed by, 'OK. Moving on.' It was only then that I realised we had been 'going for a take', as they say.

But the person who helped me most was Liz. She had endless patience in those early days. When I screwed up she never tutted or got angry. She was always there, trying to boost my confidence. She used to laugh and say, 'We don't want any acting in this next scene.'

Sometimes, if I was saying three sentences, I might pause between them and Liz would think I'd forgotten the next line. She'd apologise for interrupting by saying, 'I'm sorry. I didn't realise you were acting.'

When you become a regular in *Corrie*, the scriptwriters invent a background for your character, which is recorded by the archivist. I've only recently uncovered mine. Here's the official background to Jack Duckworth and how he met and married Vera:

Born at 4 Whittle Street, Rochdale, to bookie's runner Harry and barmaid Maggie. Harry was also a rag and bone man and Maggie was the local layer outer, helped by his sister Daisy. The family moved to 16 Butler Street, Weatherfield, in 1950. Jack left school at fourteen and went on the buses as a clippie. He left to do his National Service in the Army for two years. Afterwards he worked briefly in a paper mill making toilet rolls before taking a job with a travelling fair. While working on the fair he used to have a woman in every town and called himself Jake Mallard so they couldn't track him down. Met Vera Burton when she was holding her friend Enid Crump's hair out of the way while she was sick over the side of the Waltzer. Vera took him home and her father discovered them making love in the potting shed. He chased Jack away. Vera told him she was pregnant so they married at the local Register Office. They walked down the aisle to 'Edelweiss' and Jack was drunk. Honeymooned in Cleethorpes. To impress Vera he added two years to his age. She then discovered she wasn't pregnant. When the fair moved on, he stayed with her and got a job driving for the Council. Terry born in 1964. They moved to 20 Inkerman Street, Weatherfield. Vera left him in 1974 but returned in 1976.

In real life I'm two years younger than Liz. So the script-writers added five years to my age to make Jack born in 1936. They added two years to Liz so Vera was born in 1937.

As our screen double act developed, Liz and I started getting requests to make personal appearances and attend charity events together. It led to a close friendship between Ali and me and Liz and Don. He would drive us to clubs and theatres, where we'd be asked to pose for photos, sign autographs or sing a few songs. These were the occasions when fans, recognising me and Liz, would crowd around, pushing Don and Ali to the sidelines. They soon learned to deal with it far better than I would have done if the boot had been on the other foot.

It was wonderful to appear at theatres where everyone was seated, nobody was getting up to fetch pints or buy bingo tickets, and nobody was shouting, 'The pies have arrived.' I usually started the performance with a few songs and jokes, then I'd introduce Liz to sing a few songs. We'd finish with a duet of 'Me And My Shadow'.

Apart from working together, we'd also spend our nights off in each other's company. Don had a dry sense of humour which tickled me. Ali gets on with most people. Although she isn't an extrovert herself, she enjoys people like Liz who are. We'd go for meals together. Liz liked to have a flutter and we'd often pop into the Albion Casino in Salford after dinner.

One night Don and I were chatting at the bar while the girls went to play roulette. Ali bought ten pounds' worth of chips and didn't know what she was doing. When I went to take her home, she'd got a mountain of chips in front of her. Wherever she placed them, a crowd of mad-keen Chinese gamblers would follow and she kept winning. Ali looked at me in desperation and said, 'How do I stop?' I told her just to pick up all her chips, leave the table and cash them in. She'd won more than £100 – a classic case of beginner's luck.

These were amazing times for all of us. Nothing quite prepares you for the *Coronation Street* effect, and it can drive you to the brink of madness. I was brought up to believe you should help people when you can, and all of a sudden everybody seemed to want a piece of us. When people asked if I could do this or that for a good cause, I found it hard to say no. It was non-stop. People would ask if I could show up for twenty minutes to pose with a charity cheque or open a new community centre, but they would want me to get to Southport or Doncaster. The pressure to be everywhere at once, while finding time to learn my lines, was driving me nuts. In the end I handed my bookings diary to Ali, and told people they'd have to ask her. That way we had a chance to cut down on all the demands being made on our time.

We also decided to choose particular charities and concentrate on helping them, instead of trying to spread ourselves too thinly by helping everyone who asked. This gave us a bit of breathing space and helped us to stay the best of pals with Liz and Don.

We were still living in Gorton at that time. Don and Liz lived about four miles away in Whitefield, then they moved to Chorlton, where they threw some great parties. I've never known anyone who can be as unintentionally funny as Liz. She can have people in hysterics and she's the only one who's not in on the joke. I've lost count of the times when she's said or done something to set everyone off, but she'd have this puzzled look on her face, wondering what we were all laughing at.

Probably the best public example of this was when we were taking part in *Celebrity 3-2-1*. It was a popular game show hosted by Ted Rogers in the 1980s. The well-known booby prize was a model toy called Dusty Bin. We'd been asked to take part in a celebrity version of the programme to raise money for charity. The show involved answering a series of questions. If you got them right, you were given clues to help you win the star prizes.

One of the questions Ted asked us was: 'What P completes the Battle of the Khyber?'

I immediately said, 'Pass.'

At which point Liz dug me in the ribs and said, 'Don't pass. I think I know this one.'

As everyone fell about laughing, Liz looked totally bewildered.

Another question Ted asked was: 'What C describes a man who works with wood?'

I suggested the answer might be 'chippy' because that's what they call joiners in the building trade.

But Liz said, 'Don't be daft. You get fish, chips and peas from the chippy.'

Liz suffers from emphysema, which left her gasping for breath occasionally. For several years, she'd soldiered on because she didn't want to let down the fans. But she'd given more than thirty years of her life to playing Vera and there comes a time when you have to put yourself and your family first.

One day, when she came to tell me she wasn't renewing her contract, I said, 'Good. I'm glad.' I didn't mean it in anything but a caring way because that woman deserves some time to enjoy life. If the bosses and the scriptwriters had decided to kill both of us off, it wouldn't have mattered. I wouldn't have wanted her to stay on just for my sake.

I thought the scenes where Vera died in Jack's arms were

very moving and tastefully done. I was glad they didn't decide to have her murdered or hit by a passing tram. There's a time for that sort of storyline but I thought the way they wrote out Vera was spot on.

I can't describe how much I've missed Liz since she left the show. Ali and I see Don and Liz from time to time. She still makes us laugh and she still doesn't know why.

CHAPTER 10

The Ladies' Man

After our appearance at the Tilsleys' wedding, it was Vera who was flying the flag for the Duckworths on screen. To be more precise, she was flying her knickers.

In 1980 Vera went to France with Hilda Ogden and Ivy Tilsley to visit Weatherfield's twin town and boost business at Mike Baldwin's factory. But they had a night on the pop with a group of ex-paratroopers, which ended with Vera's knickers flying from the Charlesville Town Hall flagpole. The women agreed to keep the incident secret from Jack, Bert Tilsley and Stan Ogden.

Hilda and Vera then fell out over a bingo card that won the jackpot. Hilda insisted the winning card belonged to Stan, but Vera claimed the prize — a holiday for two in Blackpool. The friendship between the two women collapsed completely when Vera refused to let Hilda join the factory girls' pools syndicate. Hilda plotted her revenge by copying winning numbers on to Vera's coupon so she'd think she'd won a fortune. It backfired when the syndicate all expected a windfall and Vera bought a fur coat before Hilda came clean. As a result she was sacked.

From that moment Vera and Hilda were daggers drawn, which led to some memorable confrontations. Hilda came out with a wonderful put-down when she said: 'Them Duckworths are like stray cats. Invite 'em in for a saucer of milk and they're asleep in your best chair in front of the fire before you can blink.'

In those days, new characters were eased in gradually so the viewers could get used to them before they went into major storylines. That's what was happening to me. I was on a sort of probation to see if the viewers liked me while the scriptwriters considered their options.

They decided the Duckworths' marriage should go through a series of sticky patches. Jack threw Vera out after finding she was having it off with a bricklayer called Harry. Vera dumped herself on Bert and Ivy Tilsley, and even entertained Harry at their house. Bert begged Jack to take Vera back, but he was having too good a time living the bachelor life. In fact, Jack was enjoying his freedom so much that Vera went back just to spoil his fun.

So the scene had been cleverly set for this warring couple to bicker away, picking on each other and playing away from home. I think the viewers accepted their extramarital affairs because they were on a tit–for–tat basis.

Jack's first screen kiss wasn't with his wife Vera; it was with the *Street*'s glamour girl, Bet Lynch. The romance started at the beginning of 1982 when Jack was working as a taxi driver.

It wasn't just Jack's first screen kiss, of course: it was mine too! Established actors are used to snogging each other, but this was another new ball game for me.

When I got my script and saw what was expected of me, I wasn't sure how Ali would take it. Julie Goodyear was one of the sexiest women on TV at that time. She was famous for her tight sweaters and leopard-skin jackets. When I told Ali, she wasn't the least bit bothered. I suppose she'd grown used to me working with glamorous women and knew she could trust me.

Jack's chat-up line to Bet wasn't the best in the world. 'I'm attracted to you like metal to a magnet,' he said. I think even in those early days the writers saw me as a rather pathetic Romeo.

I needn't have worried about that first kiss. Our lips had barely touched when the director shouted, 'Cut.' Our next scene wasn't in the bedroom; it was the morning after. I think Bet regretted falling for Jack's charms, but she felt better when Vera confided that she was seeing a construction worker called Vic.

On the night she'd been seeing Vic, Vera told Jack she'd been out with Bet. But Jack revealed his stupidity when he said, 'You can't have been. I was with Bet last night.' It was a classic own goal.

This time it was Vera's turn to throw Jack out. And this time it was Jack's turn to ask the Tilsleys to give him a roof for the night. And this time it was Ivy who ordered Vera to take Jack back.

There wasn't much to admire about us Duckworths. We were always squabbling and being unfaithful to each other at every opportunity. Jack was a lazy sod and Vera was a loud-mouth. Yet, because of the clever writing, viewers seemed to warm to us. It may be because we never did harm to anybody but ourselves. Whatever the reasons, I'm eternally grateful that the public, by and large, took us to their hearts. It was at the end of 1982 that I was offered a one-year contract.

1983 was a dramatic year for *Corrie*. The biggest storyline to capture the public's imagination was the love triangle between Ken Barlow, his wife Deirdre and her lover Mike Baldwin. Deirdre's dilemma sent the ratings soaring and it seemed everyone had an opinion on the subject. Sir John Betjeman, the Poet Laureate and a keen *Corrie* fan, thought she should stand by Ken, but there was a woman walking around the Granada studios with a placard which read: 'Go with Mike. I would.'

Speculation reached fever pitch until the night Deirdre made her choice. The reconciliation with Ken was screened on the same night Manchester United played Arsenal. Old Trafford was packed with 56,000 fans and when the electronic scoreboard flashed the news 'Deirdre and Ken united again' there was a huge roar that echoed round the ground.

It was 1983 when Peter Adamson made his last appearance as Len Fairclough after 1,797 episodes. Doris Speed also made her final appearance as Annie Walker after 1,746 episodes. Doris, or Miss Speed as everyone called her, had been in the show since the first episode on 9 December 1960. Peter had first appeared in 1961.

There were debuts for Kevin Kennedy as Curly Watts, for Bill Waddington as Percy Sugden, and for Mike Le Vell as

Kevin Webster. It was also the year that Nigel Pivaro made his first appearance as Jack and Vera's son, Terry Duckworth.

Originally they'd chosen a blond-haired lad from Sheffield called Tony Pitts for the part. But then, for reasons which were never explained, a young dark-haired Mancunian actor called Nigel Pivaro took the role instead and he's been the only 'our Terry' to appear on screen.

Liz and I were a bit worried about working with a 'real' actor. We'd heard he'd been trained at RADA. We were both concerned about what Nigel would think of us when he discovered our trick for remembering the lines.

Although I had a hopeless memory, Liz wasn't much better and neither of us wanted to hold things up with a series of retakes. We found a neat way to be reminded of our dialogue was to stick little notes on the props. They would have a couple of words written on them to trigger our memories. As we talked over breakfast, there'd be a piece of paper stuck to the cornflakes box or the sugar bowl.

Nigel had no trouble with his lines so he'd join us for breakfast, pick up the cornflakes, shake them into a bowl, and put them back anywhere on the table. During rehearsals I told him to make sure he put the cornflakes back where he'd found them. He did this but put them the wrong way round. So I told him it was vital he put them back *exactly* as he'd found them. Nigel must have thought this was something to do with the ban on commercial advertising but then Liz told him to be careful when he moved the sugar bowl. Nigel was baffled until he spotted our crib sheets. Then he burst out laughing. Apparently they don't teach you this at stage school.

The funniest time was during a scene in which he was

checking on a chicken in the oven at Number 9. Nigel corpsed with laughter when he opened the oven door. When he'd finally stopped chuckling, I asked what was wrong. He pointed to Liz and said, 'She's only put a crib sheet on the chicken's arse.' And then the whole studio was in fits.

Nigel was a lovely lad and he became like a real son to Liz and me. A few weeks before Terry made his screen debut, the Duckworths were involved in an hilarious episode which showed the imagination of the scriptwriters at their best.

Bet Lynch was looking for love as usual. There was something familiar about one of the eligible gents in the video collection at the Bill and Coo Dating Agency she visited. Although he had a mock American accent, wore a cream jacket and called himself Vince St Clair, there was no mistaking the face of Jack Duckworth.

Bet always loved a good plot so she tipped off Vera, who wanted to hang Jack from a lamp-post by an intimate part of his anatomy. Instead Bet persuaded her to bite her tongue and lay a trap for him. Through the agency, Vera made a date with Vince at the Rovers in the name of Carole Monroe. Jack felt safe because he knew Vera would be at the bingo that night.

'Carole' was waiting at the bar wearing a red wig. Jack fell for it hook, line and sinker. He sidled up to her with a box of chocolates. As he started to introduce himself in his phoney Yankee accent, Vera hit him over the head with the box and chased him all the way home. The Rovers' regulars cheered wildly to see Jack get his just deserts. Fans to this day tell me it was their favourite scene from *Corrie*.

The arrival of three new young characters in the show – Terry, Curly Watts and Kevin Webster – gave the writers fresh options. They also brought a lot of fun and laughter to the Green Room. But Mike Le Vell, who came in as Bill Webster's son Kevin, didn't make the best of impressions when he bumped into me on his first day.

I was walking out of the car park when Mike asked me where he should put his car. I told him to park it next to my blue Volvo. As he swung it by the side of mine, he put a dent in the door. Mike was full of apologies. He must have been a bag of nerves anyway, as he was an 18-year-old lad from stage school who was about to appear in *Coronation Street*. Now he'd dented a cast colleague's car on his first day at work. I told him not to worry because I was selling it anyway. As it happens, the dealer who was buying it off me wasn't bothered. Mike and I soon became good friends. He'd been born and raised in the same sort of streets as me.

Kevin Kennedy, who was brought in to play binman Curly Watts alongside Chalkie Whitely and Eddie Yeats, was a great practical joker. With his lean and lanky body, straight blond hair in a fringe and glasses, Curly was always going to be a figure of fun. And Kev didn't need to alter his appearance to play the part. He loved to make people laugh so if his looks helped that along, Kev was happy. There was one occasion, though, when his sense of humour got me in trouble with our director.

When Jack and Vera moved into Chalkie Whitely's house at Number 9, they also inherited Chalkie's racing pigeons. He'd won £3,500 on a five-horse accumulator and emigrated to Australia to live with relatives. Fred Gee, cellarman at the Rovers, challenged Jack to race a couple of the pigeons: Fred's won and Jack's died.

According to the script, Curly was supposed to come through the door with Jack's dead pigeon in his hands. I was to say, 'What's the matter with him?'

Curly was supposed to reply, 'Gone to Jesus.'

But Kev had decided to turn the scene into something like the Monty Python dead parrot sketch. He prodded the model of a pigeon twice with his finger, as if to prove it was dead, then looked heavenwards as he said, 'Gone to Jesus.'

I was in hysterics. There is absolutely nothing worse in acting than trying not to laugh. The more you try, the worse it gets. Kev, being a true professional, could switch it on and off at will, but the more I saw his deadpan face, the more I giggled. People were losing patience.

Finally, our director, Mary McMurray, called a halt to the merriment. She said, 'I'm ashamed of you. That kind of behaviour is not on. We'll come back to you when you've collected yourself.' It was like being hit with a bucket of cold water. Mary was a wonderful director and her red card was just what I needed. I realised I'd been in danger of getting sacked for stupidity.

It's amazing how some actors can keep straight faces. In an earlier scene with Curly, I'd been holding a real pigeon in my hands as we talked across the breakfast table. As the cameras rolled, I could feel bird shit oozing through my fingers, but Kev kept the conversation going. As soon as the director shouted, 'Check that,' Kev convulsed with laughter. I thought he was going to need an ambulance, or at the very least a change of pants. But by the time the mess was cleared and we were ready to roll again, he'd completely recovered.

It may not be a coincidence that Kev Kennedy was with

me during two of my funniest off-screen experiences. In one of them, we were raising money for Soap Aid and needed to travel between the Isle of Man and Liverpool for two separate appearances. A light aircraft took us from Ronaldsway Airport in the Isle of Man to Speke Airport in Liverpool. A fast car took us to the gig in Liverpool, where we were booked to entertain the crowd.

I sang 'One Voice' with the St Winifred's School Choir, backed by Mike Timoney, and Kevin sang with a rock band. Then we jumped into the car for the journey back to Speke for our return flight. At Ronaldsway, a helicopter had been booked to take us to our hotel. The weather was appalling and we had a bumpy ride.

The pilot was an ex-RAF chappie with a cultured accent. When he started his descent into a field two miles from our hotel, I asked him to take us to the car park. But he must have figured it wouldn't be safe to land there because we were being buffeted by the wind.

When I pointed to the distant hotel, he said in a posh voice, 'It's not a yo-yo.' Then he dropped us in this field in the pouring rain in the middle of nowhere and took off.

Kev and I spotted a minivan in a lay-by next to the field so we headed for it. As we got nearer, we could see the van was rocking from side to side. Kev didn't hesitate. He knocked on the steamy window. Eventually, the window came down and there was a glimpse of hastily covered flesh in the back.

A woman's voice asked, 'What's going on? What does he want?'

The driver, still tucking his shirt inside his trousers, said,

'You're not going to believe this. It's Jack Duckworth and Curly Watts and they want a lift.'

He must have been a very understanding man because he told us to get in and got us back to our hotel in time for our next appearance.

The other occasion when Kev and I had an off-screen adventure was while I was singing with a band called Take Ten. They'd been formed around 1977 by a bass player called Gerry Jones, from Sale. Gerry had played with the Jack Anderson Band when I'd suffered my near-fatal heart attack the year before and collapsed on stage.

While I recovered, Jack was forced to hire a replacement singer. Meanwhile Gerry had decided to form his own band of young musicians. He asked me and Chris Marlowe if we'd sing with this newly formed group called Take Ten. We used to play at the Sale Hotel on Tuesday nights in the late 70s, and later at a pub in Reddish, Stockport, called the Ash. Gerry is now in his early seventies and lives in an apartment in Tenerife, where I still see him from time to time. He plays bass in a Spanish orchestra now and has a great life out there.

Back in the early 80s, Take Ten had a booking in Cumbria. They asked me if I'd sing with them. I asked Kev Kennedy and Nigel Pivaro if they'd like to come and watch. We were staying with some of the band members at a small hotel called the Three Wheels at Shap. After the show, we got back to the hotel around midnight and discovered we had no key to get in. It probably goes without saying that a large quantity of drink had been consumed.

Nigel spotted our bedroom window was open and decided that with a few helping hands he could climb up one of the three wheels that gave the hotel its name. He was clinging to the wheel with one hand and reaching for the window ledge with the other when we heard a creaking noise. Like a slow-motion film, we looked on in horror as this wheel came away from the wall.

Nigel managed to jump clear at the last moment as the wheel came crashing down and burst into fifty pieces. We managed to distribute them among the flowerbeds before the door opened. Using our acting skills, we looked a picture of innocence as the manager let us in through the revolving door of what had now become the Two Wheels Hotel.

One of our group started sniggering and set off the others. We must have gone round those doors three times before we could keep straight faces and get to our rooms. Then we exploded in another set of giggles as somebody started singing 'Three Wheels On My Wagon'.

I still chuckle at my adventures with Kev Kennedy. I couldn't believe it years later when I heard they'd decided to write Curly out of the show. How they would create such a wonderful, well-liked character, played by a brilliant young actor, and then write him out of the programme is a mystery to me. I hope they'll see sense one day and beg him to come back. It'd be worth it just for the effect he had on the Green Room. There was always plenty of laughter when Kev was around.

Bill Waddington came into *Corrie* in 1983 as Percy Sugden. Bill had worked as an entertainer during the Second World War in a troupe called Stars in Battledress, as he never tired of telling us. He was a lovely old chap, but he thought he could amuse us in the Green Room by playing his ukulele.

He liked to strum George Formby numbers, but he wasn't quite as good as he thought.

One day I introduced Bill to a talented musician and asked the musician to play a tune on Bill's ukulele. He gave a brilliant 30-second performance until I stopped him and said to Bill, 'That's ukulele playing.' It was probably a bit unkind to an old soldier but at least it had the desired effect. He never brought his ukulele into the Green Room again.

Apart from working in *Corrie*, Bill also bred horses. He told me one of them was running on a Saturday and it was a dead cert. I told him I wasn't interested because I was a very bad loser. When I was eighteen I'd lost all my week's wages in a game of three-card brag. I told Bill it had put me off gambling for life. But Bill insisted his horse couldn't lose and persuaded me to give him a fiver to back it.

On the Monday morning I held out my hand for my winnings only to be told, 'It fell at the first fence. The jockey broke his shoulder.' Bad loser that I am, I muttered it should have been his neck.

The next time the horse ran, it won at 33–1. Bill was delighted. I asked him if he'd put anything on it for me and he just shook his head. He had a bit of a reputation for being careful with his money. It probably started one day when he sold Mike Le Vell a headache tablet for ten pence.

Bill soon became a *Street* stalwart as Percy Sugden. The viewers loved the way he fled in terror whenever Phyllis Pearce had her predatory eyes on him. Phyllis, with the blue rinse and foghorn voice, was played by a lovely lady from Yorkshire called Jill Summers. She'd been a soprano singer in her heyday, then her voice suddenly dropped three octaves and she found a new career as an actress. Phyllis, a widow, had decided that Percy, a widower, should become Darby to her Joan. Somehow, Percy always managed to wriggle away from her.

We were all reminded of our precarious position as *Coronation Street* actors at the end of 1983, when Len Fairclough died in a car crash. Peter Adamson, who'd played Len for twenty-two years, had always been kind and helpful to me. It was Peter who first introduced me to Sir Laurence Olivier, telling him, 'Bill's just joined us in the *Street*.' But Peter fell foul of the *Street* bosses when he sold an article to a freelance journalist without permission. He was written out of the show in May. Any chance of a reprieve ended with the news that Len had been killed when he fell asleep at the wheel and his van crashed into a bridge that December. You take people as you find them and he was always a perfect gentleman in his dealings with me. I was sorry to see him go.

The year ended on a sad note when Violet Carson died on Boxing Day at the age of eighty-five. She'd last appeared in April 1980, after making 1,148 appearances as the formidable Ena Sharples.

CHAPTER II

Comings and Goings

When you're working in a soap opera like *Coronation Street*, it's in the nature of things that people will come and go for a variety of reasons. Sometimes the actor dies or decides to leave the show to work elsewhere. Sometimes the bosses think the actors' performances are below par and they're written out. The one reason I've never been able to understand is that the writers can't think of what to do with them. We've lost a few popular characters because of this and it's always mystified me.

The year 1984 was great for me personally. After appearing in 64 episodes between my debut in 1979 to the end of 1983, I was in 84 episodes in that one year. That put me in second position behind Betty Turpin, who'd been in 86 episodes, with Vera in ninth place on 67 and our Terry eighteenth with 61.

But it was a gloomy year for *Corrie*. First they lost Elsie

Tanner in January, when actress Pat Phoenix decided to quit. The writers left the door open for Elsie to return by having her emigrate to the sunshine of Portugal.

The same month it was announced that Bert Tilsley, played by Peter Dudley, had died while suffering from a mental illness at a hospital in Southport. Peter was an exceptional actor who'd played Bert for four years. In April, Jack Howarth, who'd played grumpy old Albert Tatlock in 1,322 episodes since 1961, died aged eighty-eight. Albert's death was announced the following month.

Then, in August, Bernard Youens died, aged sixty-nine, after appearing in 1,246 episodes as Stan Ogden. Bunny, as he was known by all and sundry, had been a newsreader and an actor in local rep before he landed the job of Stan in 1964. With wife Hilda, played by Jean Alexander, the Ogdens had become national treasures. But Bunny had terrible health problems towards the end. He'd suffered a series of strokes and a heart attack. Bunny loved the show so much he had speech therapy so he could carry on playing Stan. I remember he called me into his dressing room one day to help him get out of his overalls. It was tragic to see such a nice man brought so low by illness. Three months after Bunny's death, it was announced that Stan had died.

At Stan's funeral, Hilda held back the tears until she was alone at home at Number 13. Then, as she handled Stan's spectacle case, the tears flowed. It was the most moving scene I'd ever watched and showed Jean's extraordinary acting ability. She said later that the tears of grief were real because she was thinking of the loss of Bunny. I cried every time I saw that scene, and still do now when it's repeated.

Above: Me with my mum, Lil, taken around 1945.
Note the Winston Churchill-like defiant scowl.
Right: My dad, Bill Piddington. This photo must
have been taken shortly before he was killed in 1944.

We didn't just lean on
lampposts in those
days . . . me and my
Aunt Margaret playing
in Butterworth Street
with our pal Rosie
Hincs.

Here's my dad, Bob Cleworth, with his mum – my grandma – who was known as 'Fairy' by everyone.

My mum's parents, John Willie Smith and his wife Adelaide. She was 'Granny Smith' to me and 'Addie' to everyone else.

Me, aged 10, with my class at Bradford Memorial School. I'm the one in the hideous pullover.

My mum, taken during the war.

Mum and Dad, Bill and Lil, taken around 1940. I'm not sure whether they were courting or just married.

Me (left) and my mate John Taylor. We must have been about seven.

Banging the drum for St Paul's Church Lads' Brigade aged 18.

The action replay of our wedding in 1962. The original film went missing so Ali and I put on our wedding day clothes a few weeks later to recapture the moment.

Me and Ali with her mum, Alice Short.

Rehearsals for the TV production of *King Lear*, 1982. John Hurt (Fool) is talking to Sir Laurence Olivier (Lear). I'm the handsome one with the bristling beard in the background.

This was taken in the '90s when Jack was landlord of the Rovers and Sir Cliff Richard was touring in the musical *Heathcliff*. The beard was supposed to make him look more rugged for the part.

Waiting in line to meet the Queen, who is shaking hands with Sally Ann Matthews (Jenny Bradley). It was taken after the *Royal Variety Performance* in London, 1989, which included a *Coronation Street* sketch.

I might not look as if I was enjoying singing here, but I certainly was. It was taken at a jazz festival in Blackpool in the '90s.

Liz Dawn and me with Frank Pearson, better known as drag queen Foo Foo Lamarr. He grew up on the same cobbled streets as me.

Liz and me with actor Ian McShane and his wife Gwen Humble, taken in 1996 when Jack and Vera were filming in Las Vegas.

'The Alzheimer's Club'. Left to right is David, Derek, me, Bryn, Peter, Tony and Jack. Sadly David died in July. I think this photo was taken in 2010 but none of us can remember!

Two of my sporting heroes, ex-England goalkeeper Gordon Banks and former world snooker champ Dennis Taylor, taken at a charity dinner around 2005.

Five generations of my family, pictured in 1990. My grandma, 'Fairy' Cleworth, is seated with my son Carl. I'm standing next to my dad, Bob Cleworth, and holding Carl's son Curtis. I couldn't do that now. He's more than six feet tall!

Me and Ali at an Aquinas Trust function about five years ago.

As Elsie Tanner sailed off into the sunset with Bill Gregory to open a wine bar on the Algarve, builder Bill Webster (Peter Armitage) moved into 11 Coronation Street, with his son Kevin (Mike Le Vell) and daughter Debbie (Sue Devaney).

I started the year with a storyline involving Fred Gee, the Rovers' cellarman, played by Fred Feast, a burly Yorkshireman. Fred had been a jobbing actor before he landed the role of Fred Gee, but his main claim to fame came about as a result of him being a paratrooper in the British Army. According to Fred, he'd used his knowledge as an ex-para to teach the Hollywood actor Alan Ladd how to jump out of an aeroplane.

In *Corrie* Fred hatched a plot with Jack to fiddle an insurance claim. The idea was that Jack would 'steal' Fred's car so he could report it stolen and make the claim. Their cunning plan was ruined when the car ran out of petrol and a policeman stopped Jack as he was refilling it.

During the filming of that scene, the car and I nearly slid into the Manchester Ship Canal. The cameramen wanted me to drive close to the edge for artistic reasons. But they nearly got an unexpected dramatic effect when first the car skidded on mud and then I did too as I got out.

In the end Fred decided to raffle the car to raise money. Nobody would buy tickets apart from Percy Sugden, who got the car for £1. Fred was furious when he found Percy had sold it for £50 to Kevin Webster, who used it for banger racing.

Fred Feast was prone to make the same sort of mistakes in real life as Fred Gee. I remember he bought a pub in the Pin Mill Brow area of Manchester. Fred thought he couldn't go wrong buying a pub – it was a licence to print money, or so he thought. When he reopened it, the pair of us performed an opening ceremony in the newly built gents' toilets. The pub was in a dodgy area and I think he had to sell it at a loss. Like Fred Gee, his heart might have been in the right place but his head for business wasn't too smart. The workload had become too much for Fred. Working in the Rovers meant he was needed to appear in lots of scenes and it was making him ill. He left the show and moved back to Scarborough.

Later that year, Jack and Vera were involved in a bitter barney over their TV licence. The detector van had caught them out and the licence was in Vera's name. Vera had given Jack the money to renew the licence, but he'd spent it on booze and betting. So Vera went to court facing a prison sentence. She was fined £150 and Jack decided to celebrate the fact that she'd avoided jail. As he came home after a night on the ale, he tripped over the telly and smashed it.

By a funny coincidence, that storyline reminded Liz Dawn that she'd forgotten to renew her own TV licence. She rushed out to get one before anyone found out. Otherwise we might have read headlines like '*Street* Actress in TV Licence Shame'.

That was the first of three bits of bad luck for Jack. He was working as a taxi driver at the time and Mavis Riley, who'd just passed her driving test, reversed into his car. Not content with having the crash damage repaired, Jack got mechanic Brian Tilsley to repair other damage caused before the accident. Mavis refused to pay for the extra work and Jack, of course, was skint. Brian kept the car until the bill was paid, so Jack couldn't work. That might have been a problem for a lesser man, but Jack was the sort who could enjoy the leisure opportunities created by not working. The only way Vera could get him back to work was by paying the bill herself.

One of his first jobs after collecting the car was to pick up Vera and Ivy Tilsley from the bingo hall. The two pals had won the jackpot, so Jack joined in the celebrations. On the way home Jack was stopped by police and breathalysed. It was positive, so Jack was fined £200 and banned from driving for a year.

It was great fun working with Lynne Perrie, who played 'Poison Ivy', as she became known. I'd met Lynne when she was singing round the clubs. In those days she was billed as Britain's 'Little Miss Dynamite'. She was our answer to the tiny American singer, Brenda Lee. Lynne told a few gags too. Sometimes, if the audience couldn't see her, Lynne would climb on a table to sing. The audience loved that. She had a bubbly personality which made people around her happy too.

Like Liz and me, she'd done a bit of work as an extra and that led to a role in a film called *Kes*, the landmark low-budget Ken Loach movie which won some top awards. That, in turn, led her to the part of Ivy back in 1971.

Just like Ivy, Lynne enjoyed a drink and a gamble. Some days she'd forget to take the various tablets she was on. She'd had heart surgery and, like me, had a collection of tablets to take on a daily basis. If she forgot to take them one day, she'd have a double dose the next. It was madness.

Lynne was the sort of woman who'd do anything for anybody, but she wouldn't take care of herself. She lived life to the full. It seemed inevitable it would end in tears. One day

I arrived at work to find Charlie Lawson, who played Jim McDonald, trying to bring Lynne round. She'd collapsed and was rushed to hospital in an ambulance. Eventually she was written out of the show in 1995. She'd played Ivy for twenty-four years and it seemed strange not having her around any more.

After Jack's driving ban, he tried to fiddle more benefits from the DSS. He removed all the family's furniture apart from the barest essentials so an official could see how strapped for cash he was as he looked after his sick family. Unfortunately for Jack, the official called again without warning and found a house full of furniture and a healthy family.

Why all these things made Jack a popular character is a mystery to me. Maybe it was because all his crackpot schemes ended in disaster.

After losing his benefits, Jack and Fred Gee started selling shirts on the market. Fred, who was working as Mike Baldwin's van driver, tried to impress a businessman they were dealing with by pretending to be Mike. But the con backfired when the deal was done and he was paid with a cheque made out to M. Baldwin. Mike found out and sacked him. That's when Fred left the show.

With Jack out of work again, Vera had a brainwave. She used her earnings from the factory to buy Stan Ogden's old window cleaning round. The price wasn't such a bargain because many of Stan's customers had either died or left the area. But it did bring some romance back into Jack's life when a friendly housewife called Dulcie Froggatt offered to fill his bucket. She was married to an oil rigger who worked away for months on end. Dulcie, played by Marji Campi, was in need of a cuddle, and Jack was just the man to give her one!

While Jack was keeping Dulcie's windows spotless, he was also on the make again. Percy Sugden's pet budgie, Randy, had escaped from his cage. Percy offered a £10 reward for the bird's return. Jack figured all budgies looked pretty much the same, so he bought one with similar colouring. He took it round to Percy to claim his reward. He might have got away with it but for two things: first, the budgie he bought was the wrong sex; and second, Randy had flown back home again.

The year ended with our Terry leaving home to live with the Ogdens. He was sick of all the rows between Jack and Vera and somehow thought he'd get peace and quiet with the Ogdens. Vera accused her enemy Hilda of stealing her son. Terry was working in a slaughterhouse so the Ogdens were getting the best cuts of meat while the Duckworths were managing on scrag ends. But Terry soon got tired of running errands for Stan, and he came back home for Christmas.

CHAPTER 12

Duckworths Top the Charts

The BBC launched *EastEnders* in February 1985, to challenge the supremacy of *Corrie* in the viewing charts. They incorporated the hour-long repeat on Sundays into their figures. With those early clashes between 'Dirty' Den and Angie Watts at the Queen Vic, *EastEnders* soon caught the public's imagination. The London-based press predicted the *Street* would be swept aside by this new kid on the block. But Granada hit back with a triple dose of Duckworths.

Mervyn Watson, who'd taken over the day-to-day production of *Corrie* while Bill Podmore oversaw other projects, left the show to produce *First Among Equals*. He was replaced by Scotsman John Temple, and his arrival coincided with a diet of Duckworths for *Street* fans. In 1985, Vera was in second place behind Ivy Tilsley (89) with 83 episodes. Terry was in fifth place with 77 and I brought up the rear in seventh place with 75 episodes.

It was a time to settle down after the deaths and departures of the previous year. Bet Lynch finally took over as manageress of the Rovers Return. Doris Speed had made her last appearance as Annie Walker back in October 1983. It was hoped at first she might become well enough to return. As time went by, it became clear that wasn't going to happen. A new boss was needed at the Rovers and Bet beat the opposition to land the job. She moved out of her flat above the Corner Shop and into the pub.

When Stan Ogden died, he didn't leave much for Hilda, but he did leave his secret racing formula, as patented by Captain Carstairs. For the first time in his life, Jack was starting to get lucky with a couple of good wins on the horses – until Vera put her oar in. She became suspicious of Jack's closeness to the recently widowed Hilda so she tore up the formula book.

Vera was off the mark about Hilda. In fact, Jack was still servicing Dulcie Froggatt and her windows. There was one scene with Marji Campi which involved us being filmed snogging in Jack's car. On the day that filming took place, I was full of the flu. I'd taken all sorts of medicine to get me fit but it wasn't working: my nose was running, my eyes were inflamed and I kept getting sick. I was terrified in case I passed my germs on to Marji. After I'd thrown up for the second time and wiped the vomit from my mouth, I asked if we could film the scene later. But Marji, bless her, told me not to worry. She'd disinfected herself and said, 'Let's just get it over with.' It's hard to resist kissing a woman after a speech like that.

Jack's window cleaning days were nearly over when he landed his dream job of cellarman at the Rovers. He decided to celebrate by paying a last visit to Dulcie. He must have thought she needed a final polish. Unfortunately, he was drunk and fell off his ladder, broke his ankle and started his new job with a sick note.

The fall was filmed in easy stages. I had to jump off the ladder for the first shot. No problem. I had to crouch at the foot of the ladder for the second shot. Fine. Then I had to sit in a rose bush for the final shot. That's when I suffered scratches to parts of my body which only Ali could treat.

I was getting on very well with our new producer, John Temple, but we had a dispute one day about Jack's cap. He reckoned I should take it off when I was standing at the bar. I told John I might not know much about acting but I was something of an expert on the wearing of cloth caps around Manchester. They may behave differently with their tam-o'-shanters in Glasgow, but there was a ritual in my part of the world which I'd learned from my dad.

If he came in and kept his cap on, it meant he was going straight out again. If he sat down and put his cap by the side of him while he ate a meal, he was going out again later. If he put it on the hook, he was staying in for the rest of the night. If he put it on the tallboy, he hadn't decided what he was going to do with the rest of the night and he was keeping his options open.

I modelled Jack's cap-wearing on what my dad used to do. Of course there were variations on this theme. I had one mate who'd gone prematurely bald at the age of twenty-six. He never ever took his cap off. I think he probably wore it in bed at night. He once resigned from a golf club because they insisted he take his cap off at the bar.

Jack sold his car to Terry and Curly, who clubbed together to pay £525 for it and began a removal business called Cheap and Cheerful.

The arrival of the Clayton family at Number 11 gave Terry a romantic diversion which earned Jack a punch in the mouth. Harry Clayton, a milkman, and his wife, Connie, had a daughter, Andrea, who was studying for her A levels. Terry took a shine to Andrea and their courtship distracted the teenager from her studies. This, and Connie's poor effort at making a silver lurex dress for Vera, led to a feud between the Claytons and the Duckworths.

When Andrea finished her affair with Terry, despite falling pregnant by him, there was a bitter row in the Rovers. Jack insinuated that Andrea had been sleeping around and that Terry might not be the father of the unborn child. Harry's response was to punch Jack in his big mouth. The idea was that Jack's false teeth would be knocked out and he'd have to scramble on the floor to find them.

Harry was played by Johnny Leeze, an old mate of mine who'd worked as a stand-up comic on the cabaret circuit. I told him to be careful with his punch because I didn't wear false teeth and didn't want to start.

Shortly after that scene the Claytons left the area. They moved to Sheffield to get away from the bad influence of the Duckworths – and who could blame them? But after they'd gone, Andrea provided Jack and Vera with their first grandchild, Paul Clayton, who was to appear in the show more than twenty years later. Johnny Leeze, a Yorkshireman, went on to appear in *Emmerdale*. It was said that the public hadn't taken to the Claytons. They'd lasted only eight months.

These things happen sometimes. Nobody knows why. Maybe the success of *EastEnders* was affecting the decisions at the top at Granada. *Corrie* had always had plenty of time for its characters to develop and take root. Now there was impatience and pressure to step up the pace of plotlines. Instead of romances slowly simmering, they were coming to the boil much more quickly.

Sean Wilson made his debut in 1985 as Martin Platt. It was third time lucky for Sean, who was another product of the Oldham Theatre Workshop. They seemed to have an endless production line, turning out top-quality young actors for *Corrie*. Sean had auditioned for the parts of Terry Duckworth and Kevin Webster before landing the role of Martin. I used to tease him about not getting the part of Terry. I said he'd missed out because he wasn't handsome enough to be realistic as Jack's son.

The Duckworths continued to dominate the show in 1986. Our Terry topped the charts with appearances in 77 episodes. I was in third place with 74 and Vera was eleventh with 67.

In 1986, one of Sean's acting colleagues from Oldham joined the show. It was third time lucky for her, too. Sally Whittaker had auditioned for the roles of Sue Clayton and Kevin Webster's girlfriend, Michelle Robinson, who appeared in only a handful of episodes. The chances are that if Sally had landed either of those parts, she would have disappeared when the characters were written out. It just goes to show how fickle fate can be.

Instead she was cast as Sally Seddon, a chirpy blonde who

made her debut in January. She was walking along the street for a job interview when Kevin Webster drove his van through a puddle and soaked her. Kevin took her home to Number 13 to dry her tights and love blossomed between them. Despite the best efforts of our Terry, who got a black eye for his troubles, Kevin and Sally got married in October.

Earlier in the year there'd been another high-speed and controversial wedding when Mike Baldwin married Susan Barlow. The simmering feud between Ken Barlow and Mike Baldwin, whose rivalry over Deirdre had more than 20 million viewers on the edges of their seats in 1983, erupted again. Mike had had Ken's wife, and now he was having his daughter – no wonder they came to blows.

You couldn't imagine Bill Roache, who plays Ken Barlow, thumping anybody – he's a perfect gentleman. He's also the cast member I always go to if I need a script problem explained to me. Sometimes I simply don't understand the dialogue and I knock on Bill's dressing-room door. He's always happy to help out.

I don't like to ask the bosses what the script is getting at for two reasons: mainly because I'd probably look daft, but also because I don't want to look as if I'm challenging the scriptwriters. They know what they're doing and I wouldn't want to suggest otherwise. So Bill talks me through the scene and it all becomes clear to me. He's a clever bloke and one of the *Street*'s bridge school.

In my early days, the main card players were Bill, Betty Driver, Doris Speed, Eileen Derbyshire, Bunny Youens and Geoff Hughes. It may surprise some people that Geoff

Hughes, who played thick-as-two-short-planks binman Eddie Yeats, could play snap let alone bridge. But Geoff's a smart cookie. You have to be clever to play someone who's stupid – unless you're me, of course.

Geoff was a relative newcomer to the bridge school compared to Bill Roache and Eileen Derbyshire, who've been playing the game in the Green Room since 1961. Eileen's been in the role of Emily Nugent and Emily Bishop for nearly fifty years. Emily's a prim and proper sensible lady, but Eileen's a great titterer.

Whenever there's a serious scene like a funeral being filmed, you'll always hear Eileen giggling away. She usually sets off her pal Barbara Knox, and then it spreads like wildfire. Before long the director has to call for order so we can look suitably solemn. I don't think they realise that Eileen's the one who started us off on a fit of the giggles. She always looks so innocent.

Jack was still dallying with Dulcie in 1986, but he'd found a new object of desire in the Rovers. Barmaid Gloria Todd, played by Sue Jenkins, started receiving red roses. It was no wonder she never suspected they were being sent by Jack. When she found out, she wasn't best pleased. When Jack got the knock back, our Terry tried his luck with Gloria. She gave him the bum's rush too.

While she was playing Gloria, Sue became pregnant and they had to shoot scenes of her from the chest upwards so her growing bump didn't appear on screen. Sue used to feel the heat in the studios and I used to waft my script in her face between takes to cool her down. Sixteen years later, when Sue's son Richard Fleeshman appeared in *Corrie* as Craig

Harris, I used to tell him I'd kept him cool before he was born.

Richard is a multi-talented lad. His father, David, and mum, Sue, are both accomplished actors. Richard can not only act, he's got a great voice and can play keyboards too. In time he should become a big, big star.

You've got to admire Jack's nerve, if nothing else. Who but Jack, while playing the field, could put his name forward as Husband of the Year?

Using Vera's name and forging her signature, Jack nominated himself for the title in a competition run by *Woman's Choice* magazine. His winning slogan was: 'My husband is husband of the year because right from the day we were married he has made my life one long honeymoon.' The prize was a brand new Vauxhall Nova car, which Vera claimed despite Jack's protests. Vera took driving lessons and amazed Jack by passing her test first time.

The storyline led to a terrifying experience when Vera drove the car with me in the passenger seat and Ivy in the back. Liz had passed her test but for years she'd driven only automatic cars. She'd long forgotten how to work a clutch and change gears, so for the filming I stretched my right leg over to press the clutch and changed gears with my right hand while Liz steered. I told Liz to press the accelerator pedal gently, but she shot off like Michael Schumacher. I nearly suffered whiplash and Lynne screamed as we sped away. I managed to knock the car out of gear and heaved on the handbrake so we stopped just before we hit a wall. Lynne was laughing hysterically in the back. I think she was glad to be alive.

Eventually we managed to complete the scene, and that night Vera took Ivy out to celebrate. They ended up in a strip club. Next day, when Jack was entertaining Dulcie in the back of the car, she found a pair of men's briefs stuffed down the seat. Jack confronted Vera with the evidence, but she was saved by Ivy, who was forced to confess she'd ripped them off a male stripper.

The affair between Jack and Dulcie eventually fizzled out through lack of opportunity. Unknown to Jack, his son Terry was proving to be a real chip off the old blockhead. Terry had taken over the window cleaning round and Jack's place in Dulcie's affections. Terry had no idea his dad had bedded Dulcie before him.

Dulcie's husband suspected Jack, and when he came home early from the oil rigs, he found the cart inscribed Duckworth outside his home and his wife in a state of undress. Terry had made a sharp exit, leaving the cart behind him in his hurry. So Dulcie's husband marched straight round to the Rovers, punched Jack in the mouth and said, 'Stay away from my wife.' When the penny dropped and a dazed Jack realised what Terry had been up to, he was outraged. It was the second time in a year he'd been thumped because of Terry.

His son agreed to take the rap to calm Vera down, but she wouldn't let it rest. She stormed round to confront Dulcie for seducing Terry. During the row, Dulcie admitted she'd slept with both father and son.

Vera went on the warpath and Jack was out on his ear again, but with unexpected charm he managed to convince Vera that Dulcie had told wicked lies only because she was jealous of their strong marriage. Jack couldn't believe his luck when Vera fell for it. But Jack had already shown his ability to get out of trouble a few months earlier when he accidentally started a fire that burned down the Rovers Return.

CHAPTER 13

Jack Burns Down the Rovers

The Rovers Return had become a national institution. It had been the most famous pub in the UK for more than twenty-five years. So it came as a shock to read my script one day and find it was going to be destroyed in a fire. Not only that – the man responsible for starting the blaze was Jack Duckworth.

Despite his many failings, Jack had somehow managed to remain popular with *Street* viewers, but I was really pushing my luck this time. I wondered whether they'd ever forgive me. When I saw the plot and realised that Jack was going to be the villain and Kevin Webster the hero, I wished it could have been the other way round. But on reflection it had to be bungling Jack who cocked up again.

For those of you too young to remember, Episode 2631, 'Fire at the Rovers', was screened in June 1986. It was written by Harry Kershaw. Viewers saw the scene being set for a fire the night before. As a pianist entertained customers, the electric beer pumps kept failing as fuses blew. It was an anti-quated system, and Jack, as cellarman, kept disappearing to change the fuses. To land the job, Jack had convinced Bet Lynch that he knew all about electrics. After all, he'd worked on the Waltzers as a teenager.

So as Jack went down to get the pumps working again, Bet announced, 'Worry not, booze artists. Cometh the hour, cometh the man with the power an' the knowledge. Super-spark'll soon have the ale flowin'.'

By 10 p.m. customers were getting annoyed as the lights kept going out, but they had a sing-song by candlelight as the pianist played on. Jack, knowing the 5-amp fuses would keep blowing, substituted a 30-amp fuse. All seemed well and he revelled in the cheers of the punters and the praise from Bet.

But in the early hours of the morning, when all the cus-tomers had gone, the pub was locked and Bet was asleep in the room upstairs, the tinder-dry cables behind the mount-ing board were ignited by the high-resistance connection. The fuse box burst into flames.

First to spot the danger was Sally Seddon as she returned home from a rock concert in Sheffield with boyfriend Kevin Webster. She noticed smoke billowing out from under the door of the Rovers. The dramatic scenes which followed were filmed partly at the Rovers and partly at a derelict pub called the Pineapple near the Granada TV studios.

Kevin hammered on the door of the Rovers to wake up Bet while Sally screamed for the Barlows at Number 1 to call the fire brigade. Percy Sugden, caretaker at the community centre and resident nosy parker, came out to investigate the racket. He showed Kevin a ladder which could be used to make an attempt to rescue Bet. After ringing 999, the Barlows evacuated their home next to the Rovers. Even our Terry made himself useful, stripped to the waist in tracksuit bottoms. He organised the moving of cars away from the fire and asked for wet towels.

It was just the sort of community action my family and millions of others had seen during the Blitz: people rallying round to help each other in a good cause. And what better cause than saving your local pub?

Kevin smashed Bet's bedroom window with a brick and climbed in after seeing her lying unconscious on the floor. She'd suffered from smoke inhalation. The firemen arrived at this point to take over the rescue and bring Kevin and Bet out safely. As the firefighters placed an oxygen mask over Bet's mouth, she started to come round. There was just time for her to crack a joke. 'Couldn't you hang on a bit, love? Let me get my face on.' Then she disappeared in an ambulance.

It took the firemen three hours to dampen the fire and the Rovers was left a smouldering ruin. Jack confessed to Terry that he'd put 'too hefty a fuse' in the box. He was worried an investigation would point the finger at him.

Luckily, Newton and Ridley Brewery accepted responsibility. They admitted the wiring should have been updated and decided to give the Rovers a complete renovation.

Bet must have known by Jack's sheepish looks that he was to blame for the fire, but she agreed to keep him on as potman with a warning. 'I've pinned up a little card next to the phone,' said Bet. 'Number on it's an electrician. If a fuse ever blows, that's who you ring.'

Jack was mightily relieved. The Rovers wasn't just his local and his living: the cellar was where he listened to the radio and made his racing selections. He also felt it his sacred duty to try out the beer to make sure it was in fine fettle for the customers. Jack took this aspect of his work very seriously indeed.

The fire scene at the Rovers, directed by Gareth Morgan, attracted 21 million viewers. It spelled the end for the Select and the Snug, but it gave the production team a chance to revamp the creaking old set of the Rovers and create a modern one-room pub. It also gave me a new title as the man who burned down the Rovers Return.

I think it was in the same year that I was asked if I could play a part in the All Stars soccer team. It was a charity outfit organised and managed by a guy called Tony Steenson, and included a lot of *Street* stars. Steeno, as he's known, was a salesman of some sort who used to play semi-professionally for Hyde United. He became a friend of our family.

In the first instance, Chris Quinten, who played Brian Tilsley, asked me if I'd turn out on the wing. He said they were a man short and had a spare pair of boots in my size. With great reluctance, knowing my limitations, I turned out for a match at Chester. I managed to avoid the ball for a few minutes and then suddenly it was heading towards me at great speed. Before I could get out of its way, it struck me on the chest and dropped to my feet. The crowd cheered my dazzling ball control. I ran about five yards with the ball and kicked it as hard as I could towards the penalty area. The physical effort proved too much for me and I collapsed to the ground. I wasn't looking when my cross was collected by Mike Le Vell, who hammered it into the goal.

That was the end of my playing career. I decided to quit while I was in front. From then on I turned up as chief coach, which meant I had to bring the beer from the bar at half-time. We had some fun times raising money for various charities. We played in Spain, Portugal, Ireland and all over the UK.

Some of the pitches were magnificent, like the Glasgow Celtic ground at Parkhead, where 35,000 fans turned out to watch us. It was the last game played before a famous terrace called the Jungle. We were supporting the main attraction: the veterans of Manchester United against the veterans from Celtic. It was a real thrill to hear the crowd chanting: 'One Jack Duckworth. There's only one Jack Duckworth.'

We arrived at Parkhead in blue tracksuits – the colours of deadly rivals Rangers. We were given green ones to wear instead and I was presented with a leather jacket with the green chevrons of Celtic incorporated into it. That memorable night at Parkhead ended with Mike Le Vell and me in a high-speed taxi to the airport because Mike had to get back to Manchester for filming. We made it with seconds to spare.

The Celtic ground was the best we played on. Others looked as though they'd moved sheep off the pitch just before we kicked off. Either way we had some great laughs.

Over the years I've coached a host of ex-soccer stars, such as Brendon Batson, Norman Whiteside, Alan Kennedy, Frank Worthington, Lee Chapman, Peter Barnes, David Cross, Martin Buchan, Asa Hartford and Len Cantello. The experienced internationals among them must have been really grateful for all the helpful advice and tips I was able to give.

The *Street* stars then were Chris Quinten (Brian Tilsley), Mike Le Vell (Kevin Webster), Kev Kennedy (Curly Watts), Phil Middlemiss (Des Barnes) and Sean Wilson (Martin Platt). Mike still plays and he's been joined by the younger cast members, such as Alan Halsall (Tyrone Dobbs) and Ryan Thomas (Jason Grimshaw). Other showbiz stars included DJ Mike Sweeney, Gary Webster from *Minder*, Patrick Robinson from *Casualty*, and Nick Conway from *Bread*. My son Carl played for the team in goal.

With my acting, singing, charity work and soccer team involvement, there never seemed to be enough hours in the day or days in the week. I'd stopped going out for a pint with the lads. There just wasn't any time. I felt like a mouse on a wheel and I couldn't relax.

Adrenalin can take you only so far, especially if, like me, you have a weak heart. I'd been struggling to breathe for a while. I used to disguise it while I was out shopping with Ali. I'd stop to look in shop windows to hide the fact that I was really trying to get my breath back.

The year before we'd moved from our house in Gorton to a new home in Bredbury, Stockport. It had twenty-seven steps leading up to the door, and it had got to the point where I could manage those steps only in easy stages.

There came a time when I could no longer hide the problem from Ali and she insisted I go to see our doctor. He referred me to a heart specialist at Wythenshawe Hospital called Henri Moussalli. After examining me, the surgeon said he wanted me to come in for an operation right away. I said that was impossible because I had two weeks of scripts to fulfil. I said I would come in for the op in two weeks.

Mr Moussalli said, 'I may see you in two weeks, if you live that long.'

I hadn't realised how serious it was: putting off the operation for two weeks was a gamble. Luckily I got away with it. I was still alive two weeks later so I went in for heart surgery.

CHAPTER 14

My First Heart Bypass Operation

I'd had the operation explained to me. Henri Moussalli made it sound like a routine piece of plumbing but instead of pipes and ballcocks they were dealing with my arteries and heart valves. I was suffering from angina, which is a closing of the arteries. This makes it difficult for your blood to circulate, causing pain throughout your body and shortage of breath. The solution is to widen the narrow arteries. To do this, the surgeons use veins they've removed from your leg earlier. Why you have extra veins in your legs that you don't need is a mystery to me, but there you are. I figured I'd leave the heart surgery to the experts.

The alternative to having the operation was for my symptoms to get steadily worse until the moment when one of the arteries sealed up completely and then it would be goodbye cruel world. I'd got to the stage where that could happen at any moment. Even for the sort of man who's scared to visit the dentist, the choice was fairly obvious.

Apart from the risk to my life, I had one other worry. I was told that if everything went according to plan, I'd be in hospital for a couple of weeks and then I'd need another four months at home to recuperate. I wondered whether *Corrie* would keep my job open or whether Jack would be written out of the show.

I knew that if I died they'd have to kill off Jack, but they might do that anyway. I had a word with Podders, the executive producer, and he assured me they'd find a way to write round Jack's absence. I was greatly relieved because I'd only given them short notice – I'd only had short notice myself.

The cast wished me good luck after I'd filmed my final scene, with me hoping it wouldn't be my final scene, if you know what I mean. Julie Goodyear joked that I was lucky having a heart problem. She said Granada allowed you half a day off for flu and three weeks for cancer, but they were quite generous for open-heart surgery. The last the viewers saw of Jack was him going down the cellar to change a barrel.

After saying what might have been a last farewell to my children, Ali drove me to the hospital. I'm not a great man for sentimental words, but I'd made a cassette of love songs that I gave to Ali. With my mate Mike Timoney, I'd recorded eleven of our favourite numbers. Mike had arranged the hit record 'Matchstalk Men and Matchstalk Cats and Dogs', sung by Brian and Michael, so he knew what he was doing. He made a great job of my cassette. It included our special song, 'Wind Beneath My Wings'. Those songs, and that one in particular, expressed my feelings better than anything I could say.

So, with a last kiss from Ali, I headed off to the operating theatre. I'm not a religious man but at times like these you offer up a prayer anyway just in case someone's listening up there. The best thing about surgery is that after your general anaesthetic, you don't worry any more. It's left to everyone else to do the worrying while you're out for the count.

Henri's original plan was to carry out four bypasses on clogged arteries that he'd identified earlier. When he opened me up, he found a fifth bypass was necessary. I was unconscious while he dealt with this extra problem.

After the operation, which lasted several hours, I was given morphine to dull the pain of having my chest cut open from top to bottom. When I did eventually come round, I was on a different planet. At first you don't know where you are and then you don't realise the operation's over. I can scarcely remember Ali coming to my bedside, holding my hand and telling me everything had gone well. Eventually, as they gradually withdrew the pain-killing drugs, I started to realise I'd cheated the Grim Reaper once again.

My family were the first to visit me, then members of the cast called. Liz Dawn was so shocked by my appearance, she couldn't look at me. She went over to the windowsill and said, 'Look at all these flowers.' She then busied herself reading out the names and messages. Later she told me she didn't want me to see the shock in her face. She said I'd lost a load of weight and looked like a ghost.

Another visitor was Eileen Derbyshire, who brought a flask of soup and some sandwiches for Ali. She said: 'Everybody brings stuff for the patient, but they forget the nearest and dearest.' It was a typically kind gesture from a thoughtful lady.

There comes a time when the joy of cheating death gives way to the pain of recovery. After making sure the operation had gone successfully, Henri went abroad on holiday. While he was away, an MRSA-type bug struck and nearly finished me off. The smell from my scar was disgusting.

Henri came back from holiday a week later and quickly identified the problem. I feared the worst and asked him if I was on the way out. He became annoyed with me for being pessimistic. He said he could sort out the infection but I needed to stop being negative.

Unknown to me, he'd told Ali that if he didn't operate soon I would die. On the other hand, he didn't know whether I was strong enough to survive another operation.

For three days I was so uncomfortable with the pain I couldn't sleep. Ali sat by my bedside, holding my hand and stroking my hair. She said she'd never been so pleased to hear me snoring as when I eventually drifted off.

I was at my lowest ebb. All my fight had gone and I just wanted the pain to be over. I told Ali, 'I'm too tired, love. I've had enough.'

She got upset and angry. 'Don't you dare say that,' she said. 'You're going to get better.'

Eventually Henri decided he could wait no longer. After another general anaesthetic, he cut me open again, took everything out, cleaned away the infected bits, put everything back inside me and sewed me up again. To everyone's relief, especially mine, the operation was a complete success. I'd spent my silver wedding anniversary at death's door in hospital. Two weeks later I was allowed home to convalesce.

The day I was released from hospital was the day Liz and

I were booked to appear at a children's charity function at the Salford Albion Casino. I asked Ali to drive me there on the way home so I could at least show my face and not disappoint the fans. Ali said I was being ridiculous, and I was. But I was insistent. I didn't realise how weak I was. When I got there, with throngs of excited people swarming round waving balloons, I lasted only three minutes. I asked Ali to drive me home.

For weeks I lay in bed reading newspapers, magazines and books, and watching telly. It felt odd to be watching *Corrie* with no Jack Duckworth around.

Little by little my strength started to return. One day I was able to walk half a mile down to the paper shop. I walked back up the hill and felt so good I ran up the twenty-seven steps to the back of our house. I hadn't been able to do anything like that before the operations. I was so excited I asked Ali to put her head on my chest. She looked worried and said, 'What's the matter?'

I said, 'Nothing's the matter. That's what a strong heart is supposed to sound like.'

After eighteen weeks away from the show, I was fit enough to go back to work. When Jack emerged from the cellar, he was 1½ stones lighter. While he'd been down there, Terry had run off with a married woman, Brian Tilsley had kidnapped his son Nicky, and Bet Lynch had mysteriously vanished.

Jack was straight back in at the deep end with a comical scene with Vera. He'd managed to install a new gas fire at Number 9 and decided to sweep the chimney. After borrowing brushes, Jack shoved them up to clear a blockage. It ended with Jack and Vera and the entire lounge covered in soot. As Jack picked up the nearest piece of material to wipe his eyes, it turned out to be Vera's new fur coat. We both looked like pandas as she gave me a mouthful of abuse. It was great to be back!

Worse was to follow. Vera's mother, Amy Burton, had fallen ill so Vera moved her into the back room. To say Jack and his mother-in-law didn't see eye to eye would be putting it mildly. As Jack explained, 'If she lived in India, she'd be sacred. She's like Boris Karloff after a busy night at the grave-yard.'

Fanny Carby, who played Amy, had a penetrating voice from her time as a stage actress. So it was easy to look irritated when the pair of them fought their verbal battles. Amy filled the house with friends, warning them to keep an eye on their handbags when Jack was around. He found a way to retali-ate. After discovering Amy was frightened of birds, he made a point of bringing his pigeons into the house.

The year 1987 ended on a sad note for viewers. The mar-riage between Mike and Susan Baldwin fell apart and in December Hilda Ogden made her final appearance. She left Number 13 to work as housekeeper at a doctor's home in the country.

Jean Alexander, who'd played Hilda with such distinction for twenty-three years, had never felt the same after the death of her screen husband, Bunny Youens. But the *Street* replaced one great actor with another. As Jean departed, another star was establishing himself in Weatherfield.

Roy Barraclough, a tremendous talent with a wicked sense of humour, had signed a long-term contract as Alec Gilroy.

Roy had already made his name on TV as one half of the two old biddies Cissy and Ada, with comedian Les Dawson. Now he was bringing his own brand of comedy to the *Street*.

Because of my heart operation, I'd missed 36 of the 104 episodes in 1987, but I still managed to appear in 60 of the remaining 68 episodes. Top of the appearance charts that year were Alf Roberts (81), Mavis Riley (76), Ivy Tilsley (76), Rita Fairclough (74) and Mike Baldwin (74).

CHAPTER 15

Three Weddings and a Funeral

The year after my heart surgery, 1988, the Duckworths were once again given a heavy workload. Vera topped the appearance charts in 90 episodes. I was in fourth place with 80, behind Betty Turpin and Emily Bishop.

There was a sad start to the year when Margot Bryant died on 1 January, aged ninety. Older viewers would remember Margot playing Minnie Caldwell. She made her debut in December 1960, becoming a regular in the Snug at the Rovers alongside Ena Sharples and Martha Longhurst until she retired in 1976. She'd made a vital contribution to the programme over the years and will long be remembered for those scenes with Ena and Martha as they swapped gossip over a milk stout.

Shortly before she died, Ali and I went to see her at a retirement home in the Wilmslow area. She was still as bright as a button. Margot was a sweet old lady, but she could surprise you with the sort of language that would make a sailor blush when she felt passionate about something.

Margot's death was balanced by three weddings in Weatherfield. First Brian and Gail Tilsley remarried in February after their divorce. Then taxi driver Don Brennan, played by Geoff Hinsliff, married Ivy Tilsley in June. In November, Derek Wilton finally married Mavis Riley after a false start four years earlier. On that previous occasion both bride and groom got cold feet and failed to turn up for the ceremony. This time they married at the Register Office and had a honeymoon in Paris. Peter Baldwin's patience had been rewarded: he'd finally been given a long-term contract after making occasional appearances as dithering Derek for fifteen years.

Behind the scenes there were changes too. Producer John Temple left to join Scottish Television and Bill Podmore, the *Street*'s longest-serving producer, retired. Mervyn Watson was brought back to produce the show under new executive producer David Liddiment. For me and Jack, though, life went on as normal.

Jack doesn't often get things right, but he was spot on with his warnings that his mother-in-law wasn't to be trusted. First Amy was caught shoplifting by Alf Roberts at his minimarket. Then she was caught with her hand in the till at the Rovers. Even Vera had to accept her mother was a wrong 'un. She packed her bags and sent her away, only to find that everything of value at Number 9 had disappeared along with her. Jack reckoned it was a price worth paying if he never had to see Amy again.

Alec Gilroy had married Bet Lynch the previous September

and was now a regular in the show, appearing in 77 episodes in 1988. It gave me an opportunity to work alongside a master craftsman. Roy knew how to set me off in fits of the giggles. I'd be ready for what he was going to say, but I wasn't always ready for what he was going to do.

On one occasion I walked into the Rovers and delivered my line. Alec jumped with surprise when I spoke. Then I saw he'd got his knife down the back of the charity box which sits on the Rovers' bar. It was completely unscripted and done by Roy to get me going.

Other times, as we were delivering our lines, he'd unexpectedly grab my hand, turn it over and empty some nuts into the palm to see if he could put me off my stroke. Once Roy came over when I wasn't looking, rapped on my head and said, 'Is anyone at home?' As I fell to the floor, helpless with laughter, I broke wind rather noisily and set everyone else off.

Julie Goodyear got in on the act too. Whenever I walked behind her or Roy near the bar, they'd do a little jump and look round as if I'd patted their bottoms.

Those were happy times. With my newly refurbished heart, I was fitter than I'd been for years, and I'd learned a new way to help me remember my lines. It always seemed strange that I'd been able to learn song arrangements far more easily than scripts. So I started recording my dialogue on a tape recorder and playing it back to myself. Hearing the words spoken a few times was far easier than remembering them from the written page. I was still at the back of the class, but no longer the dunce in the corner.

Although the newlywed Alec and Bet were running the

Rovers, Alec also had a theatrical agency which arranged bookings for cabaret acts at pubs and clubs. When a rival agent was desperate for a singer as a last-minute replacement, Alec agreed to do him a favour. He said he knew an up-and-coming vocalist who was destined for stardom. The name of this new Sinatra? None other than Jackie Duckworth Junior.

Jack had always fancied himself as a singer, and Alec told him it was his big break to open a new club. We never heard him sing, but we heard the consequences and saw his torn jacket. For once Vera was supporting Jack as she complained to Alec, 'I don't care how bad he was. They'd no right to set the dogs on him.'

At the time I was still singing in cabaret at night, so I'm not sure what sort of effect this storyline had on attendances at the clubs where I appeared. Who knows? Some people might have come along to laugh at my dreadful voice only to be disappointed to find I was a decent singer.

Nigel Pivaro, the dashing young actor who played Jack and Vera's son Terry, was anxious not to get typecast in his role as a womanising villain. He'd ask to be written out from time to time so he could pursue other roles on stage and try his hand at other jobs in the theatre.

Once, while he was away from the *Street*, he got his fingers burned. Nigel had saved from his *Corrie* earnings to put money into a play which he performed in at the annual Edinburgh Festival. The critics loved it and it was turned into a film but Nigel didn't get a part in the movie.

In 1987, while I was recovering from my heart surgery, Terry had run off with Linda Jackson, the wife of his army buddy, Pete Jackson. Pete was played by Ian Mercer, a young actor who was to return to the *Street* in 1995 as Gary Mallett.

Having split from Linda, Terry came back at the end of 1988 to cause more mayhem. First, he turned up in Don Brennan's taxi unable to pay the fare. As usual, Vera had to shell out. Then, while working as Mike Baldwin's driver, he used the company Jag as a babe magnet. It misfired when an angry husband sprayed 'Stay Away From My Wife' on the side of the car and Terry was fired. He left Weatherfield for Bournemouth.

Meanwhile, Jack's face took another battering when Vera crashed into a lamp-post. She'd been taking him on a picnic to put the romance back into their marriage when it happened. Jack's nose was broken and he sued Vera's insurance company for compensation. While waiting for his windfall, Jack accompanied Don Brennan to a casino where he blew the housekeeping money.

When the insurance cheque came through, Jack couldn't cash it because he didn't have a bank account. Vera cashed it for him, then bought a new bed, a microwave and a washing machine. Jack was left with just £15. The year ended as the previous year had begun: with Jack nursing a sore face and licking his wounds.

There'd been rumours running around for some time that *Corrie* was going to expand to three episodes a week. They were dismissed by Granada as idle speculation. Then, in 1989, the idle speculation was confirmed as true.

The year started and finished with a death. Actor Chris Quinten, who'd played Brian Tilsley since 1978, had gone to Hollywood and married American TV presenter Leeza

Gibbons. He'd wanted to divide his time between Los Angeles, where he was trying to establish himself, and *Corrie*. But the bosses decided otherwise, and Brian was stabbed to death outside a Manchester nightclub in February.

It was ironic that Brian should die outside a nightspot because Chris had opened a nightclub in Manchester called Quintens. It seemed to go well at first, but then it started losing money. It was to Chris's credit that he worked his socks off, doing personal appearances here, there and everywhere to pay the bills before the club finally closed.

I'm sorry the marriage and the Hollywood dream didn't work out for Chris. In Los Angeles there's an actor behind every bar and McDonald's counter. The only job he landed was a walk-on part in *RoboCop 2*.

He was a nice lad. I met him again ten years ago at a charity bash in a London nightclub. He's one of those guys who always cheers you up because he's got a permanent smile on his face. He was working as a disc jockey and public relations man. I was pleased to see he was still earning a crust. We had a laugh about my soccer skills.

At the end of 1989, one of *Coronation Street*'s all-time villains died when Alan Bradley was killed. Alan, played by Mark Eden, was a sinister character. He became known as 'Bradley the Beast' by the tabloids. He was a devious, double-dealing cheat who'd wormed his way into the heart of Rita Fairclough. The fact that Rita was such a well-loved woman and a vulnerable widow, made Bradley's behaviour even more despicable.

In fact, Mark Eden was a top bloke. He was the long-term boyfriend of Sue Nicholls, who'd appeared on *Corrie* since

1979, first as Audrey Potter, then Audrey Roberts. Mark and Sue later married.

Mark had been a pop singer in his youth. In the late 50s and early 60s he used to have a fan club of teenage girls, in the era of Terry Dene and Marty Wilde. I'm told Mark is also a gifted pianist. We were always planning to appear on stage together somewhere and it's one of my regrets that we never got round to it.

He'd transformed himself into a terrific actor, proving that less is more. Instead of looking villainous in an obvious way, he had an air of quiet menace. It was in the cold, unblinking eyes that you could see evil lurking. I remember one scene where he picked up a sandwich from a plate and ate it without taking his eyes off Rita. It was thoroughly creepy and made the hairs stand up on the back of my neck.

After trying to rape Dawn Prescott and murder Rita, Bradley attempted to kidnap Rita in Blackpool and was knocked down by a tram. If there was a competition for all-time soap villains, Bradley the Beast would be right up there.

No wonder Mark got abuse away from the studios from *Corrie* fans who found his character so believable. I had it bad enough for nicking money from Vera's purse and putting a smile on Dulcie Froggatt's face. It must be far worse if your character attempts rape and murder and you play the part so convincingly.

Despite this storyline dominating the show that year, there was still plenty of work for the Duckworths in 1989. Jack was joint top alongside Audrey Roberts with 91 appearances, and Vera's 88 took third place.

From the Duckworths' viewpoint, 1989 would probably

best be remembered as the year they put stone cladding on Number 9 and Jack broke his glasses. Jack and Vera were so proud that the cladding made their home stand out from the rest. The neighbours might have been horrified, but that was clearly because they were jealous.

The saga of Jack's glasses began, literally, by accident. They were a prop pair, and I knocked them on the floor one day and stood on them. The storyline had started with Jack giving customers the wrong change because of his failing eyesight.

He told Vera his body was changing for the worse. Jack said, 'Me 'air's fallin' out. Me teeth are goin'. I'm not as randy as I was. And I've got athlete's foot.' Vera insisted he visit an optician, and he returned to work with a new pair of glasses.

About two weeks after Jack got his new specs, I was in my dressing room reading a script with my own glasses. When I was called for the next scene, I trod on Jack's glasses, which had somehow fallen on the floor. The arm was completely off. People were running about trying to find me another pair, but I told them not to bother. I asked someone to get me some Elastoplast and a pair of scissors from the first-aid box. Then, during a scene with Vera, Jack stuck the broken arm of the glasses back on again. While he was talking to Vera, he was supposed to be studying the gee-gees. Instead I sat there putting plaster on the specs.

As you might expect, Jack never got round to getting them properly mended, and for years I walked round Weatherfield wearing them. It got to the stage where, away from the studios, 'I see you've got your glasses mended' became as popular as 'Where's your Vera?' among the fans' repartee.

When I went on a promotional tour to Canada, I was doing a photo-signing session in Ottawa, when I looked up and saw the next twenty people in the queue were wearing black-rimmed glasses held together by a strip of Elastoplast. When I visited Japan, too, there was a giant billboard in the centre of Tokyo of Jack, wearing a simpering smile and the dodgy glasses. I've no idea what the Japanese caption said.

Eventually it was decided the joke had gone on long enough and Jack got a new pair of glasses. In the show, Vera was supposed to have got so fed up with them that she threw them on the floor and jumped on them. In reality, she saved Jack's dodgy glasses and we sold them for £1,600 at a charity auction.

Jack still saw himself as a ladies' man in 1989, until he got the ultimate put-down from Rovers' barmaid Tina Fowler. Tina, played by Michelle Holmes, was happy for Jack to buy her drinks, but turned down his offer of romance in the back seat of his car. She jumped on a passing bus instead. Vera accused Tina of trying to steal her husband. Tina told her not to be ridiculous, adding that no woman in her right mind would be attracted to Jack.

As a matter of fact, I have had one or two fan letters over the years. Unfortunately, they were all from ladies of a certain age who wanted to mother me. I showed them to Ali and we had a good laugh. I never received the naked photos or items of underwear which TV stars are supposed to get. Instead I got letters from blokes asking me to visit their local pubs for a drink.

Liz had a few secret admirers though. There was one very persistent bloke who called himself Buffalo Bill. Liz didn't write back because she didn't want to encourage him. Eventually he grew tired of the lack of response and a final letter told her, 'You've got a mouth like a cow's arse.'

The year 1989 saw the arrival of Jim McDonald, an ex-soldier, and his wife Liz. They were played by Charlie Lawson, who came from Ulster, and Beverley Callard, from Yorkshire. They moved into Number 11 with their twin sons, Andy and Steve, played by Nick Cochrane and Simon Gregson.

It was also the year they introduced the character Reg Holdsworth. Actor Ken Morley, as Reg, became a cult figure as manager of the supermarket Bettabuys. Before coming to *Corrie*, Ken had played in that hilarious sitcom *'Allo 'Allo!* He shared the gift of comic timing that Roy Barraclough had. He also did brilliant James Mason impersonations.

Ken was another man with an expressive face who could crack me up, but I got my own back on him during a scene at Number 9, when Reg came round for dinner. Vera, who worked at Bettabuys, was keen to impress her boss so she made a shepherd's pie. Jack showed her up by putting the meal between two rounds of bread and creating a sandwich. The mincemeat squirted in every direction, including my hand. Ken was a snappy dresser just like Reg, so I couldn't resist the chance to pat him on the shoulder, leaving brown fingerprints on his jacket. When the scene was finished, Ken gave me that withering look he'd perfected so well, then joined in the laughter.

My last scene of 1989 was another comical situation involving Derek Wilton. He'd taken a job selling novelties to toy shops. During Chuckles' Novelties' Christmas party, Derek had dressed as Father Christmas. He'd been accidentally locked in the warehouse and escaped by climbing on to the roof. As Jack was walking home from a drunken night out with Curly, he glimpsed Derek in his Santa outfit. Befuddled, Jack gazed in wonder, then caught up Curly and said, 'I've just seen Father Christmas.'

It was a great line, but it was in danger of being ruined by some over-enthusiastic lads who were watching us on location in Pendleton, Salford. All the efforts of the technicians and directors to keep them quiet had failed. We were in danger of having to scrap the scene or shoot it elsewhere. I walked over to them in a last-ditch attempt to save the day. I asked them to give us a break for one minute. A couple of the ringleaders said: 'All right, Jack. We'll keep quiet for you.' The crowd-control power of Jack Duckworth saved the day.

CHAPTER 16

A Visit from the Prime Minister

From time to time, filming is put on hold while we have VIP visits. It gives us an opportunity to meet people like Her Majesty The Queen, which is a great honour, of course. It also means we have to put in overtime to catch up later.

At the start of 1990, a pair of newlyweds moved into 6 Coronation Street. Des Barnes, played by Phil Middlemiss, and his wife, Stephanie, played by Amelia Bullmore, were described as yuppies. The press said it was an attempt by *Corrie* to go upmarket. Jack and Vera campaigned against efforts to gentrify the area, although their graffiti would have been more impressive if they'd known how to spell yuppies.

The Barneses' arrival scene coincided with the visit of Margaret Thatcher, then the Prime Minister, which must have been something of an ordeal for Phil and Amelia. Imagine starting your first day at work in a new job and being watched by the PM!

I was behind the bar of the Rovers with Roy Barraclough as Alec Gilroy, when Mrs Thatcher and her entourage approached. I asked Alec if we should charge her for a drink in an unscripted chat. Alec replied, 'Oh, yes. If you give one a free drink, they'll all want one. She pays for her own.'

In fact, Mrs Thatcher had a quick look round the Rovers and disappeared without bothering to stop for a drink, so I never met her. She was especially impressed with the corner shop bearing the name Alf Roberts. As a little girl in Grantham, Lincolnshire, she'd lived above the grocer's shop run by her father. His name was Roberts too.

I missed out on the Queen's visit to the set in 1982 because months previously I'd booked a recording studio for the day of her visit. I couldn't let a group of musicians down so I had to be a few miles away when she called. It wasn't going to be a formal presentation; it was just a social gathering where we'd be in the Queen's presence. I asked our props man, Vinny, if he'd like to mingle with Her Majesty. He thought I was joking until I handed him my ticket and explained that I couldn't attend.

I hope the Queen wasn't too disappointed by my absence, but I suspect that means there'll be no knighthood for Jack Duckworth. I was introduced to her in 1989 when the *Corrie* cast played a scene during the *Royal Variety Performance* at the London Palladium.

I'd met Prince Charles when we did some work for the Prince's Trust. In 2000 he called into the Green Room to meet the cast of *Coronation Street*. The scene that was being shot involved Vera being ill in bed. As he approached her bedside, the prince said to Liz, 'Hello. How are you?'

Liz replied, 'Have you brought me any grapes?'

The prince's face was a picture. He roared with laughter. That's my Liz.

We were filming a special one-hour programme live and Prince Charles asked if that meant we would be paid more money. I asked Charles Allen, one of Granada's executives, if we would get more money for being live. He shook his head and said, 'No.'

'There's your answer,' I told the prince.

'Oh well,' he said, 'it was worth a try.'

He seems a very nice man, and I'm not just saying that to curry favour, Your Royal Highness. I also admire his father, Prince Philip. He gets some stick in the newspapers from time to time for making what they call 'gaffes' but he's just got a dry sense of humour.

I'd done some work for the Duke of Edinburgh's Award scheme, and I was given a guided tour around St James's Palace. I told a group of children who were there to receive their awards how I'd just come back from Canada, where children's achievements were reported in the newspapers. I said it would be wonderful if British newspapers carried some good news once in a while. It was all off the top of my head because I hadn't been warned I might have to make a speech. The Duke congratulated me on what I'd said and told me he agreed wholeheartedly.

I was also impressed with Prince Andrew when he paid a visit to a charitable event for underprivileged children. Ali and I were mixing with these kids when the prince went past in a luxury barge along the Manchester Ship Canal. He'd been heading for a marquee where the charity organisers had laid on food and drink for their VIP guests, but Prince Andrew saw the kids waving to him and must have asked the skipper to drop him ashore.

The prince didn't wait for the boat to moor; he just jumped ashore when the boat was a few feet away. I'll bet his royal protection crew were having kittens. If you fell in the Ship Canal in those days, you were as likely to be poisoned as drowned. The prince spent a lot of time chatting to those kids and clearly made their day. It'll give them something to tell their grandchildren.

On another occasion I met Princess Anne at a function when I was standing between Ali and Liz Dawn. It gave me a chance to say to the princess, 'I'd like you to meet both my wives.'

There have been a few visits to the studios from the worlds of Hollywood and pop music. Dustin Hoffman came to see us while he was promoting his movie *Tootsie*. It was a film about a drag artist, but I was relieved to see he'd come dressed as a bloke.

I've met Sir Cliff Richard a few times at charity functions and he came to the set and posed for a photo with me behind the bar of the Rovers. He was wearing a beard at the time because he was appearing in the musical *Heathcliff*. The beard was a bit of a change from his normal clean-cut image.

We also had a visit from Status Quo when they made a cameo appearance in the show. When I walked into the Green Room, they immediately started talking in the Duckworth growl. Francis Rossi warned Rick Parfitt if he carried on talking like that, he wouldn't be able to sing when they did a gig that night.

The storyline involved Les Battersby going to shake Francis's hand and accidentally dragging him off the stage. It turned out they were playing at a gig nearby so they agreed to appear at Les's wedding. I absolutely love their music so it was a real thrill to appear alongside Francis and Rick. They seemed equally thrilled to be appearing in *Corrie*.

Quite a few top-notch celebrities would like to be in the show if they got the chance. Sir Laurence Olivier wanted to play an extra in the *Street*, so anything's possible. What never ceases to amaze me is that when I start to introduce myself to these A-list celebrities, they already know who I am and the character I play. The most extraordinary thing is when they ask if they can have their photos taken with me.

I remember when Liz and I were due to go to Las Vegas for a *Corrie* special. We were shooting a scene in an aircraft back in England as part of the video. It was a spoof on the famous Cinzano advert starring Joan Collins and Leonard Rossiter. The advert always ended with Joan accidentally throwing a drink in her face as her seat tilted backwards. Jack and Vera re-enacted that scene as Joan walked past our seats. After we'd filmed it, Liz was asking me if I thought Joan would mind if we had a photo taken with her. As we discussed it, Joan came over and asked us if we'd mind posing for a photo with her. I have to pinch myself sometimes.

When I saw Joan in a TV studio a little later and said, 'Hello', she beamed and said, 'I didn't think you'd recognise me.' Can you imagine anyone failing to recognise Joan Collins? You'd have to be dead.

To celebrate our thirtieth anniversary in 1990, Granada organised a special show, presented by Cilla Black. She came into the Duckworths' sitting-room set and, before I could warn her, she sat on the sofa. A cloud of dust rose and I had to explain that Vera wasn't the best of cleaners.

The year began with Deirdre Barlow, played by Annie Kirkbride, filing for divorce from Ken and starting an affair with an electrician called Dave Barton. Dave had rescued Deirdre's daughter, Tracy, after she'd started a chip pan fire. Dave offered to fit a new kitchen and he and Deirdre became lovers. In fact, Dave Barton was played by an actor called Dave Beckett, who was Annie's lover in real life. They'd lived together for years, so their love scenes didn't need much acting or directing.

Annie is one of the best-loved members of the *Corrie* cast. She's a gentle, caring soul who'll do anything to help people. I once saw her coming out of the disabled toilets wearing a pair of marigolds. She'd been cleaning them. There's a smoking shelter outside for those who want to nip out for a ciggie. Annie made cushions for the chairs, decorated the shelter and brought a piece of carpet for the floor. That's the way she is.

Towards the end of 1990 Jack was involved in a storyline in which he sold a 1957 motorbike to Jim McDonald. Jim knew enough about machines to open a repair shop and Jack's bike was something of a classic.

Vera hated the bike, and threw bits of it, which Jack had stripped down and cleaned, out of the kitchen window. It was a scene I'd watched my mum perform in real life thirty years earlier in our two-up and two-down in Butterworth Street. My dad had stripped down a bike and left the spare parts in the kitchen sink. Mum chucked them over the wall so Dad could never get that bike to go.

Despite Vera's best efforts, Jim found the spares, got the machine working and Jack drove it with Vera riding pillion. It was twenty-five years since I'd ridden a bike. Liz hadn't got a clue. When we approached a corner to turn left, I leaned into the corner as you're supposed to, but when Liz felt the bike lean left, she tilted to the right and nearly put us in a skip.

The year ended with Vera trying to breathe life into her marriage to Jack by taking him on a second honeymoon. Jack wasn't too keen on the idea of a romantic weekend.

He did make an effort though. For Christmas he bought Vera an Alsatian called Boomer. It should have been company for Vera, but it ate the turkey. Jack tried to train Boomer the Barbara Woodhouse way, ordering him to 'Sit' in a commanding, masterful voice. Boomer responded by growling menacingly, and Jack beat Vera to the top of the stairs with the dog after them. Boomer kept them both prisoners in their bedroom all day, snarling and baring his teeth every time they moved. Jack thought he'd bought the Hound of the Baskervilles. In fact, he later learned that Boomer was short for Boomerang. He got the name because he was always being returned to his shady owner by dissatisfied customers.

CHAPTER 17

Married to Royalty

In 1991 Mervyn Watson left to work for the BBC. He was replaced by Carolyn Reynolds, *Corrie*'s first female producer for twenty years. Newcomer Sarah Lancashire arrived in the show in January to play a dizzy blonde character called Raquel Wolstenholme for a month. Raquel was so popular with the viewers that the new producer had the sense to bring her back at the end of the year and sign her on a long-term contract.

Sarah's father, Geoffrey Lancashire, had been one of the early writers of the show. She also had her comic timing off to a fine art, just like Roy Barraclough and Ken Morley.

Sarah had been a vocalist as well as an actress, singing in a band called Titanic, which she claimed cheerfully had sunk without trace. I'd sung in a band called Take Ten with her husband, Gary, who played flute, clarinet and sax, so we had plenty to talk about.

One day I took my little granddaughter, Naomi, Sara's daughter, to the studios to meet the cast when she was five. She was fine with all of them until I introduced her to Raquel, then she burst into tears. The same thing had happened to my son Carl when I'd introduced him many years before to a drummer called George Walker. Carl looked up to George so much that he was overcome with emotion and howled his head off. Likewise, Raquel was Naomi's idol, so meeting Sarah was too much for her. But Sarah knew what to do. She went to her dressing room and came back with a bag full of Raquel's costume jewellery. She showed Naomi these little pieces and won her round. They quickly became firm friends after an embarrassing start.

Jack and Vera were soon involved in a comical storyline that started with the death of Vera's mother, Amy Burton. For all Amy's faults, and there were many of them, Vera was saddened by her loss. It would be fair to say Jack got over the tragic news quite quickly. 'Oh dear, what a pity, never mind' would sum up Jack's attitude.

At the subsequent funeral, Vera saw Joss Shackleton, whom she knew as Uncle Joss. But Joss, played by Harold Goodwin, explained that he was Vera's real father. Just before she died, Amy had asked Vera to look after Joss, so that was a possible explanation.

Jack thought Joss was just a chancer on the make, but Vera insisted on moving him into the back bedroom at Number 9. Once he'd got his feet under the table, Joss, a retired barber, let Vera into the family secret. (If you're reading this, Your Majesty, I can only apologise and say I'm not responsible for writing the storylines.) According to Joss, he was the illegitimate grandson of King Edward VII, making our Vera a cousin of the Queen.

Jack thought this was an hilarious piece of nonsense and decided to play an April Fool's joke on Vera. With the help of Joss, who had copperplate writing skills, they sent her a card pretending it had been written by the Queen. Vera fell for the hoax hook, line and sinker. But when Jack yelled, 'April Fool' and told her it was all a wind-up, she refused to accept it. She believed the lie and refused to believe the truth – typical.

For many years afterwards, whenever the Queen's name was mentioned in *Corrie*, Vera would smile knowingly and adopt a wistful look. Jack would spot the expression and roll his eyes as if to say, 'Here we go again.'

Off screen Harold Goodwin, who played Uncle Joss, was a great character. He'd appeared in more than eighty films going back to the black-and-white days. He had some fascinating tales to tell about his times in war movies with the great actors of that era.

After Joss had been reminiscing about his days in service, Jack decided to apply for a chauffeuring job, which was advertised with a housekeeper's post for Vera. They went along for an interview with references forged by Joss. They landed the jobs, but when the stately home was burgled they came under suspicion. Although they were innocent of the burglary, their false CVs cost them their jobs.

You can't keep a bad man down and Jack tried another scam that summer when water flooded his house. To exaggerate the insurance claim, Jack tore wallpaper off undamaged walls and splashed water in rooms where there was no supply. An assessor was unimpressed and refused to pay out any money. During the flood, Uncle Joss returned to his own flat and wasn't seen again.

Later that year, Mavis Wilton discovered a fox had made his home in her garden. She was delighted and named him Freddie. Jack was less than pleased when it killed two of his pigeons. He set out on a fox hunt, borrowing Boomer's owner and the Alsatian as they tried to run Freddie to ground. Mavis dispatched husband Derek to draw the scent of the hounds away from their home. Mavis stayed behind to protect Freddie like a mother hen protecting her chicks. When Jack attempted to enter her garden, Mavis was waiting with her frying pan. He ducked and it was Boomer's owner who was flattened by the pan-wielding Mavis.

Thelma Barlow, who played Mavis, and Peter Baldwin, who played Derek, were a perfect comedy couple. She'd got mousey Mavis off to a T, while Peter's portrayal of dithering Derek provided great entertainment. Why they decided to kill Derek off later I will never know. Thelma left the show soon afterwards. The pair of them are sorely missed.

Thelma is a brilliant actress with a flair for comedy. She showed what an accomplished actress she is in the Victoria Wood sitcom *dinnerladies*. I've got the boxed set and I've watched every episode about twelve times. I laugh out loud every time. I always thought if Julie Walters ever came to work at *Corrie* as Victoria Wood's other creation, Mrs Overall, my career would be over. I'd be speechless with laughter every time she came on set.

It was Thelma who helped me out when I was in agony with a pain in my right shoulder. I'd hurt myself diving into a swimming pool in Tenerife. The pool was shallower and I was heavier than I thought. My right hand hit the bottom and sent a jarring pain up to my shoulder. At work the following week, the only way I could get comfortable was by lying on the hard floor of my dressing room. Thelma saw me there as she walked past and asked what had happened.

When I told her, she gave me the name of an acupuncturist, Mr Palmer, in Northenden, Manchester. I had a treatment on the Tuesday and again on the Thursday, and by the Saturday I was pain-free and playing golf in the Isle of Man. I've given shallow pools a wide berth ever since.

In 1992 we had three weddings and two funerals in *Corrie*. The show was still flying high in the viewing charts, but we were attacked by Lord Rees-Mogg, chairman of the Broadcasting Standards Council, for being old-fashioned. He also criticised the low number of ethnic minorities who appeared. His remarks caused a public outcry and I was pleased to see the press come out in our favour.

The best piece came from *The Times*, of all newspapers. Patrick Stoddart wrote: 'The millions who watch *Coronation Street* – and who will continue to do so despite Lord Rees-Mogg – know real life when they see it even if it is heightened and sometimes lightened in the most confident and accomplished soap opera television has ever seen.'

I've always thought of *Corrie* as being warm like an old overcoat. If it's old-fashioned is that such a bad thing? There are plenty of people out there, both young and old, who would like life to be like it is in *Corrie*. I can still watch *Corrie* with my grandchildren if I choose without wondering if someone's going to get their kit off or come out with language which would embarrass them and me.

Even as some of the storylines have become darker to show the harsher realities of life, the gallows humour is never far beneath the surface. I think it's a northern trait always to see the funny side of everything. It's probably something to do with our wet weather: every dry day is an unexpected bonus for us.

Jack and Vera were still busy in the show in 1992, with me clocking up 121 appearances in fourth place behind Gail Platt (130), Raquel Wolstenholme (127) and Mavis Wilton (123). Our Vera was fifth with 115 appearances.

The year began with a sad storyline when Liz McDonald went into early labour. Little Katie McDonald was born prematurely and died the following day, leaving Liz and Jim devastated.

Then there was a catfight between Raquel and Angie Freeman over Des Barnes. Angie, played by Deborah McAndrew, lost her job as barmaid at the Rovers when she found Des had been cheating on her and tipped a pint over him. Footloose and fancy-free after his wife Steph left him to run off with another man, Des was becoming a randy Romeo. Raquel not only won Des's heart, she landed Angie's job after she was sacked.

After environmental health officials had told Alec he needed a brand-new kitchen if he wanted to serve food, custom fell away at the Rovers. He decided to introduce an exotic attraction to bring in the punters. His master plan? A mouse-eating spider.

Now I'm not afraid of spiders but this was the daddy of them all. It was about the size of my hand and kept in a cage. Alec's clever idea backfired when the spider escaped. It reappeared during an environmental health inspection and Alec had to squash it with his bare hands. The story provided great entertainment – but not for one new member of our cast.

Sarah Lancashire was truly terrified of even the smallest spider, so this was her worst nightmare made flesh. When she heard about the storyline, the colour drained from her face. She looked as though she was going to faint. Eventually she managed to ask if they were planning to use a real spider. When told that they were, she shook with fear. I don't think telling Sarah this spider only ate mice was a great help.

People who suffer from arachnophobia will sympathise with Sarah's plight. She didn't want to share a building with a spider, let alone a TV scene. The director managed to find a way to shoot the scenes so that Sarah and the spider were never in the same room together. Even so, she would sidle up to me and ask if the spider had been taken away. The conversation always went the same way.

SARAH: Has it gone yet?

ME: Yes, love. You're all right.

SARAH: Has it left the building?

ME: Yes. It's gone home.

SARAH: Do you promise?

ME: Yes, love.

Then she would try to compose herself. There were some who thought it was funny at first and made jokes about it. When they saw her in tears, it made them realise what an ordeal it was for her. I felt sympathy for Sarah and knew just what she was going through. Never was an actress happier to see the end of a plotline.

I'd had some experience of this fear of spiders. My son Carl hates them. I played a joke on him once by telling my grand-daughter Naomi to drop a tomato stalk on Carl's lap. He jumped up and left the room like Linford Christie. When he came back and found out what I'd done, Carl glared at me and said, 'Don't you ever, ever, do that again.' Carl's a strong, brave lad and normally he's got a good sense of humour, but I realised then I'd overstepped the mark.

After a slow start with the girls, Curly Watts was beginning to catch up Des Barnes in the Don Juan stakes. He'd taken a long time to 'break his duck', as he put it, but once started there was no stopping him.

As Reg Holdsworth's deputy manager at Bettabuys, Curly had saved enough to put down a deposit on 7 Coronation Street. This brought an end to his brief time as Jack and Vera's lodger. It also gave him more opportunities to have fun with the ladies.

Just as Jack had done ten years before, Curly joined a dating agency. Instead of giving himself an exotic name like Vince St Clair, Curly called himself Gerald Murphy. A meeting was arranged with a woman called Janet Shaw, who turned out to be his ex-fiancée, Kimberley Taylor.

This was a reprise of Vince's meeting with Carole Monroe, but this time it ended in smiles instead of tears. The engage-ment was revived. And, unlike previously, Kimberley's mother, Brenda, played by Marlene Sidaway, approved of the relationship. She thought Curly was a better prospect now that he had his own house – until she found Angie Freeman's black bra lying on a sofa. We were left to suspect Curly was relieved when Kimberley broke off their engagement again.

The first wedding of the year came after our Terry brought his pregnant girlfriend, Lisa Horton, to meet Jack and Vera. Terry was on bail on a charge of causing grievous bodily harm and Lisa, played by Caroline Milmoe, was determined to stand by him. After coming to blows with Jack in the Rovers, Terry's bail was rescinded and he was held in custody.

On his wedding day, Terry arrived in handcuffs accompanied by warders. In a moment of weakness, they allowed him to take off the cuffs for the wedding photos. Jack could have warned them what would happen next, as Terry legged it. He was on the run for a while until he tried to get a sub from Vera. Reg spotted him at Bettabuys and called the police. Terry was jailed for three years. Every cloud has a silver lining though. Jack earned £100 from the newspapers for selling Terry and Lisa's wedding photos.

After the traumas of 1989 with Alan Bradley, viewers were happy to see Rita find love again. It came in the shape of retired toffee salesman Ted Sullivan. Ted, played by Bill Russell, was her knight in shining armour who'd come to rescue her from falling for Reg Holdsworth. In fact, I remembered Bill from the days when I'd seen him playing a knight on telly when I was a kid. He'd been the star of a weekly series called *The Adventures of Sir Lancelot* in the 1950s. Rita's happiness was short-lived because Ted was already suffering from a brain tumour, and he died in her arms in a moving scene which left everyone reaching for their hankies.

On a cheerier note, Mike Baldwin married his off-and-on girlfriend Alma Sedgewick. We all knew that was going to end in tears eventually, but at least Alma had found happiness for a while.

At the time Ted Sullivan was dying, a new character was born. Terry's wife, Lisa, gave birth to a boy called Tommy. I remember playing a scene with baby Tommy, played by Darryl Edwards. It was ideal for an actor with a bad memory like me, because I had a chance to invent my own script. I had a few basic lines to say, but mainly I was just chatting to my grandchild about life.

I told the director I didn't want to rehearse. I'd go straight for a take as soon as they handed baby Darryl to me. I told Tommy to remember that whatever happened in his life, his granddad would always love him. It was the sort of conversation you would expect in real life between an adult and a baby who can't really understand what's going on. With close-ups of Tommy and Jack, it worked really well and everyone was chuffed with the results.

Before the year was out, Lisa had started seeing Des Barnes, and Vera warned Terry in prison. She said she thought Lisa was falling for Des. As a result, Des got a nasty beating from Terry's mates. Lisa was horrified to learn she'd married a thug. She left the Duckworths to return to live with her parents in Blackpool. Des tracked her down and brought her back to Weatherfield – with fatal consequences. Caroline Milmoe, who played Lisa, was a lovely, sweet girl. I always felt sorry for her being tarnished with the Duckworth name.

There was some light relief towards the end of 1992, when Jack took a job moonlighting as a pall-bearer. He was off sick from the Rovers with a bad back but he was caught out when Alec attended a funeral where Jack was carrying the coffin. Jack realised he'd been spotted and just managed to get the funeral director to take over from him as he made his getaway. Roy Barraclough had decided to carry a bag of sweets as Alec gave chase. It created the comic effect of sweets flying everywhere as he pursued Jack.

As Jack drove away in the hearse, he saw Vera walking along the pavement. He slid down in the driving seat as he passed her, so she stared in astonishment as a driverless hearse went by. Jack just had time to get home and lie under a blanket on the settee seconds before Alec could get there to challenge him. He managed to convince Alec he'd been mistaken and even got an apology out of him. But as Alec was leaving, the blanket slipped aside to reveal Jack's black funeral shoes. It was one of the last scenes I played with Roy, and his exit was a great loss to the *Street*.

I'd watched him twice in plays at the Oldham Coliseum and he was absolutely brilliant. One of them was a one-man show. In the first half he played a man who was dying. After the interval, he played the dead man's sister. The second half had been going for twenty minutes, when a bright spark sitting in front of me turned to his wife. In a stage whisper he said, 'By heck, it's Alec again.'

I thought the *Street* bosses should have moved heaven and earth to keep Roy, but they sent Alec off to Southampton to become entertainments director of Sunliners Cruises, ending his marriage to Bet. I was sorry to see Roy go, but I have happy memories of 1992. It was the year I was the subject of *This Is Your Life*.

CHAPTER 18

This Is Your Life

For those readers as old as me, you may remember the early days of *This Is Your Life* when Eamonn Andrews used to ambush people live in the street and stick a microphone under their noses. He'd be disguised as Father Christmas or a policeman and the audience would get a live performance from his 'victim'. After a couple of early disasters, they changed the format so that the ambush was filmed live and then spliced to a filmed gathering of friends and families with tales to tell. It was screened later with any embarrassing expletives edited out.

By 1992 Michael Aspel had replaced Eamonn as the man with the big red book. I'd seen him in action a few times when he'd surprised cast colleagues like Roy Barraclough, Annie Kirkbride and my screen wife, Liz Dawn.

In the earliest days, it wasn't just celebrities who were the subjects of the programme; sometimes it was a tireless charity worker or an unsung ambulance driver. But, sad to say, over the years the TV company discovered viewers were switching channels if the star of the show was unknown. People would watch the first two minutes, see it was a firefighter they'd never heard of who'd rescued seventeen people from a blazing building, and turn over. Life shouldn't be like that but it is. By the 1990s, the only people to feature in *This Is Your Life* were celebrities. Soap stars seemed to be top of the pops.

I'd long thought the victims must be really stupid not to realise they were being set up. How on earth could you swear an entire family to secrecy? Even if you managed that, how would you avoid somebody making a mistake? Wouldn't all the people close to you start behaving suspiciously?

We'd been watching the show one night and I was having dinner later with Ali and our friends Mike and Doreen Yates. I said they'd never catch me like that. It must have been all Ali could do to stop choking on her food, because she knew what I didn't: I'd already been selected as a victim and she was in on the conspiracy. When I look back now, I can see the signs. Hindsight's a wonderful thing.

It seems the plot was hatched three or four months before-hand. Sue Green, one of the programme's researchers, had discreetly approached Ali. She wanted to know whether the closest members of my family were prepared to assist the programme-makers in total secrecy. I'd told Ali in the past that I never wanted to be the subject of the programme. I said it would be hugely embarrassing. I'm pleased she had the good sense to ignore me because it was a great honour to be chosen and it became one of the highlights of my life.

Ali was allowed to confide in my son Carl and daughter Sara but no one else at that stage. Sara has never been able to keep a secret in her life, so how she bit her tongue I'll never know. As the day approached for the confrontation by Michael Aspel, it seems I was being followed round by a team of sleuths who were monitoring my movements to make sure I didn't twig what was happening.

Ali had collapsed with a viral infection and hurt her back in the fall, so she was recovering in Tameside General Hospital, Ashton. I was visiting her whenever I could. But she also had an extra visitor I knew nothing about: Sue Green, who was obtaining a list of friends from my distant past. The sleuths made sure that Sue was disappearing out of one door as I was entering by another.

The penny should have dropped one day when Sara said she had to take our pet dog, Cindy, to the vet. There was nothing wrong with Cindy but I was too concerned about Ali to pay proper attention. In fact, Sara was going to one of their secret meetings and invented the vet story as a cover.

On the day it happened, I was supposed to be filming a scene as Jack with Peter Baldwin as Derek at the Rovers. I was pulling him a pint when Vera came in with some news about something that was happening in Canada. She had to use the name of the city Saskatchewan, but she mispronounced it. Liz apologised and they went for a second take.

Unknown to me, they were creating an opportunity for the *Corrie* camera crew to be replaced by the *This Is Your Life* team. Liz stumbled over the pronunciation again and I went to sit down at the back while she got ready for a third take. Meanwhile, the director had said, 'Checking that.' Instead of staying where I was, I started walking off the set in the direction of Michael Aspel. He was hiding just out of sight, but Julie Goodyear spotted the danger and headed me off.

The tech team said they were ready to go for another take. As Liz came into shot again, I saw this bloke coming on set out of the corner of my eye. I thought he was going to ruin the scene. Then I recognised Michael Aspel with his big red book. My first thought was to wonder who he was after and why I wasn't in on the secret.

When he said, 'Bill Tarmey, this is your life,' I nearly fell through the floor. Julie was laughing like a drain. I turned and said, 'You sod.'

Liz had given up trying to keep a straight face and now she was laughing too. I turned to Liz and said, 'And as for you . . .'

I was in a state of shock. I said to Julie, 'What's this all about?'

She said, 'You deserve it. Enjoy it, Tarmey.'

Then, still shaking with the shock of it all, the filming stopped and I was led to a dressing room in the bowels of the Granada TV studios. There I found a smart set of clothes which Ali had arranged to be delivered. There were sandwiches and drinks, including my favourite – Guinness.

I peeped out of the dressing-room door and there was nobody around. I wondered if I was going to be the first subject of *This Is Your Life* to have nobody bother to turn up. Eventually. my favourite dresser, Roy, came in to make sure I was OK. I offered him a Guinness, but I didn't have one. It might have calmed my nerves but I wanted to stay sober. Then the make-up lady came in to put a bit of touch-up on my forehead to stop the studio lights bouncing back into the cameras.

For ten minutes after that I was left on my own, thinking how this had happened to me. It was totally surreal. I looked back on my life from that two-up and two-down terraced street, from being hopeless at school and learning to be an asphalt spreader – now this.

Eventually an assistant came and led me towards Studio 12, which is like a small theatre with a stage surrounded by seats. As I waited outside the door, I heard the *This Is Your Life* theme and I was told to go in. There I was met by Michael Aspel and led to the stage as the audience applauded.

I remember going over to Ali and kissing her. They'd brought her from her sickbed and asked if she wanted to sit in a wheelchair, but she wasn't having any of that.

Although I thoroughly enjoyed the show, I was still in a daze. I can remember it only in flashes. Some of my old school pals, such as Billy Taylor, Ian Ball and Tom Jones, were there, mates from the Church Lads' Brigade and asphalters, like Tucker Cloran and Andy Cunningham. They told the story of my pretty cup and the individually wrapped sandwiches.

Dave Livesey, the neighbour who'd saved my life after the heart attack, told Michael what had happened and his race against time to get me to the hospital. Henri Moussalli, who performed my heart bypass operation, made a fine speech. He said he'd had my heart in his hands and it was a heart of gold – a poet as well as a heart surgeon. Gordon Banks, the fabulous England goalkeeper, was there to talk about my charity work.

Friends from the world of music, such as Mike Timoney, George Walker and Paul Atherton came along. Faith Brown, the impressionist with a magnificent voice and matching bosom, described how I'd been her compère at the Condron Club. She was worried because she had a sore throat and I'd told her, 'Don't worry. When they see that chest they'll forgive you anything.' She recalled how I'd played the bongos and tambourine at the back while she was performing.

Most of the *Corrie* cast were there. I remember Bill Roache said I was a good lad. Julie Goodyear was there in a stunning dress with a plunging neckline which showed off Newton and Ridley to spectacular effect. She let the dress do the talking for her.

Last but not least was my lovely family. I remember my dad said something and he tried so hard to sound posh. My brother Alan and I couldn't stop giggling.

Finally, Michael asked me if I'd sing my special song, 'Wind Beneath My Wings', for Ali. By great good fortune, Mike Timoney and the lads had brought their instruments along and had set up on stage. They'd gone up a note too high for me, but I tried to concentrate and give it my best shot. I had to look away when I saw the tears rolling down Ali's cheeks. Then I saw Liz and Julie crying too. Surely it wasn't that bad!

At the end of the song, Michael gave me the book and I got a standing ovation. I was still feeling numb. The book contains the script for the night. A week later another book arrived at my home with photos taken during the night and a video of the programme.

Straight after the show they held a party for everyone, with loads of free food and drink. Some of my old mates who

My first appearance in *Corrie* in 1979 at the wedding of Brian Tilsley and Gail Potter.
I'm at the back with our Vera. Behind us are Ena Sharples and Albert Tatlock.

Me as 'Jack the Lad' in 1982.

Jack put a twinkle in the eyes of Dulcie Froggatt (Margi Campi) in 1984.

I think Jack wanted to put some colour into the cheeks of Tina Fowler (Michelle Holmes) as well in 1989.

Jack and Vera with our wayward son Terry in 1988.

Jack doesn't look too sure about the stone cladding at Number 9 in 1989.

When Doug Murray claimed he'd lost everything in 1993, he walked into the Rovers in his boxers, cap and socks to make a point.

In 1992 our Terry's wife Lisa brought Jack and Vera joy with the birth of their grandson Tommy.

Jack and Vera were thrilled in 1995 when they became landlord and landlady of the Rovers.

Flying home from Las Vegas in 1996, Jack and Vera bumped into Joan Collins. The scriptwriters copied Joan and Leonard Rossiter's famous advert for Cinzano. Instead of Joan, it was Vera who got soaked when Jack accidentally tipped her seat back.

Tony Blair was the leader of the Labour Party in 1996 when he called at the set to meet Jack, Vera and Raquel. A year later he was elected Prime Minister.

When Jack had a chance to ride a racehorse in 1996 it was only going to end one way . . .

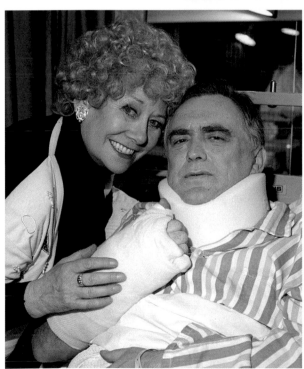

. . . and here I am later in hospital with Vera.

In 1999 Jack suffered a heart attack after his landlady, Eunice Gee, pounced on him. Jack had to have a heart by-pass operation – I've had two!

Jack as a lady bowler, playing for the Rovers' Ravers, 2004. Fiz and Hayley also in shot.

One of my favourite bands, Status Quo, played a cameo role in *Corrie* in 2005. Here's Jack in the Rovers between Rick Parfitt and Francis Rossi.

Jack's secret life as a nude model was bound to come back to haunt him in 2006. This was the moment Vera found out in an art gallery.

Jack heard in 2008 that his offer to buy a bungalow in Blackpool had been accepted. Vera was thrilled but didn't live long enough to make her dream move.

Our Terry tries to look sincere as he consoles his dad at Vera's funeral in 2008. Jack can see right through him.

Jack looked as proud as Punch in 2009 when he gave away the bride as Molly married Tyrone. It was all too much for Tyrone, who fainted when Molly arrived.

I shed real tears when Vera died in 2008 and at her funeral. It was the end of a double act that had lasted 29 years.

Jack and Vera on the beach at Blackpool in 1993. Behind their rows there was a real love affair going on.

hadn't got up to say anything were there too. If I have one regret from a brilliant night, it's that I didn't get a chance to speak to all the friends who'd come along. Some got little more than a wave and a smile, and I apologise to them. It just wasn't possible to get round to talk to everyone, and I hope the ones who missed out weren't offended.

Ali was looking very tired. It must have been quite an ordeal for her coming there from her sickbed so I took her home while the party was still in full swing. When we got home, I was tired but the adrenalin kept me awake.

It may sound ridiculous, but I've always had trouble recognising the fact that I'm famous. In my heart I know I'm a fraud. I'm just a pillock who comes into a studio to say some words that some other clever person has written. For years I'd managed to get away with it but I'd always been waiting for the bubble to burst. After *This Is Your Life*, I thought that if it all ends tomorrow, at least I was famous once.

CHAPTER 19

Making Music

After *This Is Your Life* was screened, I was asked if I'd sing with the Hallé orchestra at the Bridgewater Hall in Manchester. This was, pardon the pun, music to my ears.

Mike Timoney had been approached by a guy we both knew called Bill Connor. Bill is a conductor, arranger and musician who had told Mike the Hallé had star guests from time to time. He'd heard me sing 'Wind Beneath My Wings' and wondered if I'd be allowed to perform in a concert.

I asked Carolyn Reynolds, the *Corrie* producer, and she gave me her blessing. After I told Bill I was up for it, the Hallé management rang. I was told they didn't have a rhythm section as such in the orchestra. I thought I'd be lost without one and said so.

Twenty minutes later I got another call asking me who I'd like so I gave them the names of my long-time mates Tommy Steer on piano, Dave Linane on bass, Dave Hassall on drums and Paul Mitchell-Davidson on guitar. Although it was a great honour to play with the Hallé, I didn't trust myself to get the timing right without people I knew around me.

Dave Linane had already worked with me in *Corrie* when he was in a trio that accompanied Jack when he sang a snatch of 'I've Got You Under My Skin' at a party in the Rovers. On that occasion, I'd deliberately got my timing hopelessly wrong, as Jack wasn't supposed to be any good. Dave was horrified then. I told him this time we'd be trying to get the timing right.

Three hours before the concert was due to start, I rehearsed with the orchestra. Bill Connor had asked me if I'd sing 'On The Street Where You Live' from *My Fair Lady* and three other numbers.

Ali had bought tickets for the entire family. As I walked on stage there was a 94-piece orchestra on my left and an audience of 2,000 on my right. As is normal, I smiled at the audience as I crossed the stage to shake hands with the conductor. Everywhere I looked I could see friends and family, smiling at me, clapping and wishing me well.

Once again, not for the first time and by no means the last, I couldn't believe my good luck. As the smile got stuck across my face, I wondered whether I should have been wearing my brown trousers. In fact, I was in the full dinner suit and bowtie. I had to come out of this dream world I'd entered, stop listening to the beautiful sound that was filling the hall and concentrate on the arrangement. Although I was terribly nervous, I enjoyed every minute of it.

That performance led to another booking with the Hallé. This time they wanted me to be narrator while they played

Peter and the Wolf. It was another amazing experience for me.

I did my best to learn the lines from the script. I also got a tape of another recording of *Peter and the Wolf* but it was by Barry Humphries as Dame Edna. It's hard to imagine a bigger contrast than between the voices of Dame Edna and Jack Duckworth. But every little helps, and I arrived for rehearsals as ready as I was ever going to be.

They had a Japanese-American conductor, Kent Nagano, who asked if I'd had a score. No. I asked if he'd cue me in, so we had a run-through. At first I was coming in too early when he pointed to the strings behind me. He gave me full hand signals when it was my turn to speak and that went fine. After the show, the conductor asked me how I'd managed to do all the different voices. I told him that ninety cigs a day helped and he laughed. Everyone was happy and no one more than me.

Another request came in for me to sing for *Children in Need.* This was a BBC programme but Granada had no objections because it was such a good cause.

I was to sing 'I've Got You Under My Skin' with the BBC Big Band augmented by the BBC Philharmonic. I'd received my arrangement for the song a week before the performance. But as I was leaving my house, the postman arrived with a letter containing a new arrangement. As I sat studying it, I thanked my lucky stars I hadn't left the house a minute earlier.

At the BBC studios, as I tried to memorise the revised version, I was asked if I'd got the new arrangement. I said I'd only got it that morning and was trying to remember it.

'Don't worry,' I was told. 'We're doing the original version instead.'

The orchestra was being conducted by Syd Lawrence, who was a legend in the music world. The Syd Lawrence Orchestra had kept the sounds of the big-band era alive for decades. I'd worked with Syd a bit prior to *Corrie*, so it was good to see him again. He pointed to the 76-strong orchestra behind him and said with a grin, 'Have you seen them all?'

I winked and said, 'Sorry, Syd. When I worked with the Hallé, we had ninety-four.' Syd's reply was unprintable.

At one stage I was asked if I'd mind singing a duet with Dame Kiri Te Kanawa, the New Zealand soprano who'd sung at the wedding of Prince Charles and Lady Diana Spencer. I said I'd be delighted but for one reason or another it never happened. Perhaps her management thought Kiri singing with Jack Duckworth might end her career.

Later, in 1993, I was approached to make a charity record with the St Winifred's School Choir. They'd already enjoyed chart success with 'Matchstalk Men and Matchstalk Cats and Dogs' and 'There's No One Quite Like Grandma'. I was fifty-one and had never had a record released. In terms of experience, these schoolchildren were way ahead of me.

It was my *Street* co-star Helen Worth, playing Gail Platt, and her pal Suzie Mathis, the radio presenter, who talked me into it. I didn't need much persuading because the choir had already proved their talent and the producer was Pete Waterman, who'd taken Rick Astley, Kylie Minogue and Jason Donovan to the top of the hit parade.

The clincher came when I was told that all proceeds from

the record would go to the Aquinas Trust. This was a charity set up by Helen, Suzie, artist Harold Riley and hotelier Shaun McCarthy to help underprivileged children who didn't benefit from any other charities. I'd had a tough childhood but we never went without love and affection. I've always been happy to do what I can for kids who are less fortunate.

Helen and I used to joke about our inability to say no to worthy causes. We'd pretend to say the word 'No', but at the last nanosecond it always came out as 'Yes'. The truth is we've always been happy to oblige whenever possible.

The song they'd chosen for us to sing was 'One Voice', a Barry Manilow number with inspiring lyrics. Even as we rehearsed the song at the school in Manchester, I was reminded of my moment of glory the year before. Michael Aspel crept up to the nun who supervised the choir and ambushed her for *This Is Your Life*.

It was great fun recording the song. They say you should never work with animals or children, but the kids at St Winnie's were a marvellous bunch. They were so professional it was a joy to work with them.

It was also an honour to work with Pete Waterman, who hosted a pop show at that time called *The Hit Man and Her*, with Michaela Strachan. Pete and I were having dinner with our wives one night, discussing our love of jazz. He said he'd always fancied doing a jazz album. What an opportunity that was for me.

I can't believe the answer I gave him. Instead of saying, 'Let's do one together,' which would have been the smart thing, I said, 'You'll never make any money with jazz.' Even today I wonder what was going through my idiotic brain when I made that remark. Talk about shooting yourself in the foot!

I revealed my stupidity to his wife one night when she said Pete was out buying trains. I thought she was talking about a train set for his back bedroom, but she said, 'No, Pete buys real trains.' I think he was bidding for *The Flying Scotsman* or some similar icon of the steam age.

'One Voice' reached about fourteen in the charts and I was asked if I'd appear on *Top of the Pops* in London to sing it live. Unfortunately, it clashed with recording *Corrie*, which had to come first. I suggested we could perform it live in Manchester and have it shown live in London, but the Beeb wouldn't budge. My biggest regret was that a *Top of the Pops* performance might have sold more records, moved the song higher up the charts and raised more money for the Aquinas Trust charity.

It would have been another feather in my cap to have appeared on *Top of the Pops*, but I wasn't being awkward. When a TV crew and other actors are relying on you, it's not on to let them down. I've had to miss family funerals because of filming. It's one of the downsides to the job, but we all understand the rules when we sign up to them.

I remember when my mum was buried at Southern Cemetery at 12.30 p.m., I had to leave the wake at the Princess Hotel off Princess Parkway, Manchester, to be back at the studios filming at 2 p.m. There was some sort of party being filmed, and I had to wear a red nose and a silly hat. I was sitting there, pretending to be happy, with tears rolling down my cheeks. Liz Dawn and Julie Goodyear, who knew where I'd been, gently led me on to the dance floor. My back was to the cameras so nobody could see my tears as the filming was done.

When my father-in-law, George Short, died, I missed his funeral because of work commitments but managed to turn up for the wake afterwards. Over the years I've had to miss other funerals, weddings, christenings and parties I'd love to have attended. But you can't be in two places at once.

It isn't that I use filming as an excuse. On one occasion I postponed a holiday to Tenerife because I'd seen a poster on a shop wall saying I'd be attending a charity event. Some local lad with good intentions had hoped I'd turn up. I didn't want to disappoint any kids who came along to see Jack, so we put our holiday back by four days.

CHAPTER 20

Soap Snakes and Musical Ladders

As the new year dawned in 1993, a new phenomenon was starting to dominate soap operas. It probably started with 'Dirty' Den Watts and 'Nasty' Nick Cotton in *EastEnders*. Then *Corrie* had 'Bradley the Beast'. The viewers seemed to like hate figures. It reminded me of the days when I'd go to watch the wrestling, where Mick McManus was billed as 'the man you love to hate'. In 1993, *Corrie* had two candidates for the most hated TV character: one was Carmel Finnan, a trainee nurse played by Catherine Cusack; the other was Terry Duckworth.

Carmel earned the public loathing by her single-minded pursuit of fellow nurse Martin Platt. She was besotted with Martin, despite the fact that he was happily married to Gail with a two-year-old son, David. Carmel tried to break up the Platts' marriage by falsely claiming she was pregnant by Martin. She caused emotional chaos before her tangled web of lies was exposed and she returned to Ireland.

As the 'nanny from hell' departed, she was replaced later that year by the 'bitch from hell' in the shapely form of barmaid Tanya Pooley, played by Eva Pope. Tanya didn't mince her words when she broke up the relationship between Des Barnes and Raquel Wolstenholme. She said, 'I'm the bitchy type, the manipulating type, the home-breaking type. I'm surprised you haven't heard about me.'

Terry's outrageous behaviour sank to new depths after his wife Lisa was fatally injured by a car as she crossed the street. Vera looked after baby Tommy at Number 9 and hoped she could gain custody of her grandson. When Terry was released from prison on parole, he told Jack and Vera that Tommy was going to be brought up in Blackpool by Lisa's parents. It turned out that Terry had sold his son to the Hortons for cash.

But it wasn't all doom and gloom in the *Street*. There was an hilarious scene involving Reg Holdsworth, Maureen Naylor, Derek Wilton and a waterbed. I never watch the filming at Granada. I try to learn my lines, perform them, then go home. That way, when I watch *Corrie*, it's as fresh and new to me as it is to millions of other viewers. So when Reg used his silver-tongued charm to lure Maureen back to his flat for a night of passion, I hadn't a clue what was going to happen next. It slowly began to dawn on me, as Derek started using a drill for a spot of DIY, that trouble was just around the corner. The disaster duly occurred in the form of a flood, when Derek's drill punctured the waterbed in the flat above just as Reg was about to have his wicked way with Maureen. It was one of the funniest moments on television – beautifully written, acted and directed for maximum effect.

Comedy actress Sherrie Hewson had recently joined the cast as Maureen, an old flame of Reg. She arrived with her wheelchair-bound mother, Maud Grimes, played by Liz Bradley. Sherrie was lucky to make an immediate impact with that scene and to play it opposite such talented actors.

Jack topped the appearance charts in 1993 with 103 episodes. It was the year Angela Griffin made her debut as hairdresser Fiona Middleton, and the year a former pop star started lodging with the Duckworths.

Coronation Street has had two actors in its history who went on to become pop stars. Davy Jones of The Monkees and Peter Noone of Herman's Hermits, had appeared in the show in the 60s before they became pop pin-ups on both sides of the Atlantic. Brian Hibbard, who came into *Corrie* as layabout Doug Murray, did it the other way round. He'd previously been a chart-topper as a singer with The Flying Pickets.

Doug was eventually evicted by Jack for not paying his rent. For a while he moved into a derelict Dormobile and at one stage he walked into the Rovers wearing just a pair of boxer shorts to prove how skint he was.

Although *Corrie* was becoming harder-edged, it still had plenty of heart. Bill Roache summed it up best when he said, 'You feel that if you got knocked over by a car in *EastEnders*, someone would probably nick your wallet. On the *Street*, they would invite you in for a cup of tea.'

In 1994 Jack was involved in a couple of daft adventures. The first involved Vera and a china dog she'd inherited from her dad. Vera had it valued at £45, but was told that a matching pair would be worth considerably more. Jack, meanwhile, went and sold it to an antique shop for £25 to finance his betting and boozing. Vera spotted the dog in the antique shop and bought it for £48, believing she now had a prized pair. When she got home and found out what Jack had done, she hurled the dog at him and it smashed to pieces.

The second crazy caper happened when Jack tried to rescue one of his missing pigeons. The pigeon, named Fergie, had flown into Curly Watts' observatory. Jack decided to climb a ladder to reach the bird. He got on the roof, but couldn't get into the observatory where Curly kept his telescope. While Jack was on the roof, Curly spotted the ladder leaning against his wall and put it away. As a result Jack spent the night on the tiles – and no women were involved! He had to be rescued next morning by the fire brigade.

The story made the national newspapers: Jack became 'The Birdman of Weatherfield'. He revelled in the publicity until Dulcie Froggatt talked about her five-times-a-night sex romps with the Birdman. Vera was not amused.

In fact, the agonised look on Jack's face as he clung to the chimney-stack was quite genuine. The old piles were giving me gyp when we filmed the scene and sitting on those tiles didn't help one bit.

I like to think it was the gentle humour in *Corrie* which helped us to beat *EastEnders* in the ratings battle. In the spring the BBC launched the third weekly episode from Albert Square. It went out at 8 p.m., straight after the *Street*. We had 16.7 million viewers, and *EastEnders* had 11.1 million. The following week, Granada screened an hour-long special directly against the London-based soap. We had 14.9 million viewers and they had 8.1 million.

In 1994 I had a personal cause for celebration. It was the year I recorded a compact disc album for EMI called *A Gift of Love*, which sold 180,000 copies. They were so pleased with its success that four months later I recorded another album, *Time for Love*, and that sold 180,000 copies too.

It had all started with the song I'd sung for Ali at the end of *This Is Your Life*. That proved to be the ladder to musical success. The father of one of the executives at EMI saw my performance and suggested he should sign me up.

I received a letter from a composer, arranger, conductor and musician called Derek Wadsworth, who was based in London. The letter arrived in the post at my house and I thought it was a hoax. Derek had a CV second to none. He'd started as an amateur with the Brighouse and Rastrick brass band before graduating to become a professional trombonist and arranger with legends such as Humphrey Lyttleton, John Dankworth, Maynard Ferguson and Charlie Watts.

In the 60s he'd become musical director and arranger to Dusty Springfield, Georgie Fame, Alan Price and Judy Garland. He'd arranged recordings for Nina Simone with the Boston Philharmonic Orchestra, and for Shirley Bassey and Kate Bush. He was musical director of the London version of *Hair*, which had included future stars like Alex Harvey, Mike Oldfield, Elaine Paige and Joan Armatrading.

He'd recorded stars ranging from the Rolling Stones, George Harrison, Rod Stewart, Tom Jones, Manfred Mann, the Small Faces, David Essex, Cat Stevens, Diana Ross, Dionne Warwick, Charles Aznavour, Randy Crawford and Simply Red to the Beautiful South and Tony Bennett.

As if that weren't enough, Derek had also conducted a 500-piece orchestra and choir at the Royal Albert Hall for the United Nations. In fact, his background was so impressive that I was totally convinced it was a wind-up organised by my mates. I could think of no logical reason why a man of that pedigree should be writing to me and suggesting we make an album together. It was the musical equivalent of Sir Alex Ferguson asking me if I'd mind missing the pub soccer match on Sunday morning and turning out for Manchester United in a Cup Final instead.

I'd taken Bill Podmore's advice and carried on singing after I'd been given a long-term contract to appear in *Corrie*. Since 1991 I'd been performing once a week in my local pub, the Broadoak. Even getting up to sing with a trio met with some opposition from Tommy, who organised jazz nights there. He preferred instrumental jazz and didn't know I'd been a professional singer.

I'd been having dinner with Ali when the keyboard player, Vinny Parker, asked me if I'd like to sing a couple of songs. Vinny and I knew each other from the days when I sang at pubs and working men's clubs. When Vinny introduced me to Tommy, he clearly wasn't impressed by my credentials as a regular in *Coronation Street*. He came straight to the point. 'I don't like singers,' he said. Against his better judgement, he decided to give me a chance as long as I promised not to sing anything by Elvis or Neil Diamond.

I sang Sinatra's 'I've Got You Under My Skin', which seemed to be OK with Tommy because he said I could do one more. I turned down his kind offer, but came back the following week to sing some more gentle jazz with this talented trio. I carried on once a week for seventeen years. Some weeks only two dozen people turned up. I never made any money. The trio made a few bob to cover their petrol costs. Basically we all did it because of our love for that type of music.

It seemed my appearance on *This Is Your Life* and the song at the end had taken me into a new league. Instead of singing for nothing in front of a small group of enthusiasts, I was being asked to work with one of the world's foremost arrangers. It just didn't ring true. Two weeks after I'd received the letter, Ali persuaded me to ring Derek Wadsworth in case it wasn't a hoax. It was lucky for me that I did.

The phone was answered by a lady called Patsy, who told me Derek was having a bath. But after a brief chat, he said he'd come up to the north-west to see me. I thought it was nice of him to come on a 400-mile round-trip to see me and wondered whether he'd be able to find Ashton-under-Lyne. He arrived with Patsy and an EMI executive called Barry McCann. We all got on well from the very start. Derek shared my love of jazz, swing and bossa nova. He'd seen me on *This Is Your Life* and thought we could work together.

I suggested we sign a contract and get on with it, so that's what we did. For three weeks we'd discuss over the phone which songs I should record. There were some I'd never heard before and he'd play them down the phone to me.

Whittling the songs down to fourteen was difficult because it meant some brutal pruning. We finally settled on 'Nobody Loves Me Like You Do', 'Somewhere Out There', 'In Your Eyes', 'Tonight I Celebrate My Love', 'It Might Be You',

'That's All', 'Save The Best For Last', '(Everything I Do) I Do It For You', 'She Loves Me', 'Right Here Waiting', 'One Hundred Ways', 'A Weekend In New England', 'If We Hold On Together' and, of course, 'Wind Beneath My Wings'.

Derek gave me a list of people I'd be working with – Dave Hartley on piano, Mitch Dalton on guitar, backing singers Sue Glover, Kay Garner and Tony Burrows. They were the best around. We were also going to have violins, violas, cellos, a harp, French horns, trombone and woodwind instruments. I felt like a kid who'd been let loose in a toy shop.

I'd asked Carolyn Reynolds, by now executive producer of *Corrie*, if it was OK for me to record an album. I reminded her of Podders' pledge that I should carry on singing, but Carolyn didn't need any persuading. She said Granada would have no objections and wished me luck.

A date was set for me to catch the train down to London. Derek met me at Euston and we were driven round to the Regent Hotel near Marylebone Station. EMI had booked me into a suite with a walk-in shower. Derek and Patsy came round and shared dinner with me while we discussed what we'd be doing in the studios the next morning.

As I caught a taxi to the studios in Barnes, I was feeling a bit jumpy by the time I arrived for a 9.30 start. But after Derek had introduced me to the sound engineer and given me a bottle of water, I was feeling better. It's important to hit the right balance between not being too tense and not being too relaxed. I think it's known as creative tension.

Anyway, after one rehearsal of the first number on the list, I was ready for a take. Afterwards Derek asked me if I was happy with it. I said yes and asked Derek if he was happy. He said he was very happy. So on we went. By lunchtime I'd recorded six numbers. After a sandwich and a half-pint of Guinness, I went back and recorded another five.

I sensed there was some unease, although nobody said anything to me. Eventually I asked the engineer if anything was wrong. He said that on the contrary, everything was going wonderfully well. It was just that they'd never recorded an album so quickly before. The previous record had been ten songs in a day, and that was Tom Jones.

I reckoned that if I came in at 10 a.m. the next day, we could record the last three numbers before I caught the 1 p.m. train back to Manchester. That's what happened and I asked Derek how he thought things had gone. He just said, 'It was knockout.'

Money can't buy the feeling praise like that from a man of Derek's reputation gives you. I'd had a wonderful time and he was pleased with the results. All we had to do now was wait to see what the public thought of our efforts.

To make sure they knew about it, I had to give interviews on TV, radio and newspapers. It was important to spread the word there was a big difference between the singers Bill Tarmey and Jackie Duckworth Junior.

EMI arranged for me to visit Canada and New Zealand, where *Corrie* was a popular show among the expats and second-generation Brits who lived there. I also visited Ireland, where *Coronation Street* is popular on both sides of the border. I'm told they like it more in the south because they can pick up the British channels without having to pay a licence fee.

I've had some marvellous times in Ireland and made some good pals there. You can go into any pub and bump into a singer, a musician, a poet, a comedian or a storyteller. The people have a tradition of making their own entertainment and joining in the *craic*. I once took the words of a popular folk song into a radio studio and persuaded the live audience to join me in singing it. You can't buy memories like that.

Friends complained that the local shops had run out of my albums. I think they suspected I'd bought them all myself. But *A Gift of Love* proved popular, for which I'm very grateful.

Plugging the album gave me a chance to meet some of the people who had been sent earlier examples of my work and never responded. They were embarrassed but that's life. The recognition of talent is just one person's opinion at a particular moment in time. Apparently the BBC gets about twenty unsolicited tapes every day from wannabe singers. Even The Beatles struggled to get started.

I was just lucky that there was an untapped market for people who liked middle-of-the-road songs with romantic lyrics. Given the right arrangements and choice of musicians by Derek, we had a big hit on our hands. I got a gold disc for passing 100,000 sales, and another one for the follow-up, *Time for Love*.

By the time we'd produced the third album, *After Hours*, EMI had decided to change the winning team. I don't want to get involved in any mud-slinging here: let's just say things didn't work out. The albums made a lot of money for EMI but not for Derek and me. We'd been so eager to sign the contract that all the costs of recording and promotion came from our royalties.

I'm sorry it ended on a sour note, but I'll always be grateful that I had my moment in the sun and the chance to work with a master craftsman like Derek Wadsworth, who sadly died in December 2008.

Achieving chart success of 'One Voice', performing with the Hallé and recording the CDs would probably never have happened without *This Is Your Life*. In a roundabout way I owe my singing success to Jack Duckworth too.

CHAPTER 21

Hello and Goodbye

After Brian Hibbard from The Flying Pickets left Number 9, the Duckworths had an even more famous lodger in the form of Dave King. He played the part of Jack's older brother, Cliff.

In the late 1950s Dave King was the biggest name on British television. He was one of those entertainers like Bruce Forsyth who could turn his hand to anything. He'd started as a stand-up comic, then switched to singing and dancing, and finished up hosting *The Dave King Show*, where he did all those things. I'd watched him as a youngster growing up and now here he was, working alongside me.

Dave told me how he'd left Britain and had his own show in America, with A-list guests like Nat King Cole and Lucille Ball. It all went wrong when the show's sponsors, a cigarette company, overheard Dave criticise their product. They withdrew their sponsorship and Dave came back to England.

I asked him what he'd been doing. 'Playing golf,' he

replied. He said he'd earned enough money to take time out to enjoy himself.

I think appearing in *Corrie* appealed to him as a fresh challenge. Cliff's arrival and departure certainly gave Jack and Vera a new challenge. When Cliff died on holiday, he left Jack £30,000 in his will. That inheritance, plus the sale of 9 Coronation Street to Gary and Judy Mallett, gave them the cash to buy the Rovers Return.

It may have been a dream come true for Jack and Vera, but I feared the worst in terms of my workload. I remember when we got our scripts, Liz rushed over to celebrate. She was so excited to find that Jack and Vera were taking over Britain's most famous pub, and from that point of view so was I, but I knew it meant we'd be needed to play in far more scenes. I warned Liz there could be a cloud to this silver lining.

Apart from the inheritance from Cliff, the other reason we were able to take over the Rovers was Julie Goodyear's decision to quit the show. She'd played Bet Lynch and then Bet Gilroy for twenty-five years and she'd had enough.

I'll always be grateful to Julie for her kindness when I first joined the show. In those early days, when I felt like an outsider, she brought me in from the cold. She was also the woman with whom I'd shared my first on-screen kiss!

Another actor I'd had great fun with also decided to leave, like Julie, to work on other projects. Ken Morley had become something of a cult figure as randy Reg Holdsworth. Their departures, and the announcement that Ivy Brennan had died, left huge gaps. In fact, Lynne Perrie hadn't been seen for a year and the news of Ivy's death only confirmed that Lynne wouldn't be appearing again.

Over the years, *Corrie* has seen so many legendary characters disappear – Jack and Annie Walker, Ena Sharples, Martha Longhurst and Minnie Caldwell, Elsie Tanner, Albert Tatlock, Leonard Swindley, Stan and Hilda Ogden, and Len Fairclough to name but a few. And they always seem to be able to unearth new characters to pick up the baton.

That's the sort of thing that happens when you're working on *Corrie*: old friends suddenly disappear and new people arrive who become friends. It's a revolving door.

Although we lost Bet, Reg and Ivy in 1995, we gained Maxine Heavey, played by the lovely Tracy Shaw, and Roy Cropper, played by David Neilson. There was also another character who'd made his debut in 1994 and was starting to develop nicely. Butcher Fred Elliott, I say butcher Fred Elliott, was played by John Savident.

Savvy, as he was known by the cast, had been a policeman before he became an actor. He'd been based at Mill Street Police Station in Bradford, Manchester, only 100 yards from where I used to live. He was the sort of burly bobby you wouldn't argue with. John Stalker, who went on to become Deputy Chief Constable of Greater Manchester (and also an actor and jazz drummer, incidentally), told me how Savvy had once saved him from a good kicking.

John was a young copper and had got himself in a situation where he was surrounded by three local thugs who were about to give him a pasting, but Savvy arrived on his bike in the nick of time just like the 7th Cavalry. He only had to say, 'Hello, hello, hello. What's all this here then?' and the thugs melted away. Perhaps that's where he developed the habit of repeating his words.

Savvy had a place in London and a flat near the Granada TV studios in the centre of Manchester, but his mum lived in Ashton and he'd occasionally pop over to my house around the corner. He drove a Morgan sports car and must have needed a shoehorn to get in and out of it. When I asked him why he didn't get a more comfortable car, he simply said he bought it because he'd wanted one all his life and he was finally able to afford it.

Savvy gave me that great big toothy smile and said, in Fred Elliott fashion, 'If you've got it, flaunt it. I say, if you've got it, flaunt it.'

I thought about Savvy's words a few years later when I had the chance to buy a Rolls-Royce. It must be every working man's dream to one day own a Roller. It's a status symbol which tells the world you've hit the big-time. Part of me was saying I shouldn't try to be flash. But I could also hear Savvy saying, 'If you've got it, flaunt it.'

In the end I decided to buy one to see what it was like to drive. The one I was offered through my mate Joe was light green with red leather upholstery and red sheepskin rugs on the floor. Although it was more than twenty years old, it was in great condition and only had about 30,000 miles on the clock. To my surprise, the insurance was cheaper than I'd been paying on my Volvo. So I told Joe to swap my Volvo for the Rolls-Royce. It was just short of seven litres and weighed two tons. After two weeks I wanted to swap back.

Nobody prepares you for how powerful they are or how light the steering is. When I put my foot down, the engine roared and I surged forwards with the G-force pushing me back in the seat. The secret was to accelerate gently and smoothly, otherwise the speedometer goes in one direction while the fuel gauge goes in the other. Once I was reminded that it was a Rolls and not a Porsche, I learned to love it. I got only about 10mpg around town, but that went up to 24 on the motorways. I used to drive it to the pub, the chippy and the paper shop.

I'd been worried that it might get scratched by people who were jealous, but that never happened. In fact, it was quite the opposite. Motorists would let me out into traffic and nobody tried to cut me up. They treated my Rolls as they would treat an elegant old lady crossing the road.

One guy I knew started to say it was ridiculous for the man who played Jack Duckworth to drive around in a Roller. I decided to lead him up the garden path. I told him there was no security in the acting game, so I'd bought it to hire out for weddings – Roman Catholics on Fridays, Protestants on Saturdays and Muslims on Sundays. Two weeks later, a mate of mine borrowed it for a family wedding. When this other chap saw it all dressed up in white ribbons, he said, 'I see your new business is going well.'

There was another occasion when I got great pleasure out of my posh new car. I was driving to work one day. It was lashing down with rain and I saw two blokes waiting at a bus stop. I pulled over and asked where they were going. They told me they were going into the centre of Manchester. I said, 'So am I. Hop in.' They were a father and son who worked in the same building on Deansgate. They got in the back and we chatted about all sorts of things. They said they were fans of *Corrie*. As I dropped them off before turning left into Quay Street towards the TV studios, I chuckled to myself imagining the scene at their office when they told their pals that Jack Duckworth had given them a lift to work in his Rolls-Royce. I drove that car for two years and it gave me many happy memories.

Corrie fans will have happy memories of Tracy Shaw. She was the sort of actress who could light up a room with her smile and big blue-grey eyes. She was obviously destined to feature in a lot of romance as hairdresser Maxine and she didn't disappoint.

Roy Cropper was a less obvious character. I used to be fascinated to watch David Neilson create his awkward mannerisms. David is a big handsome bloke, but he seemed to be able to shrink when he turned into Roy. He'd stoop and develop this crablike walk as he shuffled around. He has a bag with a key on a piece of string. David created that prop because he said his mum used to have one.

The other newcomers to the *Street* were Gary and Judy Mallett, played by Ian Mercer and Gaynor Faye. Strictly speaking, Ian wasn't a newcomer because he'd already appeared in *Corrie* in 1987 as Pete Jackson, an army mate of Terry Duckworth. True to form Terry had run off with Pete's wife, Linda. The producers always hope that viewers won't notice these things. I bet they do. Gaynor is the daughter of scriptwriter Faye Mellor, who's written a lot of gritty TV dramas over the years.

The Malletts soon made an impact after buying Number 9 off the Duckworths. Within days neighbours were complaining about Gary practising on his drum kit, and then Judy erected a neon sign which read 'Santa's Nookie Nest'. We should have known how subtle their tastes were when they were attracted to the stone cladding.

As the year drew to a close, Betty Turpin was reunited with an old flame called Billy Williams, with whom she'd shared a moment of passion on VE Day in 1945. Now a widow with a reputation for making the best hotpots in Lancashire, Betty was a good catch and she married Billy, played by Frank Mills, in style.

She was given away by her son, Gordon Clegg, who'd once been a *Street* regular, running the corner shop. Actor Bill Kenwright had become a theatrical impresario away from the cobbles of Weatherfield. He was now a multimillionaire, and later became the boss of Everton Football Club. But he told me how he'd loved working with Betty and had been happy to come back to *Corrie* as a one-off for her wedding.

As one wedding was taking place, a divorce created an opportunity for another craggy face to return to the show. Bill Webster, played by Pete Armitage, had supposedly gone to Germany to work as a builder, but came home when his marriage broke up. Jack employed him as a cellarman at the Rovers.

For one scene, in which Jack and Bill were supposed to be building a wall, Granada had hired a trowel expert to show us how to do the job. Like me, Pete had worked in the building trade. So we both picked up the trowels and did a few fancy tricks with them like western gunfighters. The trowel expert said, 'I don't think I'll be needed here' and walked away.

In 1996 Granada decided to make and screen four episodes a week. That decision caused another leading character to disappear. Sarah Lancashire, who was widely loved as Raquel, the dumb blonde with the heart of gold, decided it was too much for her. Raquel had only just married Curly Watts in December 1995, in the show's first hour-long special. She left a week before the first fourth episode was transmitted in November. Like the rest of the cast, I was sorry to see Sarah go but I was pleased to see her making a successful TV career away from *Corrie*.

Jack's electrical know-how was brought into question again when Gary Mallett electrocuted himself while using a faulty socket after the central heating broke down at Number 9. The whole house needed rewiring, but the Duckworths refused to pay for it. The row between the Duckworths and the Malletts was eventually settled.

Gary formed a syndicate to buy a racehorse which they called Betty's Hot Shot. This led to another scene involving Jack and a horse. It brought back uncomfortable memories of my experience all those years ago with Bracken – and this time there was no Laurence Olivier around to cheer me up.

The scenes were shot at stables owned by the former England soccer international Francis Lee near Styal, Cheshire. I knew Frannie from my days as compère at the Manchester City Social Club, where he'd been both a player and a pantomime artist. Frannie stood on the sidelines sniggering as I tried to play the part of Jack Duckworth sitting astride a highly strung racehorse. It was a close call as to which of us was more highly strung, but I think the horse just about edged it.

It was a real racehorse and, as I mounted it, I could see its skin jumping with nerves. They also had a saddle on a fake horseback, and a horse double with a stunt rider. It should all have gone perfectly – and eventually it did, but there were a lot of anxious moments. The stunt rider had been filming the Mel Gibson movie *Braveheart* the week before – from Hollywood to Weatherfield in one gallop.

In the script Jack falls off the horse, Betty's Hot Shot. Sitting on the saddle on the fake horseback in the trailer, I managed that quite convincingly. I'd been hanging on by my thighs and managed to lean over to my left and fall out of shot. Unfortunately, the stunt rider, re-enacting the same scene, had fallen to the right so I had to record it again. This was done to the accompaniment of chortling from Frannie. The fall ended with Jack being carried off on a stretcher and hospitalised for six weeks.

Later that year, our Vera claimed she'd seen the ghost of Ivy and called in an exorcist. Jack was more opportunistic about Ivy's spectre hanging round the Rovers. He tried to cash in by calling in the press to write about his haunted pub. Jack even started wearing T-shirts advertising free spirits.

I don't regard myself as superstitious but I do believe in ghosts because I've seen one. I was working at a nightclub in Denton when it happened. A new owner was taking over and he'd decided to replace me and the trio with a pop band. Just before the handover took place, I was finishing my drink at the end of the night. The manager was cashing up the tills. As I sat there finishing my drink, an old man with a dog walked past me. I said, 'Evening' but he didn't reply. He just carried on walking into the kitchen area.

When the manager returned, I asked him, 'Who was the old guy with the dog?'

He said, 'Oh. You've met Harry.'

I hadn't a clue what he was talking about. He told me

Harry was their resident ghost. He and his dog had been seen regularly. I told the manager this wasn't a ghost, it was a bloke with a dog and he'd gone into the kitchen, but the manager showed me the kitchen was locked. When he brought a key and unlocked it, there was nobody there.

I had a similar ghostly experience when the family lived in a bungalow in Bredbury, Stockport. I'd come home and Ali was the only other person in the house. She had been tidying up and she complained that I'd sat down on our bed and left the indentation of a bumprint on the cover. I assured her I hadn't been in the room, let alone sat on the bed.

At night in the bungalow we would hear strange noises. I thought they were just the sounds of settlement you get in houses from time to time. But one day we found the heating clock scrunched up in a way that couldn't have been accidental. I told Ali we had a ghost.

She's not easily frightened, but she was very annoyed. She shares my view that there are more things going on in this world than we'll ever know about. So she went round the house saying, 'OK, I know you live here. But this is my house. I don't want you frightening the children and I don't want you damaging things.' After that, occasionally we would feel something cold brushing past us but we never had any more trouble. When we sold the bungalow we told the buyers we had a ghost but it was a kind ghost.

Our only other brush with the supernatural came when we had the greengrocers' shop in Gorton. I came back from the cash and carry and Ali asked me if I'd deal with a woman in the shop. She was wearing a headscarf and shawl like Gypsy Rose Lee and she said, 'Can you cross my palm with silver?'

I told her I had no money but she just stared at me and asked again.

In those days we didn't have a pot to pee in or a window to throw it out of, as they say in the building trade. I opened the till, took out a shilling and told her that was all I had to spare. Then she said, 'One day you will get your own band.' I thought she must have been talking to someone up the street who knew I was a singer. Then she went on to tell me I'd become comfortable but I'd have to work for whatever I got.

Many years later I was telling this story to Russell Grant, the roly-poly astrologist, when we were doing a TV show. A friend rang Ali and told her that I was on TV talking to Russell about the gypsy woman who visited our shop. Ali asked her friend to hang on while she answered a knock at the door. Two gypsies were standing on the doorstep offering to tell her fortune – spooky or what? One of the women told Ali she couldn't see any cancer in the house, but she could see a stick. Nowadays Ali, who suffers from back troubles, uses a stick. Ain't life strange? She bought a beautiful large embroidered tablecloth from them and we have it to this day. I reckon our brushes with the supernatural are more credible than Vera's sighting of Ivy Tilsley.

Later in 1996 our Terry returned, and before long he'd got yet another girl pregnant. This time it was Tricia Armstrong, played by Tracy Brabin. She was a young mum whose husband was in prison. It wasn't long before Terry turned his attentions to Curly's wife Raquel, who was sacked from her job as barmaid at the Rovers because of the trouble he caused after she rejected him. Raquel then told Curly she was leaving him to take up a job as a beautician in Malaysia. Their parting scenes were beautifully done and there wasn't a dry eye in our house as we watched it.

By the end of 1996, another new face had appeared in the show. Steven Arnold made his debut as Ashley Peacock, the nephew of butcher Fred Elliott. Three years later he would marry the lovely Maxine.

CHAPTER 22

The Mad Axeman

A new producer joined the *Street* in 1996. Brian Park was soon nicknamed 'The Mad Axeman' by the tabloid press because he let it be known a lot of characters were for the chop. His explanation was: 'Decisions have to be taken to create space and give the show some oxygen. Some characters have run their course.'

Well, we're all entitled to our opinions. My opinion was that there was no need for the wholesale carnage which followed in 1997.

On his first day at work, Brian told Peter Baldwin he'd decided to kill off Derek Wilton. Derek was one of life's losers but his misfortunes cheered everyone else up. Peter was an accomplished actor who'd brought a lot of laughter into our lives as Derek for the past twenty years. It wasn't enough that Derek had to be written out of the show, with the chance of a return when another producer came along;

Derek was going to die, boosting the viewing figures for one episode, so Peter left the show with no return ticket.

Jill Summers, the actress who'd played Phyllis Pearce in 528 episodes, died in January that year. Her death meant an end to Phyllis's prolonged pursuit of pensioner Percy Sugden. I used to give Jill a lift to Manchester's Midland Hotel, where she stayed when she was filming.

Next to go was Joyce Smedley, played by Anita Carey, who worked as a cleaner at the Rovers. Joyce was out walking her dog Scamper when she was knocked down and killed by car mechanic Tony Horrocks. Tony, played by Lee Warburton, had a breakdown because of what he'd done and left to live in Leeds. So that was two characters and a dog out of the show for the price of one storyline.

I was so upset at what was happening that I went in to the producer's office to see Brian Park. The press had published a list of characters on his hit list. I said, 'You know that list. Well, put me on it.' Then I swept out of the room with my boss looking mystified. I thought I'd rather make a living by singing than by staying in a situation where all the actors were in fear of losing their jobs. The smiling assassin, as he was also known, seemed to be revelling in his ruthless reputation.

We all know that acting is a precarious profession, but it's still a hard pill to swallow if you're doing your job well and you lose it through no fault of your own. These were people with mortgages and gas bills to pay, and there was no redundancy cheque. In some cases, work was going to be even harder to find because the actors concerned could be considered typecast by appearing in Britain's most watched TV programme.

Brian Park never spoke to me about my visit to his office and the subject was never raised again. He could easily have taken me at my word and added Jack Duckworth to his list. For a few weeks I wondered whether my script would one day read: 'Jack is struck by a bolt of lightning.' With hindsight, I'm glad it didn't happen, but I felt strongly at the time and had my say.

After Joyce Smedley's death and Tony Horrocks' departure, Derek was next to go. He died of a heart attack during a road-rage incident. Thelma Barlow, who played his widow, Mavis, took her protest at what was happening a stage further than I did. She quit the show after twenty-five years. It was a sad loss of a well-loved character and a beloved colleague. She's been in a few radio plays since leaving the show, as well as the Victoria Wood sitcom *dinnerladies* which I love so much.

There was a bit of brief cheer among the doom and gloom when Fred Elliott married Maureen Holdsworth, but even that didn't last long. Days after the wedding, Maureen realised she'd made a big mistake and ran off to Germany with Bill Webster. So we lost Sherrie Hewson and Pete Armitage as well.

Next for the chop was Don Brennan. The script had already cost him an amputated leg after a car crash. Then it called upon Don to lose his marbles as well. In the end he drove Alma's car into the viaduct at high speed, and actor Geoff Hinsliff left the show in a blaze of madness as the car turned into a fireball.

We lost two more characters that year. Bill Waddington made his last appearance as Percy Sugden, the prickly pensioner who was always sticking his nose in and telling us how he won the war, and Billy Williams, Betty's new husband, dropped dead of a heart attack, so that was the end for Frank Mills, and Betty returned to widowhood.

The show lost one of its original actors when Ivan Beavis died. His character, Harry Hewitt, had been killed back in 1967 when a jack slipped and he was crushed beneath a car he'd been repairing.

The show also lost shopworker Anne Malone, played by Eve Steele, and one of the McDonald twins, Andy, played by Nick Cochrane. Three of the long-standing writing team, Barry Hill, Adele Rose and Julian Roach, departed too.

Among all this upheaval, another Duckworth baby arrived on the scene. Single mum Tricia Armstrong, played by Tracy Brabin, had enjoyed a one-night stand with our Terry during one of his flying visits to Weatherfield. The result was baby Brad Armstrong, half-brother to Jamie Armstrong, Paul Clayton and Tommy Duckworth. Jack had built up a good rapport with Jamie, played by Joey Gilgun.

Jack never saw Tricia, Jamie or Brad again after they moved to the other side of town, but I do see Joey Gilgun from time to time. He's now a strapping six-foot tall, bewhiskered young man starring in *Emmerdale*.

Terry never took much interest in his son Brad before the Armstrongs moved, but he did take a keen interest in the till at the Rovers. Unlike Vera, Jack could always see what a low-life Terry was. Jack's sure he gets it from the Burton side of the family.

When he offered to carry the takings to the bank, Jack set a trap for Terry by giving him a bundle of cut-up newspapers in an envelope and telling him to hand it over unopened. Terry came back furious. He'd ignored the instruction – as Jack knew he would – and opened the envelope. He caused a scene, which ended with Terry getting thumped by Tricia's new boyfriend, Ray Thorpe, played by Chris Walker. To add insult to his injury, Jack kicked him out and told him never to darken the Duckworth door again.

In exchange for all these exits, the Street's new blood arrived in the form of single mum Zoe Tattersall, played by Joanne Froggatt, and the Battersbys. Les Battersby (Bruce Jones), his wife Janice (Vicky Entwistle), and their daughters Leanne (Jane Danson) and Toyah (Georgia Taylor) were described as 'the neighbours from hell'. They moved into 5 Coronation Street, after it was bought by the council. I'll say this for them: they made the Duckworths look respectable.

The highlight of the year for me was a singing tour with the Andy Prior Big Band. I'd managed to persuade Granada to let me have an extended holiday. I'd known Andy's dad, John Prior, who was an outstanding musician. His son proved to be a chip off the old block, with a few skills of his own. Andy can play trombone, tell jokes, do impressions and conduct an orchestra. On top of that he can sing Frank Sinatra numbers in such a way that if you close your eyes you'd think Ol' Blue Eyes really was back.

We toured sixteen venues throughout the UK, attracting an audience who'd largely grown up through the big-band era. Some brought youngsters with them and I'd like to think they'd learn to appreciate that sound too. The nearest we got to my home town of Ashton was a gig at Oldham. Ali bought a wad of tickets for friends and family. We had a full house that night – apart from one empty seat next to my darling wife.

Ali had got so used to buying two tickets for the pair of us that she'd counted me into her reckoning. She hadn't worked out that I'd be unable to take my seat in the audience on account of my being on stage singing!

A couple of years later, John Prior told me Andy's band had broken up. He asked if I'd sing with them again if they could be persuaded to re-form. I happily agreed to work for nothing. Andy had played with and conducted American bands in the States and earned massive respect over there for his talents.

I enjoyed recording a one-off show with the Andy Prior Big Band for Granada, but it went out at 1.30 in the afternoon instead of in a night-time slot and few people saw it. I watched the programme and Ali asked me what I thought. I told her the band was great but the singer looked too fat and too old to be singing romantic ballads. I decided not to sing on telly again.

Another happy memory for me from 1997 was when they decided to produce a special for the DVD market called *Coronation Street: Viva Las Vegas!* The story was that because Jack had lied about his age, the marriage to Vera might not be legal. If you cast your minds well back, you may recall that when Jack was working on the fairgrounds, he'd pretended to be older than he really was so he'd seem more sophisticated and worldly-wise. This meant he'd made a false statement on the wedding certificate which might have invalidated their marriage. Jack reckoned this made their Terry what he'd always thought he was.

To be on the safe side, Vera suggested they go on holiday to Las Vegas and have another wedding ceremony over there. I don't think Jack was too keen on the wedding idea, but all the glitz, glamour and gambling won him over.

Three days before we headed out to the States we filmed the sequence with Joan Collins on an empty plane. Then we were off to the US of A.

I'm not sure what clothes Liz had packed for herself, but I think she'd thrown in a few woollies and the odd cardigan in case it got nippy. She was amazed to find Nevada was so hot. I told her the clue had been in the fact that we were heading for the Nevada Desert and, in my limited experience, deserts tend to be hot places.

We were there for two weeks and I spent the first one alone until Ali joined me. They gave me a suite the size of a football pitch to stay in. The bed was far bigger than the bedroom my parents used to share with their three youngest kids in Butterworth Street. You could have got a soccer team in my bath.

I had a maid called Maisie, who used to come in twice a day to clean the room. She was black, looked like Olive Oyl out of *Popeye*, and talked with a Southern drawl that sounded straight out of *Gone with the Wind*. I told her to concentrate on making the bed, cleaning the shower and the area in between. I explained I was scared to go any further into the room in case I got lost and couldn't find my way back. Everything there was on a grander scale than you get back home. If you ordered a burger, it was big enough to feed a family of six.

We'd taken our own team out there, led by director Brian

Mills and floor manager John Friend Newman. Brian knew our strengths and weaknesses so I was pleased to be working with him.

The Americans also had a team of technicians working with us. I think we might have had to strike a deal with their union to enable the filming to take place. We got on really well with those guys. Liz would amaze them by bringing them coffees and sticky buns from her trailer between scenes. Like me, she had a trailer the size of the average house. The crew told us that American TV and film stars used to stay in their trailers, come out when called to deliver their lines, and then disappeared back into their trailers. They weren't used to being asked, 'How many sugars, love?' by people like Liz. Having said that, I don't suppose there is anybody like Liz anywhere in the world. Brian also surprised the American crew members when he invited them to join us all at the bar after filming had finished and we bought them rounds of drinks. It was a happy time all round.

According to the plot, Jack and Vera fall out when she insists Jack leave a one-armed bandit he's been playing. Jack's convinced it's about to drop the million-dollar jackpot, and so is an American gambler, who's waiting to pounce. The moment Jack leaves the slot machine, the American jumps on to the stool he has just vacated and drops the jackpot with his first coin.

Back in their room, an unholy row breaks out over whose fault it is. Somehow Vera blames Jack and hurls his suitcase out of their room. As I was running out to avoid the flying suitcase, I caught my left hand on the door lock. It pierced me on the bridge between thumb and forefinger. The colour drained out of the faces of the American crew when they saw I was stuck to the sharp lock.

Gingerly, I pulled my hand away, expecting a fountain of blood to spurt out. I was taking anticoagulants because of my heart condition and they thin your blood. This made it slow to congeal, and on a previous occasion I'd bled like a stuck pig with a minor scratch on my nose. I feared the worst and told everyone to stand clear. It was an anticlimax when I didn't produce more than a smear of blood, so I just asked for a plaster.

The nurse who was on stand-by insisted on ringing the nearest hospital. She also called for an ambulance. I think they were terrified in case I sued someone for negligence. While we were finishing the scene, a doctor and a nurse arrived. He was picking at the edge of my plaster, but I ripped it off to show him the damage. He reckoned I'd need six stitches in the wound. He seemed to think I'd require some kind of anaesthetic to stand the pain of having six stitches. But I said loudly, 'Us Brits are not big Jessies,' and that seemed to lighten everyone's mood.

I enjoyed playing the part of the tough guy like John Wayne. The truth is that the stitches were no problem, but when he put the antiseptic on afterwards it was all I could do to stop squealing like a schoolgirl. I'm afraid they might have heard a gentle whimper.

Later they filmed the wedding in the Little White Chapel, where Liz and I exchanged vows as Jack and Vera. Afterwards I was talking to the actress who'd performed the ceremony. She informed me she was a real pastor and not an actress. My question for any legal experts out there is this: are Liz Dawn and I married? Could we be charged with bigamy?

After the Vegas special, Jack and Vera headed from the bright lights back to the cobbles of Weatherfield. The year 1997 ended with Jack using a dating agency again. Golden Years had been set up by Alec Gilroy and he was paying Ken Barlow to escort lonely ladies to dinner. Jack overheard the details and went along to pose as Ken.

He was taken upstairs by sex-mad Renee Turnbull, who was desperate for Jack's body. Renee was played by Lynda Baron, the object of Ronnie Barker's lust as Nurse Gladys Emmanuel in the sitcom *Open All Hours*. As Jack fled, clutching his shoes, he dropped one like Cinderella at the ball when the clock struck twelve.

Unfortunately, the shoe I dropped fell forward, causing me to slip on it and go crashing down the stairs on my back. For a moment I thought I'd broken it. As the crew rushed to help me, I told them to leave me for a minute while I got my breath back. Then I allowed them to haul me carefully to my feet. I was just badly bruised and we managed to re-shoot the scene without any further stunts from me.

Later Renee arrived in the Rovers, clutching Jack's shoe and looking for her Prince Charming. That earned Jack another earbashing from Vera.

By the time 1997 ended, another actress oozing sex appeal had arrived in the show. Natalie Horrocks, played by Denise Welch, claimed, 'I'm not pulled as easy as a pint of Newton and Ridley's.' But you could have fooled the women of Weatherfield, as she jumped from one bed to another. Natalie was the mother of mechanic Tony Horrocks and she took over his share of the garage. She became Kevin Webster's partner in more ways than one.

Another newcomer arrived in the form of eco-warrior Geoffrey 'Spider' Nugent, played by Martin Hancock. He was Emily Bishop's nephew and moved into her spare room. He attracted the attention of Toyah Battersby and they became lovers.

At the start of 1998, Brian Park left *Corrie* to set up his own production company and was replaced as producer by David Hanson.

The year started with a sizzling storyline which gripped the nation. A cad called Jon Lindsay, who pretended to be an airline pilot and single, had captured the heart of Deirdre. He was a con man with a wife and kids. Deirdre eventually saw through his lies. But when she used a bank card he'd given her to withdraw £5,000 he owed her from their joint account, it turned out the account belonged to a Captain Jenkins.

Deirdre was charged with obtaining money and property by deception. While she was being held in prison for three weeks, viewers were caught up in the drama. People were sporting 'Free Deirdre' T-shirts and stickers on their cars. Prime Minister Tony Blair even raised the matter in Parliament, to much amusement, when he called on the Home Secretary to intervene.

One critic wrote: 'Now the dividing line between *Coronation Street* fiction and real-life fact has not so much blurred as completely disappeared up the nation's aerials.'

When the 'Justice for Deirdre' campaign finally ended with her release, four different newspapers claimed victory for themselves – and there was me thinking it was the scriptwriters.

CHAPTER 23

Lusty Jack and a Bedroom Siege

When you're filming four episodes a week, as we were, time flies by. It certainly did for Des Barnes in 1998. He started the year by proposing to the Rovers' pretty barmaid Samantha Failsworth, played by Tina Hobley. She accepted but got cold feet. She moved in with Natalie Horrocks, who succeeded in getting them back together. But then Sam began an affair with handsome mechanic Chris Collins, who was also having an affair with Sally Webster. Are you following all this?

Des found out about Chris and Samantha's secret when he kicked down a door at Chris's flat and found them in bed together. Des should have known better than to go kicking down doors. Five years earlier he'd burst into another bedroom and found his girlfriend, Tanya Pooley, in bed with his boss, bookie Alex Christie. Finding Samantha in bed with Chris was only the start of it for Des.

After a whirlwind romance with femme fatale Natalie, he

married her. Would they live happily ever after, we wondered? Not for long, they wouldn't.

When Natalie's son, Tony, returned to Weatherfield, he was being pursued by drug dealers because he owed them money. Des intervened in a fight and got beaten up for his troubles. He just had time to regain consciousness and tell Natalie he loved her before dying of a heart attack. Cue violins and pass the tissues.

We were all sorry to see Phil Middlemiss go. We'd lost another popular character, a good colleague and a key member of my All Stars soccer team.

While all this was going on around them, the Duckworths became involved in a row with Alec Gilroy, who'd bought the Rovers off them when they ran out of money. Jim McDonald was hired to mend the rotten staircase between the Rovers' bar and the accommodation above. Alec refused to pay the bill, claiming the stairs were still Jack and Vera's property. Jim lost patience and removed the stairs, trapping Vera in the flat above. Firemen had to rescue her from the bedroom window. Jack finally settled the bill and Jim returned the stairs.

When Jack suffered leg pains, the doctor demanded he change his unhealthy diet and give up smoking. Vera sent him to a hypnotist for help. Jack had fun pretending he'd been hypnotised into a former life as Lusty Jack, a seventeenth-century squire. I used my impersonation of Robert Newton as Long John Silver to create Lusty Jack's voice. In fact, I might have been impersonating Tony Hancock impersonating Robert Newton.

It gave Jack an opportunity to pinch barmaids' bottoms while supposedly under the influence of his ancestor, Lusty

Jack. He got away with it with Natalie and Samantha, but when he fondled Betty, she gave him a smack which would have brought any man out of a trance.

When the Duckworths got into financial troubles again, Alec bought the tenancy of the Rovers off them as well. While they were on holiday in Blackpool, Alec had the locks changed. They rushed back and took possession of their bedroom, but Alec turned off the heating and tried to starve them out. Alec became frustrated because residents rallied round to supply them with food. Eventually he sold the pub to Natalie and moved to Brighton.

Meanwhile, the *Street* had a new villain in the handsome form of Greg Kelly, illegitimate son of Les Battersby. He had an affair with the smitten Maxine but then turned his attentions to Sally Webster. Greg, played by Stephen Billington, proved to be a violent crook as well as a love-rat. With a dad like Les, who could have doubted it?

During 1998 there had been three other significant additions to the cast. Jackie Dobbs, played by Scouse actress Margi Clarke, had befriended Deirdre while she was on remand in prison. Jackie moved into Deirdre's flat with her 16-year-old son Tyrone, played by Alan Halsall. He was to become a surrogate son to Jack over the years after his mum left Weatherfield.

The other arrival was a quirky character called Hayley Patterson, played by Julie Hesmondhalgh. Hayley was a bit of a shy, oddball character and we found out why later. It seemed a romance made in heaven when a love affair started between her and the *Street*'s other oddball, Roy Cropper, but the course of true love didn't run smoothly for them.

David Hanson's spell in charge ended in 1999 when Jane McNaught became *Corrie*'s twenty-ninth producer. David had steadied the ship after the big changes which had been made under Brian Park. Jane had worked on the *Street* before and was a lifelong fan of the show so we looked forward to a period of calm and stability.

Unfortunately, the year got off to a tragic start when life imitated art. First, Alf Roberts died from a heart attack at Nicky Tilsley's eighteenth birthday party; six weeks later, Bryan Mosley, who first played Alf in 1963 and became a regular in 1971, died from a real heart attack.

Bryan was a lovely bloke with a kind, gentle nature. Before joining *Corrie* he'd starred in the classic movie *Get Carter*, featuring Michael Caine in the title role. Bryan played a crooked businessman who got thrown off a car park roof by Carter. Some actors would have bored the pants off colleagues with their 'me and Michael Caine' stories but Bryan wasn't a boastful man. In his younger days, he'd been a qualified fight arranger under the stage name Billy Windrush!

He was a regular churchgoer and he told me that his congregation had prayed for me while I was having heart surgery in 1987. When I came back on set after recovering, he gave me a prayer, which I have copies of to this day. It reads: 'God grant me the serenity to accept the things I cannot change, courage to change the things I can, and wisdom to know the difference.' Bryan advised me to read it as often as I could and I took him at his word. You don't have to be religious to understand the common sense in those words.

Bryan had already suffered a heart attack and had been advised to take things easy by the doctors, so he asked to be written out of the show. When he acted the heart attack scene for transmission on New Year's Day, we would never have believed that he would die from a heart attack on 9 February.

The memory of what had happened to Bryan came back to me when I received a script in which Jack suffered a heart attack. I asked Ali if she thought they were tempting providence, but she sensibly said acting a heart attack should be easy for me because I knew what the real thing was like.

We all missed Bryan's cheerful humour. I recall fondly a cruise which Ali and I shared with Bryan and his wife Norma on board the *QE2*.

I've been lucky enough to be a guest of Cunard on a few occasions. I avoid appearing in cabaret, but I'm happy to sing a few songs in the lounges when the mood takes me. There's always some musician I recognise from my days on the cabaret circuit. One night I was about to sing 'My Funny Valentine' with a trio when Petula Clark asked if she could sing it with me.

She was one of my all-time heroines. She's got a fabulous voice and it was a magical moment to perform a duet with her. Pet had been the star of the cabaret earlier in the night. The next night I was singing 'Mean Woman Blues' in the same cocktail bar, and Pet and her backing singers came up and did backing vocals for me.

It wasn't all plain sailing though. On one trip a Force 8 gale blew up as we were going across the Bay of Biscay. I'm lucky that I don't get seasick, but I was surprised by the amount of pitching and tossing that was going on.

As I held on to the bar, I asked the chief engineer, 'Don't they have those equaliser things?'

He said, 'You mean stabilisers, and they only work when they're in the water.'

As the year unfolded, Natalie Barnes was earning a reputation as a merry widow. Our Vera didn't mince her words. She said, 'Natalie Barnes is that hard-faced, if she fell on the pavement she'd crack a flag.'

After attending the court hearing of the men who'd murdered Des, she ended up in bed with his brother Colin. Then she employed Vinny Sorrell as her new cellarman at the Rovers and had a night of passion with him too. To be fair to Natalie, she wouldn't sleep with just anybody: she turned down Jim McDonald.

It was a year of sex scandals in Weatherfield. Roy Cropper had fallen in love with Hayley Patterson only to discover that she'd started life as Harold Patterson. This caused Roy to have second thoughts for a while – and who could blame him? But love, as they say, conquers all. They got together after she'd had a sex-change operation. I was to undergo a sex change of my own a few years later!

A female curate at St Paul's Church, Weatherfield, agreed to perform a ceremony in the church, but Les Battersby tipped off the press and ruined their big day. It ended happily though when the curate performed a service in their flat surrounded by well-wishers.

Another sexual twist came in the curvy shape of Linda Sykes, played by Jacqueline Pirie. Mike Baldwin cheated on wife Alma with sales rep Julia Stone, who seduced him. He'd no idea she was an ex-prostitute who was planning to blackmail him. After Alma left him, young machinist Linda offered comfort and they became lovers. But when Mike's illegitimate son, Mark Redman, came to work at Underworld, she fancied him too. Linda finished up getting the spring and autumn double up with Mark and Mike, just before Mike proposed to her.

It all ended in tears, as we knew it would, on Mike and Linda's wedding day. Mark had agreed to act as best man. At the reception he felt compelled to tell his dad he'd had sex with his new stepmother.

With all this rampant passion going on around him, the scriptwriters decided Jack wasn't getting his fair share. An amorous landlady called Eunice Gee, played by Meg Johnson, tried to put that right. Jack and Vera had moved into Eunice's bed and breakfast accommodation on Park Road, Weatherfield, after moving out of the Rovers. As they sat on the sofa together, Eunice couldn't hold back her secret lust for Jack a moment longer. She made a lunge for him – and he suffered a heart attack.

He had to have a triple bypass operation. It proved successful, which was a blow to our Terry, who was hoping to cop for a few bob in the will. Instead, he sold Vera a second-hand car which had been a salvage job. Vera was involved in a crash and her passenger, Judy Mallett, hurt her leg. Judy later collapsed in her backyard while hanging out the washing. It turned out she'd had an embolism as a result of the leg injury, and her husband, Gary, blamed our Terry for her death.

When he called round to see Jack and Vera on Christmas Day, Gary punched Terry and Vera smacked him round the face. Until that point she'd always supported Terry and taken his side, but this time he'd gone too far. She disowned him.

I still see Nigel Pivaro from time to time. He works as a reporter on my local newspaper these days and he pops round from time to time. He calls me 'Dad' and always asks after his mum, Liz. People still shout abuse at him when he's out and about at the shops. Nigel just laps it up. He loves playing a nasty character.

By the end of 1999, though, our Terry had a big rival in the Mr Nasty stakes. A new, snarling villain had emerged by the name of Jez Quigley.

CHAPTER 24

The Millennium Year

When I was introduced to new cast member Lee Boardman, he was perfectly charming and polite. He was the sort of well-mannered man fathers want their daughters to bring home for tea. But when I saw his performance as drugs dealer Jez Quigley, I could hardly believe the transformation. Evil seemed to ooze from every pore as he forced first Leanne Battersby, then Steve McDonald, into his violent world.

Lee was so convincing as the cold-blooded killer Jez that I found it hard to have friendly chats with him at first. The Jez character was so believable that you didn't want him near you. It showed me how easy it is for fans to think they're meeting the *Corrie* character and not the actor who plays him.

Of course it didn't take me long to snap out of the imaginary world, and Lee became a popular colleague among the cast. We all admired the way he could be laughing and joking as himself one minute, and all snarling menace as Jez the next.

His reign of terror in Weatherfield lasted a year. He was acquitted of the murder of Tony Horrocks, which made him even more threatening – he could get away with murder. Leanne fled the country to escape his clutches, and Jez had Steve McDonald beaten up for defying him. But the attack on Steve sealed Jez's fate. Ex-soldier Jim McDonald attacked the brutal thug. Jez ended up in hospital and died from a ruptured spleen. It brought an end to some terrific, terrifying performances from Lee, but I think *Corrie* fans breathed a collective sigh of relief when they heard he was dead.

While all this murder and mayhem was going on, Jack was quietly getting himself his ideal job – as a lollipop warden on Rosamund Street. Apart from the early start, the hours suited him fine, and he's always had a soft spot for kids. Of course he also got school holidays off, which allowed him and Vera to visit their grandson Tommy in Blackpool.

After their bust-up with Terry, Jack and Vera transferred their affections to Tommy and to their teenage lodger, Tyrone Dobbs. Tyrone had adopted a stray greyhound called Monica as a pet. She'd raced once as Tyrone's Torpedo, but became lame after being hit by a car.

As I said earlier, actors are warned never to work with animals or children. Monica was living proof of the reason why. Time and again she would wander off as we were film-ing. We had to have pieces of chicken in our pockets to keep her still, but as soon as the cameras started rolling she would stroll out of shot. Eventually I stood on her lead to keep her still while we finished the scenes.

The storyline with Monica enabled Tyrone to find love in

the shape of kennel maid Maria Sutherland, played by Samia Ghadie. They became engaged.

Meanwhile, the tangled love lives of Martin and Gail Platt were upstaged by the news that Sarah Louise Platt, played by Tina O'Brien, had become pregnant at thirteen. The turmoil created an opportunity to turn their ten-year-old son David into a little monster, a role which Jack Shepherd took on with relish.

Away from Weatherfield, I had the chance to fulfil a long-awaited ambition to visit my father's war grave in Uden, Holland. I'd put off going there for many years because I didn't want to upset Bob Cleworth, the man who married my mum and raised me as his own alongside my younger brothers and sisters. I didn't go to see my dad's grave in Holland until after Bob's death. I didn't want him to think I was in any way ungrateful for all that he'd done.

A few years before he passed away, I'd asked him if he would mind if I changed my name from Piddington to Cleworth-Piddington. My thinking was that I didn't want to show any disrespect to the father who'd been killed in the war but I wanted to show Bob how much I loved him and appreciated all he'd done for me.

I asked him over a pint in his local pub, the Princess, in Manchester. When I asked him if he'd mind, he didn't answer at first. Then he got up and went to the gents' toilet. He came back after about five minutes and said, 'I'd love that, son.'

Bob was from the old school of men who didn't show their emotions in public. I think he'd gone to the toilet so I wouldn't see his tears. I could imagine him, wiping them away and composing himself before he came back out, beaming with pride.

After that day, I'd go regularly to see Bob in his local and make a point of kissing him on the top of his head in front of all his mates. Bob used to pretend to fight me off, pulling away and saying, 'Give over,' but I think he secretly enjoyed my show of affection for him.

In 2000 I was filmed for a one-off TV programme called *Jack and Bill*. I arranged to go to Holland with the production team. I took with me my cousin, Wilf Piddington, and my youngest brother, Alan Cleworth. It was my way of uniting both families.

I also invited Alan Hart, a *News of the World* reporter, who'd found out the details of my father's death and where he was buried many years before. He'd unearthed the facts about Bill Piddington's death and his grave number, and passed the information on to me, but he'd respected my privacy and hadn't published the details. I was grateful for that. We'd become friends over the years, and he's helped me with the writing of this book.

I learned that my father had been an ambulance driver during the war. He'd taken part in the Normandy landings and followed the Allied advance as the German Army retreated. In October 1944, he was with a group of soldiers on the front line near a convent in Veghel. The Germans launched a mortar barrage. My dad was hit by flying shrapnel and killed.

One of Dad's comrades wrote a poem about his death during the battle of Arnhem which was forwarded to me. An excerpt from it reads:

That was the start of the Arnhem Battle
Where thousands of our Paras were mown down like cattle.
The futility of Arnhem and the awful loss of life
Made us sick and sorry throughout their days of strife.
We were in the Dempsey corridor trying to come to their
    aid,
As day by day their hopes began to fade.
As they evacuated Arnhem, and this they did by night,
They brought back many wounded so we worked through-
    out and no respite.
We treated them and comforted as well as we could,
And did all the things that good Medics should.
Then on our way to Veghel and tragedy in store,
We opened up in a convent when the guns began to roar.
As shells exploded overhead, the very air was filled
With shrapnel flying everywhere and Bill Piddington was
    killed.
I laid out Bill and we buried him beside a busy road
And our carpenter made a wooden cross to mark his last
    abode.
We were glad to be on the road again, with Veghel out of
    sight,
And as long as I live, I'll not forget that night.

The account might not win any poetry prizes, but I think it paints a picture of the scene and the horrors of war.

My dad was removed from the makeshift grave referred to in the poem, and taken seven miles away to Uden, where he was reburied in a war graves cemetery with hundreds of fallen comrades. As I went to look at his grave, the cameras filmed me. We hadn't even noticed the time, but by a coincidence a nearby church started to chime. It was 11 a.m. – the traditional time for observing a minute's silence on Remembrance Sunday. Afterwards I signed the visitors' book. Where there was a space for comments, I just wrote: 'At last.'

I was introduced to the Mayor of Uden, who asked if I'd like to visit the convent where my father had been killed. I thought the emotion would be too much for me. Looking back now, I wish I'd gone. But the trip did put to rest a few ghosts from my past.

This segment was included in the 30-minute programme, which showed me working on the set of *Corrie*, singing with the jazz trio at my local, the Broadoak, recording for my latest album and relaxing at our holiday home in Tenerife.

As the year 2000 drew to a close, Sue Cleaver made her *Corrie* debut as divorcee Eileen Grimshaw. And another character first seen in 1994 was becoming more prominent. The Granada casting department had discovered yet another gold nugget of comedy acting in Malcolm Hebden, who plays Norris Cole so brilliantly.

CHAPTER 25

Fun at the Allotment

Viewers may have thought our Terry couldn't stoop any lower after he'd sold his own baby to his in-laws, the Hortons. They'd be wrong. Our scriptwriters devised a way in which the Duckworths' son could become even more despicable.

The story started with the return of Andrea Clayton. She'd had a fling with Terry but left the area when she became pregnant by him and realised he was a dodgy lot. She came back to Weatherfield to find him in desperation because her son Paul Clayton, now a teenager, needed a kidney transplant. Surgeons were looking for a suitable donor and Terry was his best hope.

After we tracked Terry down, he drove a hard bargain. Jack had won a fortune on the greyhounds, but Terry demanded £25,000 up front before he would agree to donate his kidney. Then, after trousering the cash from Jack, he did a runner. Terry had left his son in the lurch and conned his dad.

Vera came to the rescue when tests showed her kidney would be a good match for her grandson Paul. She volunteered and Paul made a good recovery. But she became desperately ill and lapsed into a coma. It was while we were shooting these scenes for a live one-hour show that Prince Charles visited the studios and Liz asked him if he'd brought any grapes.

Due to a misunderstanding at the hospital, Emily Bishop visited Jack and told him that Vera had died. He rushed to the hospital to find her alive but still unconscious. When she finally came round, Jack was waiting at her bedside. She eventually recovered and he presented her with tickets for a three-week cruise round the Caribbean.

I thought the scenes were exceptionally well crafted because they showed the depth of true feeling between Jack and Vera. They may fight like cat and dog, but behind all the bickering there's a genuine love affair going on. Marriage is a battleground for them but when the chips are down they're always there for each other.

Of course, it wasn't long before Jack was up to his old tricks again. When Vera suspected he was going deaf, Jack discovered his ears simply needed de-waxing. He couldn't resist the temptation to ignore her by pretending he was still deaf. When Vera found out, she shouted at him louder than ever.

While this was going on in Weatherfield, I was given an opportunity to fulfil another ambition by singing with the BBC Big Band, again at the Bridgewater Hall. It was a marvellous opportunity to get out of my scruffy Duckworth clothes, put on a tuxedo and bowtie, and sing with one of the country's best swing orchestras.

There was also a comic element to the night. An old friend of mine called Mike Yates came to the concert with me. Mike, who is sadly no longer with us, had been a stand-up comedian on the club circuit and often drove me to gigs.

He was one of those men who could turn his hand to anything, and when we arrived at the theatre we overheard some of the staff talking about a leak in the ladies' toilets. Quick as a flash, Mike said, 'I'll sort it for you.' Next thing I know he's paddling into the ladies in his dinner jacket, carrying a box of tools. When I came off at the interval, he had his thumbs up. For a moment I thought he was giving me encouragement. Then I realised he meant he'd fixed the toilets.

The next night I got a great review in the *Manchester Evening News*. Under the headline 'A Satin-Smooth Jack Purrs Along', they compared me favourably with Frank Sinatra and Harry Connick Junior – praise indeed. The review read: 'But though the between-song chat came in the accustomed arid Ardwick crackle we know and love from *Coronation Street*, when the band struck up Bill's voice transformed into a transatlantic purr.'

When I read the review to Mike, he asked: 'Did they mention my plumbing?' There was a real truth behind Mike's joke question: without him and his plunger, the night would have been a disaster.

Back on the *Street*, it was the Duckworths' forty-fourth wedding anniversary. Jack, romantic devil that he is, surprised Vera with a fish and chip supper in the potting shed next to his new allotment. After the seduction with fish and chips, Jack tried to make love to Vera on the shed floor, but his bad back let him down for a bit of an anticlimax.

The storyline that Jack's old pigeon-racing pal had left him his allotment created a couple of comical *Corrie* moments. The first of the funny plots was the secret distilling of poteen in the shed. Jack's mate offered to do all the donkey work for Jack's vegetable growing if he could use the shed for making illicit whisky. The secret came out one hot day when the brew overheated and caused a huge explosion, which happened as Vera was walking past.

Liz rehearsed the scene carefully twice because we knew we were going to get only one chance at filming the explosion – Granada's budget doesn't run to two explosions for one scene. Each time Vera reached a certain spot, the director clapped his hands to indicate the blast. Vera was supposed to turn and gasp. Liz had it off to a T.

When they went for a take and Vera hit her marks, they detonated the explosion and Vera was seen shooting through the air and landing on her arse. I rushed over to help Liz to her feet and luckily she wasn't hurt. As she dusted herself down, she said, 'They frightened me to death. I thought he was going to clap again. Nobody told me there was going to be a real explosion.' Priceless.

The other funny scene at the allotment happened two years later, when Jack allowed a girl called Maz, who owned the neighbouring plot of land, to use his greenhouse in exchange for some of the produce. Maz pretended she was growing tomatoes, but in fact she was cultivating cannabis. When Maz offered Jack and Vera lager and chocolate brownies, the unsuspecting Duckworths found themselves eating hash cakes.

I've never bothered with illegal drugs in real life. The legal ones, like cigarettes and alcohol, are more than enough for me. Of course growing up in the Swinging Sixties in the world of showbiz, there was plenty on offer. I've had and still have many friends who are regular users. Some take them for medicinal purposes to ease pain; some are looking to get high. I don't pass judgement on them, but it's not for me.

I had to ask a mate, who shall be nameless, how to play a stoned Jack Duckworth. I was advised, 'Play pissed but slower.' I told Liz what I'd been told so we both slurred in slow motion.

Jack and Vera had no idea what had happened, so when Maz gave Vera her secret recipe for chocolate brownies, together with cannabis as the special ingredient, Vera cooked a batch. She thought the cannabis was some sort of herb.

She handed them out at the church fund-raising meeting in the cafe. Shortly afterwards the police raided the allotments and discovered cannabis growing in Jack's greenhouse. Maz disappeared and Jack was charged with cultivating the plant. He pleaded not guilty but was convicted and fined £200. Jack's not been back to the allotment since, and I suspect he might be banned because of his drugs conviction.

CHAPTER 26

Back from the Dead

Between the allotment explosion and the discovery of cannabis, Jack lost his job as cellarman at the Rovers. At least Jack can claim he was sacked in style. Lillian Spencer, the relief manager at the Rovers, was played by one of Britain's best-loved comedy actresses, Maureen Lipman.

It was a blow to his pride when Lillian made Jack redundant on the grounds of old age and ill health. Jack was supposed to have been born on 7 November 1936, so he was sixty-six years old at the end of 2002 – five years older than me. That didn't stop our Vera storming into the pub and giving Lillian a piece of her mind.

Maureen has proved herself on stage and screen over the years, and I love the series she's done with Anne Reid called *Ladies of Letters*. Anne also appeared in another favourite of mine, *dinnerladies*, and is still remembered by *Corrie* fans as

Valerie Barlow – a part she played for ten years until her death by electrocution in 1971.

In real life, my health was starting to suffer again and I'd asked the producer to give me a lighter workload. After my heart bypass operation in 1986, Henri Moussalli had warned me that the symptoms of angina – hardening of the arteries – would return in ten to twelve years. By 2002 I'd gone sixteen years and the old breathlessness and pain were starting to come back. Also by this time, poor Henri had died of cancer.

I'd stayed in touch with Wythenshawe Hospital, always supporting their Heart Start Appeal whenever I could, but I hid from them how bad I was feeling. I tried to ignore it as long as I could. To be brutally honest, I was a bit frightened of having the operation again in my sixties. There was no way I could keep the symptoms secret from Ali though, and she kept pestering me to go for tests.

In 2004, I eventually gave in and had a medical examination at the Alexandra Hospital in Cheadle, Stockport. Their verdict was that I needed to come in within a week. I'm not sure whether the scriptwriters had time to invent a reason for Jack's absence, but I was out of the show for eight or ten weeks.

This time I needed four new bypasses, and they used veins taken from my right leg to do it. For the second time in my life I got hugs and kisses from my nearest and dearest, and I wondered whether I'd ever see them again.

The operation seemed to go well and I remember recovering in my private room, watching Tim Henman competing at Wimbledon. It was tense stuff and maybe not the best thing for a heart patient to watch.

I was wired up to a machine measuring my heartbeat, and it puzzled me when two nurses ran in to ask if I was all right. They left, but a few minutes later they ran back in again looking alarmed. That's the last thing I remember until I woke up in the intensive care unit – I recognised the ceiling was different from the one in my private room.

It seems that my heart was beating irregularly and they'd had to use a defibrillator machine to steady the rhythm. Apparently my heart stopped beating at some stage and the medical team had to press hard on my chest to get it started. I was oblivious to all this going on around me, of course. It was my family and friends who were suffering, wondering whether I'd pull through.

Only when I started to recover and had a pain in my back did I learn that it was caused by the efforts to bring me back from the dead using the medical version of jump leads. The doc told me my heart had stopped more than once. I didn't bother to ask him for the exact number of times. I was just glad to be alive.

There was a further scare when I developed an allergy to the drugs they were giving me to stabilise my condition. I was having the most terrible nightmares both day and night. I could see the floor and ceiling moving. It was like being in one of those horror movies. They decided to stop the drugs, which were having an hallucinogenic effect on me.

They offered to install a pacemaker to control my heartbeat, and I told them to go ahead. By this time you could play noughts and crosses on my chest anyway so one more little scar wasn't going to make any difference.

I was in for another five days. You can tell you're

improving at the Alex because you're moved nearer and nearer to the exit door. Eventually, I was allowed home for another month to recuperate.

My screen wife, Liz, was also suffering from health problems. Like me, she'd been a lifelong smoker and was paying the price. Her breathing was affected by emphysema, which would leave her gasping every now and again. We discussed how long we could carry on in *Corrie*. She wanted to devote more time to her family, and I felt the same way, but we both agreed to soldier on for the time being.

CHAPTER 27

When Jack Became Ida

John Stevenson is one of my all-time favourite *Coronation Street* scriptwriters. I'm told it was John who first saw the possibilities to develop the characters of Jack and Vera.

He used to be a showbiz writer for the *Daily Mail* before becoming one of *Corrie*'s key writers. He'd joined forces with another *Street* scriptwriter, Julian Roach, to write the Granada sitcoms *Brass* and *The Brothers McGregor*, which proved hugely popular.

John was a local lad and we became good friends. But I always worried when he rang me. He only called when he'd got something spicy or dicey in mind. When John started to explain how he had an idea for Jack to manage a 'ladies' bowls team, I was way ahead of him before he got to the punchline. I told him, 'I always knew you wanted to get me in a frock.'

In fact, the full plotline he was planning was *Corrie* comedy at its best, and I had no hesitation about agreeing to appear in drag. It all started with Jack trying to raise a bowls team from the Rovers, but not enough men were interested. Hayley then revealed she used to be a top player in the 1980s and suggested they recruit a women's bowling team. She was joined by Eileen, Janice, Fiz, Sonia and Shelley to form the Rovers Ravers.

Barman Ciaran McCarthy, played by former Boyzone singer Keith Duffy, bet Jack £50 they wouldn't win when they reached the cup semi-final. After the Ravers won, Jack and Ciaran agreed to go double or quits in the final.

Jack's plans were knocked sideways when his star player, Hayley, was told she couldn't play because she was born a man. Eileen Grimshaw, played by Sue Cleaver, came up with the brainwave that Jack should dress up as a woman and play instead of Hayley.

I'm not sure whether John Stevenson got his inspiration from pantomime, Shakespeare or the cross-dressing Corporal Klinger from M★A★S★H. Either way, Jack finished up in blonde wig, make-up and a dress.

As Jack stared into the mirror at the clothes factory, he said to himself, 'I've been out with worse.' At that moment the boss, Danny Baldwin, played by Bradley Walsh, came into the room. Jack hurriedly put his cigarette out of sight and when Bradley asked this strange woman her name, she replied, 'Ida Fagg.' It was the first name that popped into Jack's head so that's the name he bowled under.

The scenes were filmed in the Eccles area of Salford. As the women were dressing Jack, Hayley described the end prod-uct as 'like a lady who's had a rough life'. Jack begged them to put less sand in his bra. He complained the weight would spoil his delivery stance.

I'd never realised what women have to put up with. The extra weight puts a lot of strain on your back. If you ever try it, lads, you'll know what I mean!

Ida Fagg was due to play Edie Bagshawe in the deciding match. As they picked up their woods to bowl, the pair of them recognised each other. They'd both done their National Service in the army together.

In those days, Edie had been a bloke called Eddie. As the fact dawned on them, Edie, played by actress Carol Macready, explained in a simpering voice that he'd changed his name to Edie and become a cross-dresser. Edie explained: 'You might get to like the frock yourself. It has its advantages. You get bought more drinks and fish suppers.' They both kept their secrets and Ida won with her final wood.

Earlier, Hayley had been seen shaving Jack's legs, and Jack turned to Hayley for help as the match reached its climax. With one decisive wood left to bowl in the match, Jack said, 'Just undo my bra, would you?' Then he sighed with relief and sent down the winning wood. Like a lot of men I know, Jack was quite an expert at undoing bras worn by others, but I can assure you it's a lot harder to undo your own – just take my word for it.

Jack was the heroine of the hour, but his troubles were by no means over. Vera came looking for him, convinced he'd been having an affair with this mystery woman called Ida. Vera followed Ida, muttering, 'I'm sure I've seen her somewhere before.' She watched as Ida entered the shed. Convinced she was up to no good with Jack, Vera waited for the guilty couple to emerge.

When Jack came out of the shed alone five minutes later in men's clothes, Vera was convinced he'd been up to mischief with Ida. But Jack showed her the empty shed and persuaded her she'd been imagining things. His final words on the subject were that Vera would never see Ida again, and the viewers knew what he meant even if Vera didn't.

It was huge fun to play those scenes. Everyone in front of and behind the cameras had to work hard to keep straight faces and avoid sniggering when they were rolling. But the biggest laugh came when a paparazzi photographer fell out of a tree on the edge of the bowling green. He'd been hiding there to try to get a picture of me in drag. We made sure he was all right and then the laughter started again. Well done, John Stevenson.

CHAPTER 28

Jack the Nude Model

The year 2005 had started with Jack breaking the news to Tyrone Dobbs that his girlfriend had been cheating on him. Maria Sutherland has been playing away from home with a footballer and Jack decided Tyrone should know the truth. It's a thankless task telling someone that sort of painful news; people tend to blame the messenger.

As Tyrone had been like a son to Jack, he felt it was his duty to pass on the information. It was a very moving scene and Alan Halsall gave a great performance as the devastated Tyrone. He looked like a whipped dog, and you wanted to give him a big hug. Jack and Vera were surprised when Tyrone and Maria subsequently got back together and announced their engagement.

Later that year, the Duckworths booked a caravan holiday in Formby on the Lancashire coast. Jack was never keen on the idea in the first place. He was even less so when Vera told him it could be their own private love nest.

Jack had taken the precaution of bringing his pigeons with him for company, and he used them to escape Vera's clutches when she became amorous. After Jack released the pigeons, Vera thought she'd got him all to herself at last. But he explained he'd have to dash back home to feed them, leaving her behind.

Jack let himself in to Number 9, where he surprised Tyrone and Maria, played by Samia Ghadie. I understand Maria was so shocked by Jack's unexpected return that she dropped the towel she was wearing. I can only assume that the towel-dropping scene was shot separately from the shot of my reaction to it. I know I'm getting old but if a pretty actress like Samia had done that, I would definitely have remembered the scene. Perhaps she gave instructions that all the dirty old men had to leave the set while it was filmed!

Tyrone and Maria begged Jack to go back to Formby and Vera so they could have the house to themselves. It had been raining for two days in Formby and Vera was less than pleased with her missing hubby.

As the beginning of a storyline which almost led to divorce for the Duckworths, Frankie Baldwin gave Vera a magazine that urged women to be more self-assertive. Frankie was played by Debra Stephenson, a brilliant impressionist who'd worked on *Spitting Image* and appeared in *Bad Girls* before joining the cast of *Corrie*. Every now and then she'd make us all laugh in the Green Room with a quick burst of Cilla Black or Shirley Bassey.

Why Frankie thought Vera needed to be more forceful,

Jack will never know. It's not as if Vera was ever the shy, retiring type. So the more stroppy Vera became, the more Jack wound her up. When she got in a taxi claiming she was going to leave him forever, he stubbornly refused to apologise. That's typical of lots of real-life couples I know: they won't back down and a little argument becomes a massive marriage-breaking row.

Jack eventually admitted he was missing his wife on their forty-eighth wedding anniversary. He tracked Vera down to Southport, where he found her sitting on a bench on the promenade, staring out to sea. She told him she was thinking of drowning herself. Anybody who knows Southport would be aware that you have to walk through miles of sand to reach the sea and then a few more miles before the water reaches your knees.

When Vera told Jack how she was planning to end it all, he replied with great tenderness, 'That'd be a hell of a long walk, lovey.'

They patched up their differences and reminisced about the last time they were in Southport. That was for a dirty weekend before they married. Ever the silver-tongued Romeo, Jack suggested they book into the same hotel and the couple sealed a reconciliation.

Their lovey-dovey behaviour lasted only a day though. When they got back, Vera bought Jack some chocolates from the Kabin as an anniversary present. As soon as her back was turned, Jack tried to get a refund so he could have a bet on the horses.

He was interrupted when an ashen-faced Norris came downstairs to say Rita was dead. In fact, she had only fallen asleep.

When Rita suddenly awoke, she frightened the life out of Jack, Norris, Sally Webster and Blanche Hunt.

The best part about the scene was that Jack had to run into Sally's arms in shock. Sally Whittaker, who plays Sally Webster, is a lovely girl. When she first joined the show I used a Manchester building site expression to give her a great compliment. I said she'd got a bum like a shirt button. Sally had never heard the saying before, but she laughed and always remembered it.

From time to time over the years she'd give me a wiggle and say, 'What do you think, Bill? Still like a shirt button?'

I think it's fair to say I don't have a bum like a shirt button, so you can imagine how I felt when I read the scripts which informed me Jack was going to apply for a job as an artists' model. Just like Quentin Crisp in *The Naked Civil Servant*, Jack was going to be paid by tax and ratepayers for baring all in the name of art.

It started when Jack decided to buy Vera a decent Christmas present. As usual he was skint and as usual he was looking for an easy sure-fire way to make money. Jack's life has always been a triumph of hope over experience!

When he spotted an advert for 'life models' at an art school, Jack didn't realise the full implications. He was interviewed by the art teacher, Hilary Sanders, played by Maggie McCarthy. When Jack heard he'd have to get his kit off in front of all her students, he was about to make a sharp exit, until Hilary mentioned the fee of £200. Now every man has his price. Jack's just happens to be cheaper than most. Hilary described Jack's body as 'lived in', which he took as a compliment in view of the £200 wages.

The scenes were filmed in a studio at Manchester University. There was a stage containing a chaise longue and below it were a series of artists' easels. My heart sank when I recognised some of the extras who were playing art students. I'd worked in cabaret with some of them. I walked over to singers Molly Coogan, Jo Lester and Maggie Cole, and told them if they started tittering I'd get them blacklisted.

According to the script, Jack comes out wearing a dressing gown, which he takes off, and adopts a reclining pose on the sofa. I was wearing my grundies underneath the dressing gown, but the camera was placed so that a potted plant would cover my embarrassment. I complained to the director, Terry Dyddgen-Jones, that it was a disappointingly small plant he'd chosen. I wondered whether some cast colleagues had been telling tales. Terry assured me that as the show was going out before the nine o'clock watershed, there was no way he was going to ruin the evenings of millions of *Corrie* fans. Terry was right. The scenes were all done in the best possible taste, as Kenny Everett used to say. It was great fun to shoot and I was relieved when it all went smoothly.

But Jack's troubles were only just beginning. After buying Vera an Edward VII figurine with his modelling fee, he made the mistake of telling her how he'd earned the money. Vera phoned Hilary and went berserk. She ordered Hilary to keep her hands off Jack.

I've always thought it's quite touching the way wives like Vera think other women are desperate to get their husbands into bed. Vera continued to regard Jack as a prize stud long after he'd been put out to pasture and not long before the trip to the glue factory.

Eventually Hilary talked Vera round and persuaded her and Jack to pose together for a painting. Meanwhile, Jack agreed to continue with his nude modelling for Hilary on the quiet. But, like all Jack's best-laid schemes, his plotting came unstuck when he and Vera visited the art gallery for the unveiling of their joint portrait.

To Jack's horror, the rest of the room was devoted to nude paintings of himself. He tried desperately to steer Vera away from them, but to no avail. She seized one of the offending paintings and crowned him with it. When we shot the scene, by pure chance, Jack's glasses slipped sideways to enhance the comic effect. I looked just like Eric Morecambe in his heyday.

This happened in 2006. By this time Jack and Vera had long since left the bed and breakfast business in Park Road, Weatherfield, and moved back to 9 Coronation Street. Tyrone and Maria had broken off their engagement and he was now going out with Molly Compton, played by Vicky Binns. Molly had been depressed because she didn't think Tyrone was interested in her. Tyrone didn't think he was good enough for Molly. Jack and Vera played matchmakers and they were delighted when Molly asked if she could move in with them and Tyrone.

I was sixty-five when Jack celebrated his seventieth birthday later that year. I can only take this opportunity to congratulate the make-up artists for making such an age difference seem credible. Vera decided to throw a surprise party for his birthday. As we all know, the trouble with surprise parties is that they usually end in tears. This one was no exception.

Vera pretended that, as Jack didn't want a fuss made of his

birthday, she'd go away to Amsterdam with the girls. They were secretly planning a surprise party. And because Vera and the girls were going to be away, Tyrone thought it would be a great idea to book a stripogram for Jack.

So surprise number one for Jack is when all the friends of the Duckworths, including Vera, turn up at the Rovers to toast his birthday. And surprise number two comes when the stripper booked by Tyrone starts to undress. There was no surprise about who got the blame: Jack, the birthday boy, who knew nothing about what was going on behind his back, was labelled a dirty old man by Vera.

Back at Number 9, Molly started to train Jack to become a better husband. She reckoned it was like bringing up a dog, using a combination of reward and punishment. For a while, it worked, but Vera soon got fed up with helpful Jack and wanted her old lazy slob of a husband back. There's just no pleasing some women.

The following year saw Vera and Jack both on the injured list. First, Vera sprained an ankle and Jack had to help Tyrone and Molly look after her. They borrowed a baby monitor so she could call for help if necessary while Jack was in the Rovers. Then Jack put his back out while moving the pigeon loft. Tyrone converted an armchair into a wheelchair by adding rollers to it so he could still get to the Rovers.

These storylines were a tribute to the many men I've known over the years who have overcome all sorts of injuries, obstacles and wives' objections and gone through hell and high water to reach their local pubs.

Eventually Tyrone and Molly got tired of looking after the invalid Duckworths. Molly contacted their eldest grandson,

Paul Clayton, to share the burden. Jack and Vera were delighted to see Paul, now played by Tom Hudson. Little did they know he'd turn out to be a chip off the old block, Terry.

Paul and Molly organised a golden wedding anniversary party for Jack and Vera at the Rovers. Paul even gave Jack a gold necklace for Vera. But just like his good-for-nothing, scheming dad, Terry, Paul was looking out for the main chance.

He'd undermined Tyrone over some missing money and then used Number 9 as security for a £30,000 loan to buy a share of a restaurant. When Jack discovered what Paul had done, he told Vera he'd loaned him the £30,000. He didn't want Vera to know her grandson was following in Terry's footsteps. Like so many women, Vera couldn't see faults in her own flesh and blood. Jack didn't want to disillusion her so he shouldered the blame for the fact that Vera couldn't have her dream home in Blackpool.

CHAPTER 29

The Death of Vera

Liz had told me on previous occasions that she was going to leave the show. For the past six or seven years, she'd said that this would be her last twelve-month contract. In 2007, I knew she meant it. Her emphysema wasn't getting any better and the years when Liz could enjoy her well-earned retirement were shrinking.

Time and again we'd discussed the situation. Liz was always worried that if they wrote Vera out of the show, Jack would be written out too. It was typical of Liz to put other people's considerations before her own.

I told her not to worry about me. If it happened, it happened. I'd passed retirement age myself in April 2006, so it wouldn't have been the end of the world if they decided to send Jack and Vera off into the sunset together.

Our *Corrie* contracts come up for renewal in the autumn and Granada starts negotiations towards the end of summer.

Even though I could sense a new determination in Liz to quit, there was still the chance she'd allow herself to be talked out of it again.

Just like Helen Worth and me, Liz had an inability to say no. I'd often find Liz at a charity bash which I knew she shouldn't have attended because of illness. Liz was so reluctant to let people down, she'd sacrifice her own social life and health so as not to disappoint others. This time she stuck to her guns. She told me that instead of signing a new twelve-month contract, she'd given them time to write her out of the show by the end of 2007.

When they told Liz that Vera was going to die, I think she was relieved. It meant that Jack would be able to carry on and that I'd be able to continue working as Jack the widower if I wanted to. Of course there's always the chance that a character can be written out or killed off at any time, but at least Liz wouldn't feel responsible for me losing a well-paid job.

After Liz made her decision and knew there was no turning back, I noticed it seemed to take a weight off her shoulders. She could finally see the light at the end of the tunnel. It must be a tremendous wrench to leave the *Street* after so many years. It's like a second family and I know it's a bit scary to think about retirement. You wonder whether you'll have regrets when it's too late to change your mind. All these thoughts would have been going through Liz's mind, but once the decision was made she seemed to relax.

When I read the script which showed how Vera was going to pass away gently, I thought it was a delightful way for her to go. The battles that Jack and Vera had fought in the early days of their marriage were replaced with a tenderness that didn't seem out of place. The story of Jack and Vera wasn't like *Romeo and Juliet.* It was more like *Punch and Judy.*

Despite the bust-ups, the affairs and the flying crockery, they'd managed to reveal a depth of feeling for each other. It wasn't sentimental. It was the sort of love affair that comes from adversity. They'd been through a lot together for more than fifty years and come out the other side. Their son Terry had been a huge disappointment, always taking from them and never giving anything back. I've known many real-life couples like Jack and Vera. You wonder why they stick together, yet when one of them dies, the survivor seems lost.

Our final scenes together revolved round the decision to sell 9 Coronation Street to Tyrone and his fiancée Molly, and for the Duckworths to buy a bungalow in Blackpool. The move to Blackpool was only six weeks away when they visited their new home. On their return to Number 9, Vera was tired so Jack sat her in her favourite chair, took her shoes off and made her comfy.

She told him to nip to the Rovers for a couple of pints while she got their tea ready. The last words she spoke to Jack were when she asked him what he'd do in Blackpool when there was only her and none of his mates around. In the past, Jack would have been horrified by the thought. But he knew that's just what he wanted now. They'd be living round the corner from their grandson Tommy, relaxing and talking about old times.

It was a sign of the change in Jack when he had a swift couple of pints and turned down the offer of a third because his tea would be ready. He walked back to Number 9 singing,

'She's my lady love' from 'Lily of Laguna'. When he saw Vera
with her eyes closed, he assumed she was asleep and told her,
'I'll just get me tea.'

But there was nothing in the oven. When Jack came back,
he tried to nudge Vera awake. He gave her a couple of
nudges. When Vera didn't respond, he realised she'd gone.

We had a problem filming that scene because of Liz's
breathing difficulties. Obviously dead bodies don't breathe,
but the emphysema made it impossible for Liz to hold her
breath for more than a few seconds.

I realised there was a way round it because in the script Jack
talked about Vera not liking to be cold. I had a word with the
director. I said if Jack put his coat over Vera, the viewers
wouldn't see she was still breathing. It worked well and I
remember feeling genuine grief as I talked to her. I'm getting
emotional even now as I cast my mind back to the scene.

Jack was holding Vera's hand and calling her his little
swamp duck. It was all beautifully written. The sadness didn't
need any acting on my part because I was suffering a real
loss – the loss of my screen wife.

When Tyrone and Molly came back from the Rovers, with
Tyrone carrying and spilling most of a pint of beer for Jack,
he met them at the back door. He led them through and
showed them Vera's body. Molly phoned an ambulance while
Tyrone fetched Paul from his restaurant. A crowd gathered
when the ambulance arrived and soon the word spread that
Vera had died.

As Vera's body was taken away by paramedics, Jack sat alone
at the table staring at Vera's empty chair. When Jack started
to cry at his loss, I was crying for my own loss because that

had been Liz's last scene. Our partnership as a soap double act was over.

Tyrone and Molly worried about Jack as he took his time coming to terms with the loss of Vera. I think it was perfectly natural that Jack should seem like a lost soul. Her death had come out of the blue and he would have been in a state of shock.

Terry turned up like the proverbial bad penny, no doubt wondering what was in it for him. He didn't even recognise his own son, Paul. He'd never seen him as an adult and Jack had to introduce them to each other.

At the funeral service I was feeling dreadful. I'd got all the symptoms of a flu virus that was doing the rounds. The scenes were being filmed in a cold crematorium. The crew kept me warm by covering me with blankets. At one stage I couldn't speak my lines because my mouth was so cold. We shot the scene in between me having fits of coughing, shivering and sweating.

The setting reminded me how things had come full circle since I'd first met Liz in a cold church at Brian and Gail Tilsley's wedding back in 1979. I remembered the heater, Vera's smouldering dress, and how I'd thrown Liz to the floor and smacked her bottom. By 'eck we'd 'ad some adventures in those twenty-eight years since, as Jack would say.

As Jack grabbed the lectern for support, he made a lovely speech about his Vera. I found it moving because of its honesty and simplicity. Once again, I found genuine emotion bubbling up inside me so there was no acting necessary.

My sombre mood was soon lifted when I saw Vera's coffin disappearing into the fiery furnace. Stagehands were hauling it away on ropes. I recognised the lads pulling the coffin and thought what a bumpy ride Vera would have been getting for her last journey. Alan Halsall, who plays Tyrone, looked at me and we started giggling. For some reason the sight of these lads pulling an empty coffin seemed ludicrously funny. I think it was just a reaction to the tension of the moment. It was our way of reminding ourselves it was only a play.

Terry took the opportunity to warn Jack not to sell Number 9 to Tyrone and Molly. It was obvious to Jack he was worried about his inheritance. After Terry had gone, Jack told Tyrone, Molly and Paul that they were his family now and he'd be ignoring Terry's advice about the sale of the house.

When Jack returned home, he picked up a photo of him and Vera together. The tears started to flow again for the last time. When Jack brought Vera's ashes back home, he put the urn on the mantelpiece and told Tyrone and Molly that she would be watching over them from now on. Jack said when he died he wanted them to scatter both sets of ashes together.

Granada threw a farewell party for Liz at the Rovers, attended by the cast. She was presented with a massive bouquet of flowers and a huge painting of Jack and Vera. Two days later Liz threw a second party for family and friends at the Old Grapes, a pub she jointly owns near the Granada TV studios off Quay Street, Manchester.

I couldn't attend the second bash because by that time I'd taken to my sickbed. But I still see Liz from time to time and she's always on the phone.

Ali and I have been out with her and Don, and they're

having a great time. They're watching their many grand-children grow up – I can't keep count of how many they've got. They're also going on lots of holidays. Liz especially likes cruises, so she's often to be found sailing the Seven Seas.

Liz has been retired for more than two years now and she's loving every minute of it. Good luck to her. She deserves it.

CHAPTER 30

Life after Death

Once the funeral was behind us, I was relieved to see that Jack still had a part to play in *Corrie*. I didn't want him to become a grumpy old man on the edge of the action. Although I'd asked the bosses to lighten my workload, I wanted to feel I was earning my corn with decent storylines. I needn't have worried. Our scriptwriters came up with some clever ideas involving Jack.

On the day Vera died, Jack had placed a bet with the book-ies. I've never understood the language of betting so when Jack says he's having an each-way Yankee, I haven't a clue what he's talking about. I say the words but it might as well be a foreign language as far as I'm concerned.

Anyway, Jack had placed a complicated bet involving several horses and forgotten all about it in the shock and confusion that followed Vera's death. The bet won Jack £3,172, but he was told he needed the betting slip to claim the money. The slip had gone missing. After much deliberation the bookie paid out, but as usual Jack didn't keep the money for long.

He found out his grandson Paul was heavily in debt to the bookie, and handed over his winnings to help out. But Paul's financial problems were far from over. He'd got involved in an insurance fraud and the restaurant was burned down to make a claim for damages. Police charged him with arson and he decided to jump bail.

Jack wanted Paul to face the consequences and serve any prison sentence. He gave him a choice: he offered Paul £10,000 to run away and start a new life, or promised him £30,000 on release if he served his time. Jack left Paul with the cash to think about it. When Jack came back from the Rovers, he found Paul had gone but he'd left the £10,000 in an envelope by the phone. It was a sign that while Paul was a wrong 'un like his dad, he did have some principles. Terry would have disappeared along with the cash, so there's hope that Paul could mend his ways one day.

Tyrone was pleased to see the back of Paul. He'd been jealous of the fact that Paul was a flesh-and-blood relative of Jack and Vera, whereas he was a surrogate son.

With Paul off the scene, Tyrone could get round to proposing marriage to Molly. The trouble was that Tyrone lacked confidence so Jack decided to lend a hand. He gave him Vera's engagement ring and told him it's what she would have wanted. Tyrone took Molly to a posh restaurant, but lost his bottle and the moment passed.

Molly's aunt, Pam Hobsworth, played by Kate Anthony, joined forces with Jack as matchmaker for the tongue-tied lovebirds. She gave Tyrone a fake Fabergé egg in which a taped message of his voice asked, 'Will you marry me?' But when he got down on one knee in the Rovers and presented Molly with the egg, she opened it to hear a message asking, 'Where do you put the batteries?' Kirk Sutherland, played by Andy Whyment, had accidentally taped over Tyrone's voice while setting up the egg.

Humiliated, Tyrone fled the pub, but Molly was delighted when she realised he'd been trying to propose. All turned out well when he found her sitting at a table for two outside a burger van decked in fairy lights. Molly opened another fake Fabergé egg, a chick popped out and said, 'Yes.' It was *Corrie* at its best – a mixture of comedy and romance that would have had viewers reaching for their hankies and saying a warm 'Aaahhh'.

Jack's very fond of Molly. Apart from the fact that she's beautiful, she also makes him his favourite meals like cheese on toast. When Molly and Tyrone fell out, Jack got them back together again. And he was chuffed to bits when she asked him if she'd give her away at the wedding. Jack had never had a daughter of his own and he wanted to foot the bill for Molly's big day. But there was another comical twist before he got her down the aisle.

Tyrone had had some extravagant ideas for making the wedding special. They involved a flock of doves and a Korean harpist. But he fell foul of a practical joke when he called at the Flying Horse on the way to the church. A couple of crooks called Dodgy Dave and Whispering Geoff pretended they were undercover policemen and arrested Tyrone for handling stolen goods. Jack, thinking they were real detectives, bribed them with £100 to let Tyrone go ahead with the wedding.

As he walked down the aisle with Molly, Jack beamed with pleasure, bowing as if all the admiring glances were for him. When Molly smiled at Tyrone as they stood before the altar, he smiled back at her. She turned to look at the vicar and when she looked back a second later, Tyrone had gone. He'd fainted and fallen forward to the church floor.

Alan played the part brilliantly. His face was a picture as he crumpled, and later when Molly brought him round. His day was complete when he heard that Dodgy Dave and Whispering Geoff were genuine crooks and not undercover cops.

The wedding reception took place at the Rovers – where else? – and Jack made another fine speech. It seems he's becoming quite an orator in his old age!

CHAPTER 31

A Companion for Jack

It was a year after Vera's death that Connie Rathbone walked into Jack's life. I knew there was something special about Connie because the casting department wanted me to do a screen test with the five or six actresses who were auditioning for her part.

I knew two of the actresses who were up for the role because I'd worked with them in the past in other shows. Our casting department were looking for some kind of empathy between Jack and Connie. They asked me which one I liked best, but I refused to answer. I said I didn't want to go down that road. I said I'd work as well as I could with whomever they chose but picking the right candidate was their area of expertise and not mine.

I thank my lucky stars that I never had to do a screen test for the part of Jack Duckworth. Otherwise I might have spent the rest of my life chucking darts in the background at the Rovers. No matter how experienced you are, an audition is a nerve-racking experience. It's all the more so when you're up for a part in *Coronation Street*, in which you'll be working with some of the most famous faces on telly.

One or two of these seasoned actresses were literally shaking with fear when they sat next to me to read their lines. It can't be easy working alongside a sex symbol! I tried to calm them as best I could so they'd be able to give it their best shot.

I'd never worked with Rita May, who eventually got the part. She'd done a lot of TV work in the past and had worked with Alan Halsall in a children's hospital series.

The storyline that brought Connie into the show started when Pam Hobsworth's scheme to make bio-diesel from chip-frying oil caused an explosion which rocked the street. It scared away Jack's pigeons and he worried whether he'd ever see them again.

Some weeks later Connie turned up on Jack's doorstep with Scarlett O'Hara, his favourite bird. She'd been feeding her at her home a few miles away and noticed the ring on her leg. It had Jack's name and address on it so she'd brought her round in a basket.

The pigeon in the basket Connie was carrying was a model, but Rita hadn't noticed. In between takes, Rita said to me, 'It's a very quiet pigeon, isn't it?'

I fell about laughing. Then I said to the crew, 'Nearly thirty years of Liz and now they've found me another one.' It broke the ice with Rita May, just as my fire-extinguishing technique had broken the ice with Liz all those years before.

Jack invited Connie in for a cup of tea and she told him her husband had recently died. Jack told her about losing Vera and they shared a drink in the Rovers. At the end of the visit, Connie gave Jack her phone number. He agonised over what to do, but Molly told him he should go for it. Vera would want him to be happy.

It was a view that wasn't shared by Tyrone, who was horrified to find Connie round at Number 9, sitting in Vera's old chair. Tyrone became jealous again, just as he had been when Paul arrived on the scene.

Jack was aware of Tyrone's feelings, so he never told him about a trip to the bingo with Connie or the fact she'd invited him to stay with her in a friend's apartment in Spain. In fact, Jack later found out the apartment belonged to Connie, who'd been trying to play down her wealth.

Jack pretended he was going to Blackpool for a couple of weeks on his own. Poor old Jack – he's the world's worst liar and he always gets found out. Tyrone isn't the sharpest tool in the box, but when he spotted a Spanish airline label on Jack's suitcase and found a pair of castanets and a sombrero, it didn't take Sherlock Holmes to solve the mystery.

Tyrone was convinced that Connie was a gold-digger but Jack soon found out that nothing could be further from the truth. Under pressure Connie eventually agreed to show Jack her home. When they arrived in a taxi and she opened the electronic gates, he found she lived in a mansion with a hallway bigger than his house. And when he saw the room with a full-size snooker table and a bar, he thought he'd died and gone to heaven. On top of that he found Scarlett, who'd gone missing again, in Connie's back garden.

By this time Jack had started to feel in the way of the

newlyweds at Number 9, but Tyrone and Molly wanted him to stay. Then Connie suggested he could move in with her. When Jack finally agreed to accept her offer, Tyrone was furious. After seeing Connie's home, though, Tyrone realised he'd got it all wrong. He apologised to her for his behaviour.

It turned out that Connie and her late husband had owned a chain of launderettes. They'd worked hard all their lives but just when they sold up to reap the rewards, her hubby had died. Connie's a wealthy widow but she hasn't forgotten her working-class roots.

Jack left most of his possessions behind at Number 9, apart from some photo albums, Vera's Princess Diana mug, his stuffed pigeon Fergie and Vera's ashes. It's a tribute to Connie's easygoing nature that she's quite happy to share her home with Jack and his late wife's ashes. In his occasional conversations with Vera, he told her, 'She'll never take over from you, love.'

It was certainly a missing pigeon and a joint sense of loss which brought Jack and Connie together initially. She and Jack both enjoy life's simple pleasures and they've got a lot in common. They're both looking for companionship rather than passion – though Jack got a bit worried when Connie's sleepwalking led her to his bedroom door at night.

I don't know what the scriptwriters have in mind for Jack and Connie as we reach the summer of 2010. I just know that Jack's a lucky lad to have found such a nice woman. As for Jack, well, he's mellowed with the years, hasn't he? It's been a long time since Bet Lynch filled his pint pot for him and Dulcie Froggatt rang out his chamois-leather. Perhaps Jack and Connie will have a future together one day. I certainly hope that whatever happens to Jack, the *Street* bosses will find a way for Connie to carry on. I think the writers and Rita have created a very warm character with a lot of potential. When you find a gold nugget like that, you shouldn't chuck it away.

CHAPTER 32

The Final Curtain

Just like Liz, I'd been planning to retire for a while before I finally decided to take the plunge. Over the years the cast and crew have become like another family to me. I've been lucky to have had several different types of family in my life.

Bob Cleworth, the man who brought me up, and his wife, my mum, were of the old school. They believed that men, and boys who wanted to become men, should never wear their hearts on their sleeves. Big boys didn't cry and real men put up with whatever life chucked at them and got on with it. To show weakness would make things worse for you. Any displays of love were done in private once a boy was old enough to wear long trousers. I'm sure my dad, who died in the war and was from the same era, would have felt exactly the same.

My parents-in-law, who were of a similar age, had a different way of showing their love. They were keen churchgoers who loved mankind. Alice, my mum-in-law, would have found some good in Jack the Ripper. She used to call me her 'Billy boy'. She and George were an affectionate couple who showed their love for each other with hugs and kisses and holding hands. They didn't mind who saw them either. I'm glad to say that's the way their children were brought up and I was fortunate enough to marry one of them.

Then there was the musical family. This was a sort of brotherhood of men and women with a shared sense of humour. There was a common feeling that maybe we'd never get the recognition our talents might deserve, but at least we were having fun not getting there. The unfairness of it all was dealt with through dark humour.

Then there was the cast of *Corrie*. On both sides of the camera, we might have had occasional squabbles among ourselves, but if anyone on the outside kicked a member of the cast, we all limped. There has always been a great team spirit within the show. It's been tested from time to time. I'd be lying if I pretended that all the cast members were liked by all the other cast members. But making four episodes of a drama every week requires the cast to work as a team and put aside any personal differences. When anyone was in trouble, whether they'd lost a loved one or were having a health problem, everybody rallied round. There was always a hug from somebody. Nobody would kick you when you were down.

There was also a great deal of patience and understanding shown to those of us who weren't from an acting background. It must be difficult for people who've worked at the Royal Shakespeare Company and the Old Vic to find themselves sharing scenes with people like me. If they've felt that way, they've never shown it. I was only tutted at once in thirty years. As I made an average of twenty mistakes a year in that time, that works out at one tut per 600 cock-ups.

Leaving a family like that can be a tremendous wrench. At the time of writing, I still don't know what it's going to feel like.

Before Christmas 2009 I'd made the decision in my head that this would be my last 12-month contract. I thought it would be nice to stay long enough for Jack to be around for the fiftieth anniversary celebrations in December 2010, then retire before my seventieth birthday the following April.

It was in March 2010 when our producer, Kim Crowther, introduced me to Phil Collinson, who was taking over from her. I said I'd like to have a word with him. We were running late that evening for a variety of reasons. One of them was that they'd changed the locks to the dressing rooms and my key didn't fit. I was in a rush to get home because we were having a joint celebration of our wedding anniversary and Sara's birthday with a dinner at the Broadoak Hotel, round the corner from our home in Ashton. So it was arranged that Phil should come round to my house for a chat a few days later.

I told him then that I wanted to leave the show. I was sorry it was going to happen on his watch but I'd had enough. I explained how Ali had persuaded me it would be nice to carry on until the fiftieth anniversary, if that's what they wanted. Phil asked me if there was anything he could say to make me change my mind. He said Jack was a much-loved character who'd be sorely missed.

I told him it was nice of him to say so but my mind was made up. I explained that I'd never enjoyed the best of health because of my heart problems, and I wanted to have some time with my feet up before I popped my clogs.

Then Phil asked me if there was any particular way I'd like to be written out of the show. I hadn't given it any thought because I wasn't expecting the question. I'd assumed the scriptwriters would come up with a variety of suggestions and they'd just pick the one they liked best that suited the general plan.

I said jokingly that I could come out of Dev's shop and get squished by a derailed tram. Phil didn't look too impressed with that idea, or the follow-up, when I said he could get rid of a few others at the same time in front of the fatal tram. I hope he realised I was joking.

It would be nice if Jack could have an heroic death, pushing Connie and a baby buggy out of the way of a runaway lorry, sacrificing his life for theirs. The camera could do a close-up of Jack's broken glasses on the cobbles to symbolise his death. That would be a nice way to be remembered. On the other hand, they might decide to have Jack move away from Weatherfield for good.

No doubt they'll tell me at the appropriate time. Will Jack live or will he die? To be or not to be – that is the question I've heard somewhere before.

The *Daily Mirror* splashed the exclusive story that I was leaving the show on its front page in April. Most of my family and friends already had a good idea what I'd been thinking.

Current cast members and former colleagues all said nice things, for which I'm grateful. Seeing the stories about Jack's departure was a bit like reading your own obituary. Hopefully there'll be a few more twists and turns in the old boy's life before Jack leaves Weatherfield one way or the other.

CHAPTER 33

Looking Forward

As I approach retirement, I'm not sure what the future has in store – I never have been. My life has been built from a series of unplanned situations which I've dealt with as they've come along. If we'd had such a thing as a careers adviser at school, I don't think singer or TV actor would have been very high on his list of suggestions for me.

So I'm looking forward to retirement in the same way: let's see what happens. I've never had a plan for my life and it's a bit late to start having one now.

More than anything, I'm looking forward to the freedom. The idea that I can wake up in the morning and not have to do anything I don't feel like doing is very appealing. It's something I've never experienced before so I'll have to see whether it's as good as it sounds.

I've joked with friends about how I might be going back to the producer in a couple of years begging for a part. I'd be asking if I could play Jack's identical twin brother. I could even dig out that blonde wig and come back as his sister.

Seriously, though, I think I'd like to pop back to the studios once in a while to say hello to all those friends I've made on both sides of the camera during the past thirty years and more. Most people who leave the show never come back. It may be out of embarrassment that they'd be a distraction and get in the way. But I don't like to think I'll walk out of the Granada studios one day and never see my *Corrie* family again.

Perhaps I could start a *Coronation Street* Old Boys' and Girls' Association, with an annual dinner at which we could all talk about the good old days with the current cast members. There'd be a few familiar faces there: Peter Baldwin and Thelma Barlow (Derek and Mavis Wilton), Roy Barraclough and Julie Goodyear (Alec and Bet Gilroy), Charlie Lawson and Nick Cochrane (Jim and Andy McDonald), Phil Middlemiss and Caroline Milmoe (Des and Lisa Barnes), Kev Kennedy and Sarah Lancashire (Curly and Raquel Watts) and Johnny Briggs and Amanda Barrie (Mike and Alma Baldwin), as well as the Duckworth family – Liz Dawn (Vera), Nigel Pivaro (Terry) and Tom Hudson (Paul Clayton).

Most of all I'm looking forward to spending more time with my real family. They've had to take second place to my work for most of my life. I've missed funerals, weddings, christenings and parties because of filming commitments. Hopefully, after I retire from *Corrie* they'll get my undivided attention. Ali and I could have more of a social life.

My son Carl is the landlord of a pub in Ashton which I visit regularly and where I catch up with some old friends I've known most of my life. My daughter Sara learned to be an expert seamstress from her mum and she has her own small business called Perfect Fit in Stamford Street, Ashton, making hand-tailored ladieswear. Sara lives round the corner and is a regular visitor to our house.

Then there are the grandchildren. Carl has a son Curtis by his first wife, Jackie, and a son Matthew by his second wife, Sandra. She has a daughter, Leigh, by a previous relationship, and Jackie has two daughters, Elizabeth and Olivia, by a later one. As far as Ali and I are concerned, all five of them are our grandchildren. Sara has two children, Naomi, nineteen, and Callum, fourteen, so that gives us a total of seven. It means we have a good chance of seeing some great-grandchildren one day. Stop press: we've just heard there's one on the way!

My old musician friends come round to my house once a week for the meeting of the Alzheimer's Club. It's not meant as any disrespect to sufferers of this illness, but we're all getting to that age when we forget things. So we can tell each other the same old stories and they still sound to some members as if they're hearing them for the first time. Somebody always brings the latest jokes along and we have a session called 'Name-dropping Corner'. It's an opportunity for us to outshine each other with celebrity anecdotes.

One of our group told the true story of how the 50s heart-throb singer Johnny Ray came to his house and his mum cooked Johnny a full English breakfast. Another talked about the time he worked with Hollywood sex symbol Jane Russell. I, of course, can't resist telling stories which begin: 'As I used to say to Sir Laurence Olivier – or Lazza as I knew him . . .'

The rule is that you can exaggerate – or elasticate, as we put it – but you can't lie. We start our trips down memory lane about 8.30 p.m. and for three hours we never stop laughing. We've come to the conclusion that we had the best of times in our business.

Customers enjoyed a golden era too. They could pay the equivalent of 12p to watch three decent acts in their local clubs. There used to be jugglers, acrobats, conjurors and sword-swallowers in those days, as well as stand-up comics, singers and musicians who could play everything from the musical saw and the spoons to the zither. You'd even get knife-throwers whose wives were strapped to a revolving wheel on stage. You often wondered whether it was wise for them to go ahead after they'd had a blazing row and he'd knocked back a couple of pints.

My only regret as I approach retirement day is that I've been unable to carry on singing in recent years. I've been suffering from shortage of breath again and have to carry an inhaler around with me. I loved singing with the gentle jazz trio at the Broadoak, but my voice was getting weaker. I didn't want to wait until people told me it was time to go. I wanted to give up of my own volition before I became an embarrassment to myself.

To some extent I feel the same way about playing Jack. I want to leave on my own terms before cast colleagues and viewers start to think it's time I called it a day.

Of course, there are some cast members who are older than me and they're still going strong. People like Bill Roache (Ken Barlow), Eileen Derbyshire (Emily Bishop), Barbara Knox (Rita Sullivan) and Betty Driver (Betty Williams) absolutely love appearing in the show. They've all enjoyed good health and can see no reason why they shouldn't carry on. Good luck to them. It's nice to have these older characters in the show because there are older characters in real life. I think viewers enjoy switching on and seeing the same old familiar faces they've seen for decades as well as the new characters whose personalities will be developing in the years ahead.

I'm in no doubt *Corrie* can survive without Jack Duckworth. Whether Bill Tarmey can survive without *Corrie* remains to be seen. I think we'll both be OK.

Leaving the show means I'll be free to advertise products. I've been unable to do that while I've been under contract to Granada. It's brought up some strange anomalies. For instance, one company wanted me to do a voice-over for their product but I wasn't allowed to do it. Instead, I rang up a local lad who did impersonations on the TV programme *Who Do You Do?* He was a mate of mine called Aidan J. Harvey, and I taught him how to take off Jack's voice. In that way, Aidan was able to impersonate Jack Duckworth's voice for the advert and no rules were broken.

From now on I'll be able to do my own voice-overs without having to pass the work on to an impressionist. You might even see my face again during the adverts while you're watching *Corrie*. Like me, you'll have to wait and see what happens next.

CHAPTER 34

Looking Back

As I've looked back on my life while writing this book, I can't escape from the fact that I'm the jammiest devil I know. I could have died on half a dozen different occasions. If it hadn't been for my mate and neighbour Dave Livesey, I could have been dead at thirty-five from a heart attack three years before a *Coronation Street* character called Jack Duckworth was even invented.

Since then I've had several more brushes with death, but here I am, aged sixty-nine, with some fabulous memories to savour. It's been great fun going back in time and remembering things which had been long forgotten. Even the bad memories, like my heart problems, had happy endings. I'm not a religious man but I certainly feel I've led a charmed life.

After that heart attack in 1976, I felt I was living on borrowed time so I was determined to make the most of it. I never expected to be around this long; perhaps that's helped me to live life to the full.

As I explained in the early chapters, my childhood took place in bleak conditions. I lost one father in the war, but that meant I gained another dad. We were short of many things in those early days, but we were never short of the most important thing that every kid needs – love. That's why I would never change a single thing about my life. The hardships early on have made me appreciate the good things I'm lucky enough to be able to afford now.

Getting up at five o'clock on a cold winter morning, breaking the ice to use the outside toilet and catching two or three buses to get to work doesn't sound like much fun, yet I look back on those days with great fondness. I found myself smiling at the memories of my time as an apprentice asphalter. The work was hard but the company was terrific. They were hard men with hearts of gold and a wicked sense of humour.

My singing days had their fair share of disappointments too, but I learned from my mistakes. I wasn't prepared to sacrifice my family life by living away from home for weeks on end. Perhaps if I'd made that compromise, I would have been successful. We'll never know. But then I probably wouldn't have taken on work as an extra at Granada TV, and I wouldn't have had the chance to play Jack Duckworth.

If I hadn't played Jack Duckworth, I wouldn't have been on *This Is Your Life*. If I hadn't sung 'Wind Beneath My Wings' to Ali on *This Is Your Life*, I wouldn't have met the extraordinarily talented Derek Wadsworth and been offered a recording contract by EMI.

It seems to me at times that life is so random you never know what lies around the corner or what to do for the best. But of one thing I have no doubt: meeting Ali was the luckiest thing I ever did. She was the one who always encouraged me. She taught me to overcome any fear of failure or rejection. You have to be prepared to fail if you want to succeed.

There must be a lot of people out there, and I could have been one of them, who think if they don't try something, they can't fail. Ali gave me the courage to try. I always knew if I tried and failed, she'd be there to tell me not to worry. There was no shame attached to failure. If I went for an audition as a singer or compère and didn't get the job, it was their loss as far as Ali was concerned. She always had faith in me.

Being in the right place at the right time seems to have been a knack I've had throughout my life. It's not something I've ever planned. When I called at the Horseshoe Club in Ashton and overheard Ian Raven talking about work as an extra at the Granada TV studios that was one lucky break. Being offered a lift to the studios and an introduction was another.

The biggest break at the start of my acting career was not having to read for the part of Jack. I'm sure that if I'd had to memorise a script for a screen test I'd have gone to pieces. I'd read for parts three times before, and the only role I got was as a slaughterman in the play *Thicker Than Water* and the director already knew me. I made a complete mess of the other two auditions.

Even landing the role of Jack might never have led anywhere. Luckily for me, Liz had started to turn Vera into a popular character, but there was no guarantee that her husband, who hadn't been seen for five years, would become a regular in the show. Fortunately, the scriptwriters, and John Stevenson in particular, saw a spark between Jack and Vera that could be developed. Bill Podmore, the producer at that time, saw it too. He was prepared to overlook the fact that I'd had no training as an actor. Just like Ali, he had faith in me.

Of course I spent the first few years thinking I was going to be found out. I feared that some new producer would recognise my failings and wonder what Bill Tarmey thought he was doing pretending to be an actor. To some degree that took some of the shine off my early days as Jack. I could never relax because I always thought the bubble was going to burst at any moment. I hope that doesn't sound ungrateful because I've had a wonderful time playing him. It's just that for a long time I felt a bit of a fraud.

The difference between my acting and my singing was that I always felt I knew what I was doing when I was perform-ing with musicians. I didn't experience any of the fear that I'd associated with acting. For that reason I think my happiest memories have come from my singing. But I'm under no illusions: it was working in *Corrie* as Jack that gave me the opportunity to sing with top bands, record top-selling albums and have a jamming session on a cruise ship with Petula Clark. I still have to pinch myself to make sure I haven't dreamed some of these amazing events in my life.

I'd watched the early days of *Coronation Street* as a teenager. Twenty years later I was performing alongside TV legends like Violet Carson (Ena Sharples), Jack Howarth (Albert Tatlock), Doris Speed (Annie Walker), Peter Adamson (Len Fairclough) and Pat Phoenix (Elsie Tanner).

I had my first sex scene with Julie Goodyear (Bet Lynch). OK – it was behind the bedroom door and wasn't filmed, but I don't like to spoil a good story. We did at least share my first screen kiss.

Johnny Briggs (Mike Baldwin) had been raised in a tough area of London similar to mine in Manchester. We both survived the Blitz 200 miles apart. But he'd enjoyed stardom longer than me and taught me how to behave and dress when the cast had to travel first class and stay in five-star hotels for awards ceremonies. That was another nerve-jangling experience when I first joined the programme, but Johnny showed me how to enjoy myself without letting the side down.

Working with Liz was another wonderful experience. She's delightfully dotty and I still chuckle at some of her antics. She and Don have become our friends for life.

I've also had some huge fun with Steeno and the All Stars football team. Unlike the rest of my family, I'm not a big soccer fan. I have to ask Ali to explain the offside law to me. But I've enjoyed the banter with the lads in the dressing room.

For the vast majority of the time, I've loved chatting to *Corrie* fans when I'm out and about. They continue to ask me daft questions as if I'm Jack Duckworth. Believe it or not, they still approach me and ask, 'How's your Vera?' to which I reply, 'Still dead.' But I understand that in some cases they're so surprised to see the man who plays Jack in their shop that they say the first thing that comes into their heads without thinking. It's quite sweet really.

Over the years I've seen youngsters come into the show

and blossom into regulars. They're middle-aged now, so I won't embarrass them by naming them but you know who you are! Others have been there since before I started and show every sign of carrying on long after I've finished. They're all very special people in their different ways and it's been a real pleasure and a privilege to work with them.

I've made friends with many of the technicians on the other side of the camera, from the props men to the make-up artists and wardrobe, from the sound and camera men to the floor managers and directors. It's they and the scriptwriters who've helped me get away with this acting lark for all these years.

The role of Jack has taken me and Ali to the far side of the world, to New Zealand and to Canada, where *Corrie* has millions of viewers. It's taken us on luxury cruises and it's paid for dream trips to Bali and Fiji. It's also taken us to Ireland, where we've made lots of friends with some of the warmest people on the planet.

I've met royalty, been introduced to prime ministers and to pop legends such as Sir Cliff Richard and Rick Wakeman. This is beginning to sound like Name-dropping Corner at the Alzheimer's Club, but I've started so I'll finish . . .

From the world of soccer I've met Sir Matt Busby, Gordon Banks, George Best, Denis Law and Bobby Charlton, Colin Bell, Mike Summerbee and Frannie Lee, and I've shared a dinner table with Big Sam Allardyce, the Blackburn Rovers' manager (whom I still owe a bottle of champagne).

From cricket I've met the marvellous West Indian all-rounder Sir Clive Lloyd and our own Freddie Flintoff. I've shared a drink and a chat with Sir Ian Botham, who asked if

I'd pose for a photo with his mum and dad, who were life-long *Street* fans.

From boxing I've met world champions Barry McGuigan, Ricky Hatton and Amir Khan, and Sir Henry Cooper, Billy Walker and Nigel Benn. They're six of the most dangerous and charming men you could wish to meet.

I've played golf with music legends Johnny Mathis, Howard Keel and Don Henley from The Eagles.

I'd been on first-name terms with most of the stars of the TV show *The Comedians* since before they were famous. I've also met Bob Monkhouse and worked on *Corrie* with Norman Wisdom, Roy Hudd and Maureen Lipman.

I've also performed with some of the unsung heroes of the musical scene who are respected throughout the business even though they aren't household names. I've sung with the Hallé, with big bands, with the Toronto Bach Children's Chorus and with St Winifred's School Choir. I've had a Top 20 single with them and had two solo albums which sold well over 100,000 copies and 'went gold'.

I've chatted to Hollywood stars like Dustin Hoffman and Joan Collins. And did I mention I'd once worked with Sir Laurence Olivier?

It's been an extraordinary adventure, but the truth is that I've been at my happiest when I've been at home with my family, or having a pint and singing a couple of songs in my local pub.

I'm tremendously proud of my wife and children. They're equally proud of my successes but they haven't let it affect them. Carl and Sara both live nearby and we've always been a close-knit family.

My home in Ashton has a bar and an indoor swimming pool, so it's a magnet for the grandchildren and my drinking mates. Most importantly, it's only five miles from where I was born and raised. I could have moved to a posh house in the country, but that's not our style. We've always been townies and we feel comfortable mixing with working-class folk like ourselves.

I own a holiday apartment in Tenerife, where we can escape when the weather turns colder. But I have problems with my breathing when planes reach high altitudes so I've cut down on my visits. Ali and I have many happy memories of our times in the Canary Islands, whatever happens in the future. We're not afraid of having to cut back when my income from *Corrie* disappears. We've lived the dream and enjoyed almost every minute of it.

The most amazing thing was that the bubble never burst. Week after week I was speaking words that talented people had written for me, and a talented director told me where to sit or stand when I spoke those words. I haven't even had to change my accent. The only acting I've ever really done was when I pretended to sing badly.

That's why I've been both proud and embarrassed when Liz and I have won soap awards. We were voted Best On-Screen Partnership in 2001 and won the Inside Soap Award for Outstanding Achievement in 2002. Liz and I blush to think what the real actors were feeling about us when we were getting these gongs. I can only say that if they ever thought we were a pair of amateurs who didn't deserve such honours, they never hinted that they felt that way.

Even at the very end, when I told new producer Phil

Collinson I was leaving, he tried to persuade me to stay. I was expecting him to be happy to see the back of me. You see, I've always known that they knew that I knew that they knew I couldn't really act. But somehow we've muddled through.

I'd like to thank all those people who made it possible. I'd also like to thank the army of *Coronation Street* fans who've supported the show by watching it over the years. And I'd especially like to thank those fans who bought this book.

Index

Danson, Jane, 216
Darin, Bobby, 45
Dave King Show, The, 200
Dawn, Liz ('Elizabeth'), 86, 92–101, 118,
    142–3, 158–9, 160, 187, 201, 239, 241,
    270, 286–7
  ad work of, 93
  awards received by, 291
  BT's ill health and, 141
  BT introduced to, xi
  BT receives support from, 96
  BT's *This Is Your Life* and, xi, 174, 175–81
  extra's work of, 93–4
  fans of, 90–1, 98, 100, 154–5
  gambling and, 98–9
  ill health of, 100, 245, 258–64
  joins CS, 90, 92, 94
  leaves CS, 100, 258–64
  other jobs taken by, 94
  real name of, 92–3
  singing career of, 92–3, 98
  stage name acquired by, 93
Dawson, Les, 63, 145
Dene, Terry, 152
Deno's Club, 78
Denos, Mr (club owner), 78
Derbyshire, Eileen, 127–8, 141
Devaney, Sue, 117
Diamond, Jack, 62
Diamond, Neil, 194
Diana, Princess, 185, 272
Dick Barton – Special Agent, 17
dinnerladies, 167, 214, 242
dirty mac brigade, 66
Dobbs, Jackie (CS), 225
Dobbs, Tyrone (CS), 44, 137, 225, 232,
    250–1, 254–7, 260–3, 266–8, 271–2
Doctor Who, 80
Dodgy Dave (CS), 267–8
Donovan, Jason, 185
'Don't Laugh At Me 'Cos I'm A Fool', 12
Douglas, Colin, 80
drag artists, 25, 160, 247–8
Driver, Betty, 87, 127
  singing career of, 70
Ducie Avenue Technical School, 34
Duckworth, Cliff (CS), 200–1
Duckworth, Daisy (CS), 97
Duckworth, Harry (CS), 97
Duckworth, Jack (CS), 16, 111
  allotment of, 239–41, 242
  AP's father influenced, 44
  bickering nature of, 5–6
  birth of, 97
  BT's ill health and, 137–8, 139–45, 146
  BT's split personality and, x

cap-wearing of, 124–5
Claytons' feud with, 125–6
CR meets, 269–73
development of, 86, 87, 96–7
extramarital affairs and, x, 103–5, 120–1,
    123, 128, 130–1, 152, 192
fame as, 68, 77
fans of, ix, x, 82, 88–91, 107, 120, 136,
    153–4, 156
first screen kiss of, 103–4, 201, 288
gambling and, 123, 150, 153
grandchildren of, 173, 190, 215
'Husband of the Year', 129
'Ida Fagg' sobriquet of, 247–9
identical twin brother of, 280
ill health of, 124, 208, 227
illicit drugs and alcohol and, 240–1
'Jackie Duckworth Junior' sobriquet of,
    149, 197
'Jake Mallard' sobriquet of, 97
joins CS, vii, ix, xi, 1, 4, 47, 77, 79, 81, 84,
    86–7, 115
leaves CS, xi
'Lusty Jack' sobriquet of, 224–5
modelling work of, 253–4
pigeon-keeping of, 15, 108–9, 144, 167,
    192, 239, 251, 256, 270
popularity of, 120
producer's hit list and, 213–14
Rovers Return burned down by, xi, 131,
    132–8
second honeymoon of, 163
second wedding of, 217–20, 221
singing skills of, 149
'Superspark' sobriquet of, 133
VD's death and, 100–1, 258–64, 265, 269,
    271
VD's last words to, 260
VD marries, 97
VD's sparky relationship with, 86
VD stolen from, 88–9
'Vince St Clair' sobriquet of, 107, 171
Duckworth, Lisa (née Horton) (CS), 172,
    173, 190
Duckworth, Maggie (CS), 97
Duckworth, Terry (CS), 97, 106, 107, 115,
    121, 122, 125, 126, 127, 130, 134, 143,
    149–50, 172, 173, 189, 190, 205, 210,
    215–16, 217, 229, 237, 257, 263
Duckworth, Tommy (CS), 173, 190, 215, 232
Duckworth, Vera (née Burton) (CS), x, 4, 16,
    115, 286
  bickering nature of, 5–6
  birth of, 97
  'Carole Monroe' sobriquet of, 107, 171
  Claytons' feud with, 125–6

Tarmey, Bill – *continued*
 shy nature of, 33
 siblings of, xi
 singing career of, x, xi, 1, 2, 3, 44–5, 53,
  57, 60–71, 72–6, 78, 88–9, 98,
  110–11, 149, 158, 164, 182–4, 193–9,
  208, 216, 236, 238–9, 279, 287
 special song of, xi, 140, 180, 182, 193, 195,
  285
 split personality of, x
 sport and, 14, 30, 33–4, 36, 42–3, 76, 135–7,
  151, 224
 stag night of, 48
 stage name acquired by, 55
 This Is Your Life and, xi, 174, 175–81, 182,
  193, 195, 199
 'Tuppenny Rabbit' sobriquet of, 22, 56, 84
 woodworking 'skills' of, 29–30
 WWII and, xi, 7, 8–9, 11
Tarmey, Mel, *see* Tormé, Mel
Tarrant, Chris, 80
Tatlock, Albert (*CS*), 47, 86, 94
 death of, 116
Tattersall, Zoe (*CS*), 216
Taylor, Billy, 31, 33, 179
Taylor, Brenda (*CS*), 171
Taylor, Georgia, 216
Taylor, Johnny, 25
Taylor, Kimberley (*CS*), 171
Taylor, Mr (storeman), 41
Te Kanawa, Kiri, 185
Teddy (dog), 28–9
Temple, John, 122, 124, 147
Tennant, Pete, 40
Thatcher, Margaret, 157–8
'There's No One Quite Like Grandma',
  185
Thicker Than Water, 80, 286
This Is Your Life, xi, 174, 175–81, 182, 186,
  195, 199, 285
Thomas, Ryan, 137
Thorpe, Ray (*CS*), 216
Three Wheels Hotel, 111–12
'Three Coins In The Fountain', 70
'Three Wheels On My Wagon', 112
Threlfall, David, 81, 83
'Tie A Yellow Ribbon Round The Old Oak
  Tree', 58
'Tiger Feet', 63
Till Death Us Do Part, 63
Tilsley, Bert (*CS*), 94, 102, 103, 104
Tilsley, Brian (*CS*), xi, 4, 79, 81, 86, 94, 102,
  116, 118, 135, 137, 143, 147
 death of, 150–1
Tilsley, Gail (née Potter) (*CS*), 79, 81, 92, 94,
  102, 147

Tilsley, Ivy (*CS*), 63, 80, 94, 102, 103, 104,
  122, 129–30, 145
 leaves *CS*, 119
 'Poison Ivy' sobriquet of,119
 remarries, 147
Tilsley, Nick ('Nicky') (*CS*), 143, 226
Time for Love, 193, 198
Times, 168
Timoney, Mike, 54, 57, 62, 78, 110, 140, 180,
  182
Tiswas, 80
Titanic (band), 164
Todd, Gloria (*CS*), 128
Tommy (jazz organiser), 194
Tootsie, 160
Top of the Pops, 63, 187
Tormé, Mel, 55, 57
Tracey, Bob, 53
Trampas (*Virginian*), 83
Trautmann, Bert, 76
Troughton, Patrick, 80
Turnbull, Renee (*CS*), 221
Turpin, Betty (*CS*), 3, 69, 87, 92, 94, 115,
  146, 206
Turpin, Cyril (*CS*), 92
Tutin, Dorothy, 81
Two Wheels Hotel, 112
Two-Way Family Favourites, 19

UCP tripe and cowheel factory, 16, 24
United Nations, 194
Unwin, Shelley (*CS*), 247

Vale Cottage, 57
Verity, Bill, 30
Verity, Jean, 30
Vic (*CS*), 104
Victor Silvester Orchestra, 70
Vinny (props man), 158
Virginian, The, 83

Waddington, Bill, 105, 112–13, 214
Wadsworth, Derek, 193–9, 285
Wakeman, Rick 289
Walker, Annie (*CS*), 3, 47, 68, 68, 86, 94,
  105, 123, 202
Walker, Billy ('Blond Bomber') (boxer), 43
Walker, Billy (*CS*), 3
Walker, Chris, 216
Walker, George, 54, 70–1, 165, 180
Walker, Jack (*CS*), 47, 202
Walsh, Bradley, 247
Walter, Uncle, 11
Warburton, Lee, 213
Warren Club, 58
Warren, Tony, 26